With the Somersets in Afghanistan

Major-General Sir W. Nott

With the Somersets in Afghanistan

The Recollections of an Officer of H.M. 40th Regiment During the First Afghan War 1838-42

John Martin Bladen Neill

With the Somersets in Afghanistan
The Recollections of an Officer of
H.M. 40th Regiment During the
First Afghan War 1838-42
by John Martin Bladen Neill

First published under the title
Recollections of Four Years' Service in the East
with H. M. Fortieth Regiment

Leonaur is an imprint of Oakpast Ltd

ISBN: 978-0-85706-489-9 (hardcover)
ISBN: 978-0-85706-490-5 (softcover)

http://www.leonaur.com

Publisher's Notes

The opinions of the authors represent a view of events in which he
was a participant related from his own perspective,
as such the text is relevant as an historical document.

The views expressed in this book are not necessarily
those of the publisher.

Contents

To Lieut.-Colonel Hibbert, C.B., 40th Regiment.

My Dear Colonel,

I know no one to whom I can more appropriately inscribe the following pages than to the Officer who, with but one short interruption, commanded the 40th Regiment during the period of which I attempt to treat, and who held the proud position of being its leader, when to its other glorious achievements were added "Candahar"—Ghuznee"—"Cabul,"—1842.

I beg you will accept the dedication of this Narrative to you as a slight acknowledgment of the numerous kindnesses I have received at your hands during the many years we have served together, and as a grateful recollection of the facilities afforded me by these kindnesses in the performance of my duties as Adjutant in the field, during an eventful period, and under circumstances of no ordinary difficulty.

I am,

My dear Colonel,

Yours most sincerely and faithfully,

J. Martin Bladen Neill.

Army and Navy Club, St. James's Square,
June 2nd,

40

Preface

The following pages would perhaps be more appropriately entitled "*Random* Recollections"—of associations connected with the great and eventful military operations, in which the writer had the peculiar good fortune to participate.

Upwards of two years have now elapsed, (at time of first publication), since General Nott made his glorious and successful advance from Candahar; and it is with a regret akin to shame that the writer finds, that among the many officers in the Candahar army, no one, not even from the general's staff, has been found to come forward and give a military account of the administration of affairs in Western Affghanistan in 1841 and 1842, by one of the most distinguished men whose deeds have for years shed a lustre over our actions in the East.

The Author is keenly alive to his own inability to do justice to the reputation of his general, and he hopes that the very imperfect and inadequate attempt which he makes to depict events connected with the name of "Nott," may be the means of rousing from lethargy some one of higher talent and more extensive information, who will, in doing justice to the "illustrious dead," confer a benefit on the public, by giving a faithful and detailed account of the actions of the Candahar Army and its distinguished leader.

Should such a result be effected, the Author will feel that although his labours have been but slight they will not have been in vain.

During the period of which he attempts to treat, the Author kept a journal, in which he carefully recorded, as they occurred, all incidents worthy of note. This journal was carried off with his baggage by the enemy in the Khyber Pass, when the campaign in Afghanistan might almost be said to have closed; and he was thus deprived of the best means of refreshing his memory. Finding, however, on his return home, that many of his letters written in India and Afghanistan had been preserved, he amused himself by devoting his leisure hours to the compilation of the following narrative, the perusal of those letters having suggested the possibility of his not altogether failing in an attempt at authorship.

While engaged in his work, he was fortunate enough to supply some of the deficiencies in his letters, from a journal of events connected with the advance of the army from Candahar, by his friend Lieutenant Carey, 40th; and since the work has gone to press, he has been enabled to make some slight alterations, at the suggestion of his old friend and comrade Lieutenant Alex. Nelson,—an officer who performed the duties of sub-assistant commissary-general to the Bombay troops in the Candahar Army, during the most stirring and arduous period embraced in the Author's narrative, with a zeal and ability which contributed much to the comfort and efficiency of the troops, and secured for him the marked approval of his general.

The Author is at a loss to express the sense he entertains of the obligation conferred upon him by Mr. Thomas Brigstocke, in permitting an engraving for his book to be taken from this distinguished artist's admirable portrait of General Nott, now exhibiting in the Royal Academy. He is fully alive to the extent of the kindness of that permission, and feels assured that the value of his work is much enhanced by the circumstance that, embodied with it is the portrait of the gallant and lamented commander of "The Veterans of Candahar."

The writer is aware that he has entered on ground which has been frequently and well described. Should he in any part of his narrative echo sentiments which have already appeared before the public, he is entirely unconscious of the plagiarism, and in such case he trusts that some satisfaction may be derived by his predecessors from the fact, that they are not singular in their views and opinions.

The Author is vain enough to hope that, notwithstanding the many faults, imperfections, and perhaps puerilities, which may be found to abound in his work, it will not prove altogether uninteresting to the general reader; he will, therefore, make no apology for intruding it on the public, but would crave leave to remark, that in the hurry and bustle of active military service, a soldier can spare but little time from the performance of his duties for collecting information unconnected with them, and that consequently—

In vain sedate reflections he would make,
When half his knowledge he must snatch not take.

June 2nd, 1845.

Chapter 1

Order to March

In the month of December 1838, H. M. 40th Regiment, then stationed at Deesa, on the north-west frontier of Guzerat, received instructions to hold itself in readiness to proceed to Lower Scinde. There it hoped to form part of the *corps d'armée* of Scinde, which, towards the end of that year, had been assembled at Bombay under his Excellency the commander-in-chief of the Presidency, Lieutenant-general Sir J. Keane, for the purpose of carrying out the policy of the Governor-general, as embodied in his Lordship's celebrated Manifesto, of the 1st of October 1838.[1]

The arrival of the order to which I have referred, caused no slight degree of excitement in the lines of H. M. 40th Regiment, and diffused among us considerable joy, in the anticipation that we were yet to share in the honours and perils of the active *corps d'armée.* Such joyous hopes of good fortune were, however, but short-lived; for, long ere leaving Deesa, we received the too certain intelligence that the 40th was destined to form part of a *corps de reserve* which was to be assembled at Kurachee, (a sea-port in Scinde, to the westward of the Indus,) under Brigadier Valiant, K. H., and which was to be stationed in Lower Scinde at different points, as circumstances might render expedient.

Continued inactive service, particularly in the East, where regiments are permitted to remain so long at the same station, is apt to produce and encourage indulgence in comforts and luxuries most unnecessary and expensive: it is, in consequence, surprising how great is the accumulation of articles, supposed at the time of their acquisition to have been essentials, which, when the order for march arrives, are

1. Appendix A.

found not only perfectly useless, but in every way cumbersome and vexatious. In this, as in other things of equal and greater importance, experience teaches, not wisdom.

It would be well were officers, both on their own account and that of their men, ever to bear in mind the necessity, and compel the observance, of the rule, that nothing is more essential—nay, more imperatively called for, than that the establishments of the members of a corps, individually and collectively, should be kept in that state which would best enable them *at once* to take the field; and I feel assured that nothing would more conduce to the attainment of this object, and be of greater service to all classes, than not only the restriction by Government of officers and men to a certain number of baggage-cattle, but the strict enforcement of an undeviating adherence to such an order.

It is no unusual circumstance for subalterns, in time of war, to have five or six camels for the carriage of their baggage; and when such is the case, and other ranks travel in a proportionate degree of grandeur, it is easy to conceive what an unwieldy mass the baggage of an Indian army becomes,—and, as a natural result, how much the duties and anxieties of a rearguard are increased.

Those officers who have ever borne part in the preparations for moving a corps in India, even from one station to another,—much more for equipping it for immediate active service,—must remember, with aught but feelings of pleasure or satisfaction, the delays, annoyances, and consequent squandering of valuable time caused by the arrangements necessary for the disposal of superfluous stores, kit, &c., and the difficulty in procuring the requisite quantity of carriage for the transport of overgrown baggage. These observations *par parenthèse*.

In a short time, by the exercise of considerable ingenuity and perseverance, our kits were reduced to what we thought marching condition, and we looked anxiously and impatiently for the day on which we were to leave cantonments. Soldier-like, after having sojourned three years at Deesa, we desired a change of scene; and yet our joy at leaving this station was mingled with no small share of regret in the contemplation of our approaching separation from the different corps composing the Deesa field-brigade, with whom we had been so long and happily associated, and between whose officers and ourselves there had subsisted a more than usual degree of kindness and unity of feeling.

Those of the 40th who served at Deesa during 1836, and the

two following years, will always recur to these years with lively emotions of pleasure, and, though not the most eventful, will class them among those connected with the most pleasurable reminiscences of their Eastern life,—embittered though the recollection be with the sad conviction, that death has been more than usually busy among the members of the old Deesa brigade, and that many a young and gallant heart which then beat high in life and hope, now rests in the silent tomb,—calm, motionless, unknowing, but not forgotten.

Considerable loss, and no little annoyance, were experienced at this time by the officers of many of the corps which now took the field, from their being obliged to leave the houses they had purchased on entering cantonments,—with no immediate, and but little distant, hope of being able to dispose of them. The system which at present obtains in India, of requiring officers to provide themselves with houses in cantonments at their own expense, I cannot but view as objectionable. In such a view, I am aware I am far from being singular'; and in embodying my opinions on this, as well as on many other subjects, I shall doubtless say much that has already been said, and in a better and more forcible manner.

It must ever be the policy and intention of Government to guard its servants, so far as consistency and a regard for the public interest will permit, against loss: and I conceive that not only would this object be effected, and thereby a great boon conferred on the officers of the army, but an immense saving would eventually be made by Government, were all houses in cantonments made public property, and the officers charged a moderate rent, on the same principle as that pursued in garrison.

It is urged by many, that the increased allowance given to officers in the field is to repay them for any additional expense they may have to incur in the purchase of houses at out-stations; but I maintain that it can only be viewed as the means of providing them with camp equipage, and of enabling them to defray the increased expense for necessary supplies, caused by the distance at which field-stations are from the Presidencies, whence those supplies generally proceed.

To suppose that officers at field-stations should dwell in tents, is to entertain an idea of the practicability of a measure amounting almost to an impossibility, as not one constitution in a thousand would be able to withstand the enervating influence of such exposure to the heat; and regiments would thus be deprived of the services of their officers, whose superintendence of, and intercourse with, the men are so essential to uphold the discipline and well-being of the army.

That it is not the intention of Government that officers should be exposed to the risk of thus ruining their constitutions, is evident from the fact that at every permanent cantonment, comfortable barracks are built for the men, and that, on the establishment of new cantonments, officers are entitled to a certain advance from Government, to enable them to build bungalows,—such advance being refunded by deductions from the pay of those officers who take advantage of this Government indulgence.

It rarely happens that an officer can rent a house in cantonments; he is therefore compelled to purchase one, which seldom costs less than from 2000 to 3000 *rupees*, or from 200*l.* to 300*l.*: it becomes, therefore, a matter of very serious inconvenience, particularly to the junior ranks, when a regiment is ordered to take the field, and no other is sent to relieve it, as was the case in 1838 with the Queen's Royals at Belgaum, and H. M. 40th at Deesa; for the proprietors of houses are thus not only deprived of the sum they expended in their purchase, and which, on the eve of a march, would be most acceptable, but they are also put to the expense of keeping up a guard, or species of private native police, to look after and keep in repair the property during their absence, or until an opportunity presents itself for its disposal.

All these annoyances would be removed by Government taking the officers' bungalows into their own hands; the deductions for house-rent would soon repay the sum expended in their building or purchase, and very little extra trouble would be entailed on the barrack-master department in the event of the houses becoming unoccupied. Add to all this, there would not be the same inducement for officers to incur (needlessly, I grant,) the very great expense many do in the outward and inward adorning of their houses,—numbers of which are furnished in a style that would not disgrace the drawing-room at home of a gentleman of good fortune. It is frequently absurd the extent to which the spirit of emulation in furnishing their houses neatly—perhaps with more truth it may be said *effeminately*—is carried among some officers, and might form a fruitful theme for commentary for those who interest themselves in the cause of extravagance in regimental messes.

Having participated largely in the hospitalities of our friends at Deesa, and having been paid the compliment of being publicly entertained at dinner by Major-General Brooks commanding, and the officers of the brigade, we marched out of Deesa *en route* to Mandavie on the morning of the 4th of January, 1839.

The *depôt*, consisting of a few sick men, and the women and children of the regiment, were left behind under command of Brevet-Captain Stamford.

On leaving Deesa, the 40th mustered six hundred and fifty bayonets, and I will venture to say there was not a smarter or more 'service-like' corps in the different armies assembled at this time. Our route at first lay through a part of Guzerat, and resembled the other portions of this province we had had already seen, being alike distinguished for its generally bleak appearance and vast extent of bauble jungle. At about forty miles from Deesa, we encamped close to the walls of Rahdunpoor, a place formerly doubtless of consequence, but now possessing little importance. The Rajah, who resides here, and whom we had frequently seen at Deesa, came out in the afternoon to visit us. He drove up to our mess-tent in what had been some hundred years ago a handsome curricle, but which possessed little of the beauty and elegant lightness of the carriages of the present day. His Highness, a handsome delicate looking youth, drove himself; and seated beside him in his *curricle* was his minister, a bloated, disgusting, sensual-looking piece of mortality. His retinue was composed of the most perfect rabble I ever saw.

Being apprised of his intention to visit us, a guard of honour, composed of the grenadiers of the regiment, was drawn up in front of the mess tent, where on his arrival he was received by Colonel Valiant, who presented the officers to his Highness. Before taking his leave, he invited us to a *Nautch* at his palace in the evening, and all off duty attended,—more for the purpose, however, of seeing the royal abode, than in the hope of deriving amusement or gratification from this most tiresome, discordant, and uninteresting source of native enjoyment and gaiety.

At this distance of time, I am unable to give any but a most imperfect description of the interior of the palace; so far, however, as my recollection serves me, it was even more paltry than the palaces of petty *rajahs* generally are,—well stocked with detached portions of old European furniture—probably procured at the sale of some deceased officer's effects—a superfluity of execrable prints, and an unlimited supply of very small and exceedingly distorting mirrors. The citadel was fast going to decay, but as far as I could judge from the hurried inspection I made, it must have been a place of considerable strength. The town differed in no essential particular from those I have seen in the East, being like them distinguished for narrow streets and close bazaars, and decidedly inferior to none in filth.

Shortly after leaving Rahdunpoor, we entered the province of Cutch. Here we found supplies of everything scarce and dear, owing to the dreadful famine of which this land had been the scene, consequent on there having been, for two seasons, such a very slight monsoon. For miles, hardly a blade of grass was to be seen, and seldom did a symptom of cultivation meet the eye. The gaunt haggard appearance of the natives, spoke painfully and forcibly of the miseries they had endured, and under which they were still labouring. Noble exertions had been made throughout India to raise funds for procuring the necessaries of life for the starving population of this and similarly afflicted districts; and although much was effected by the princely sum realized by the subscriptions of those possessed of such means of relief, yet, as in all similar cases, it was vain to hope to minister to the wants of all. Sickness, ever the attendant on famine, was making dreadful ravages; hunger was the incitement to crime; and well authenticated cases of mothers offering their children for sale from actual want, were not unfrequent.

From the proximity of Deesa to Cutch, it was natural to suppose that we should suffer to some small extent from the influences of the famine with which this neighbouring province had been visited. This we experienced not only in the difficulty found in procuring cattle in sufficient numbers to move the camp-equipage of the 40th, but also in the enormous charges for them, each camel costing us upwards of a *rupee per diem*, while those of the Bengal division under Sir H. Fane were, we understood, procurable for nine *rupees per mensem*,—a rate of hire which I believe in the northern provinces is considered rather exorbitant.

Continuing our route, we crossed part of the "Run of Cutch," a desert waste, the mirage on which is one of the most curious and magnificent sights I have ever seen. The whole country had the appearance of a vast extent of water, and every object around presented itself in a peculiar and strangely enlarged shape,—the smallest twigs and bushes assuming the character of the most beautiful and lofty trees, raising a visionary forest, the effect of which was most pleasing and grateful to the eye. The appearance of the camels in the distance was particularly striking; their legs being concealed from view by the effects of the mirage, they seemed to glide along the imaginary lake like mighty vessels, accounting probably, as some writer has observed, for this animal being called the "*ship of the desert.*"

So complete was the deception relative to the appearance of water, that on one morning after a very long march, I have a perfect recollection of seeing many of the men going off after breakfast for the purpose, as they supposed, of enjoying a bath,—this lake, much to their chagrin, and the amusement of those too knowing or too lazy to accompany them, turning out a Will-o'-the-wisp.

There was little else in the general appearance of the country to interest, differing slightly as it did from the low brushwood-studded plains of Guzerat, with which our eyes had been so long familiar. The jungles were well stocked with game, especially when near a river. We found numbers of wild hog, but owing to the thickness and extent of the cover, it was almost impossible to *ride* them, so our sport was limited.

With the exception of Addysir and Anjar, we passed no town of any size. The supply of water was good at the daily halting-places laid down in the route furnished by the quartermaster-general; and the encamping grounds were good and extensive.

When within a few marches of Mandavie, our Commandant, Colonel Valiant, received instruction to the effect that opposition might be expected to our landing at Kurachee, and—as the immediate occupation of that sea-port would much facilitate the operations and expedite the progress of the *corps d'armée* which had landed at Vikkur, near one of the mouths of the Indus, and was slowly advancing on Hyderabad,—calling on him to move forward the reserve as quickly as possible. Having made a forced march, we reached Mandavie on the morning of the 27th of January.

In concluding this chapter, I may be excused for indulging in a piece of regimental vanity in stating that H. M. 40th had now finished a march of upwards of two hundred and forty miles, during the performance of which not one case of drunkenness had occurred, and only one instance of misconduct—and that of a very trivial nature.

Chapter 2

Arrival at Mandavie

On marching into Mandavie, we found awaiting our arrival, H.M.S. *Wellesley*, seventy-four, bearing the flag of His Excellency Rear Admiral Sir Frederick Maitland, one of the H. C. steamers, the transport ship *Hannah*, and a considerable fleet of country boats, for the conveyance of stores, ammunition, horses, &c. A company of European artillery, (Bombay,) under command of Captain W. Brett, which had marched from Bhooj, as also the 2nd Bombay N. I. Grenadiers, under Major Forbes, which had been embarked at Bombay in the H. C. steamer, and which were to form part of the Scinde reserve force, had likewise arrived.

The beach at Mandavie was the scene of much confusion: ammunition and warlike stores of every description were lying about; officers, and subordinates of public departments, were moving to and fro, intent on their various avocations; while regimental officers, during their short respite from duty, were rushing frantically about in the hope of procuring boats to carry their baggage and horses to Kurachee,—a matter of no easy accomplishment, as so many of the country craft were required for the public service. At length all the material was shipped, and it was found that boats sufficient remained for all private purposes.

The company of artillery was directed to repair on board the transport ship, and H. M. 40th to embark in the evening in H. M. S. *Wellesley*. The *bombardiers* certainly had the best of it in one point of view at least, having more room and being enabled to take their baggage with them. Whereas, we of the *royal army* were allowed to take on board the flag-ship a very reduced portion of kit, and as may be supposed, having a body of six hundred and fifty men with us and more than a proportionate number of officers, we were considerably crowded.

Holding the staff-situation of adjutant, my time from the moment of arrival at Mandavie was completely occupied, in conjunction with the quartermaster, and Lieutenant Jerningham, R.N. of the flag-ship, who was our most invaluable colleague in carrying out the arrangements made by our respective chiefs for the embarkation of the 40th in the evening. This service was commenced about eight p. m., under the immediate superintendence of Lieutenant-Colonel Powell of the 40th, who had that morning joined and taken command of the regiment, Owing to the scarcity of boats and the distance at which the *Wellesley* was anchored from the shore, the last detachment did not get on board until nearly two o'clock on the morning of the 28th.

Our reception from our gallant brethren of the sister service was most gratifying; every endeavour was made by them to render our situation as comfortable as possible. The novelty of our position tended in some degree to reconcile us to the difference of sleeping on *terra firma* with lots of elbow-room, and being stowed away as thickly as possible in a cock-pit, several feet below the level of the sea, and where the few rays of light that entered only served to make the darkness more visible. But not the least amusing part connected with our temporary residence in the midshipman's palace, was the awkwardness of the landsmen in their attempts, sometimes unsuccessful, to get into the hammocks, affording infinite source of good-natured merriment at the expense of the "*sodjer officers*"

The day after our embarkation, the Admiral set sail for the Hujamree mouth of the Indus, off which we anchored: from the poop we could plainly see several tents of some portion of the army. Shortly after our arrival we were joined by H. M.S. *Algerine* and one or two of the Honourable Company's cruisers.

During our *séjour* at this place, we were in great anxiety in consequence of the disappearance of Captain M'Gregor, commanding the transport *Hannah*, (Captain Brett, of the artillery, and another officer whose name I forget. It happened that in the evening they had gone out in one of the ship's cutters to amuse themselves; and while rowing about at a considerable distance from the shipping, a strong breeze sprung up from the shore, which, with the assistance of a powerful current, carried them, unknown to us, far out to sea. Blue-lights and other signals were made during the night; morning came at length, but the boat and crew were nowhere to be seen: the wind having, however, subsided, it was hoped they would soon appear, but not doing so, a schooner was dispatched in search, which, after cruising about for a time, fell in with our friends, for whose safety we began to be most apprehensive. During the height of the storm, they had succeeded, by a piece of great good fortune, in laying hold of a passing *pattimar,* in which they passed the night, and were enabled to return. It never would have done on the eye of our brilliant and eventful achievements at Minhora, to have lost our commandant of artillery.

On the evening of the 31st of January, we received our final instructions, which were, "to proceed to Kurachee and take it." We accordingly immediately weighed anchor and set sail for that port. On the evening of the 1st of February, we anchored within seven or eight hundred yards of the small fort of Minhora, which guards the entrance to the harbour of Kurachee,—rather a dangerous proximity to the enemy's stronghold, especially had his ordnance been good—which fortunately for us was not the case.

Immediately after anchoring, our boats were lowered, and we proceeded to prevent any communication with the harbour from the numerous fishing-smacks and country craft. While employed in this service, our boats were several times fired on from the fort, but with no effect. Everyone looked anxiously for the morrow, anticipating from the hostile feeling already shown by the garrison, that the *reserve* would open the campaign.

Morning at length broke, and the sun burst forth in all that glorious effulgence which can only be witnessed in the tropics; there was not a breath to ripple the sea, or disturb the vast uniform brightness of its glassy surface. The white walls of the little fort, perched on its rocky cliff, stood erect before us, and the city of Kurachee in the distance, with its long chain of bold, beautiful, but sterile hills in the background, all contributed to form a picture of no ordinary grandeur.

The calmness of the scene was broken by the preparations on board the flag-ship, where the crew were busily engaged, "clearing for action," while the soldiers and marines were taking a quiet but minute inspection of their flints and ammunition.

The *amusements* of the day began about eight o'clock in the morning, when a flag of truce was sent on shore under charge of Lieutenant Jenkins, I. N., accompanied by Captain Gray, H. M. 40th regiment, as interpreter:—the instructions of these officers were, to require the immediate and unconditional surrender of the fort. Compliance with this *modest* request being refused, preparations for landing the artillery and four companies of the 40th, under Lieutenant-Colonel Powell, K. H., were immediately commenced; and this object was effected on the western side of the fort, under cover of H. M.S. *Algerine* and H. C. S. *Constance*, which stood in for this purpose. A second flag of truce was now sent, but with as little success as the first. The *Killadar*, Wussul Ben Butcha or some equally unpronounceable or unwriteable name, admitted that he was perfectly aware that his fort must fall to so superior and well equipped a force; but he could not, consistently with his reputation as a soldier, and his *faith* as a Belooch, be guilty of the double crime of disobedience of orders, and surrendering his post. He offered, however, to send down to Kurachee, from the Governor of which he felt assured he should receive instructions to deliver up the fort at once. All this was very fine and very specious, but the old Admiral was not to be *done*; he said he would admit of no temporising, and ten or fifteen minutes were given to the *Killadar* to consider; at the expiration of which time, that functionary still refusing to accede to our request, the *Wellesley* opened her broadside on the fort with admirable precision.

A second division, composed of the remainder of the 40th, was now ordered on shore, under Major Hibbert; this I was permitted to accompany,—leave to join the first having been refused me, although, from my immediate commanding officer having gone in command of it, and the grenadiers, the company to which I belonged (being only acting adjutant)—forming part of it, I had anticipated having the honour of accompanying the first division. As it turned out, however, I saw as much of this affair by remaining on board the *Wellesley* to perform the duties of adjutant-general,—Captain Valiant, who was acting in that capacity, having landed in command of the Light Company,—as if I had accompanied the colonel; for, before reaching the shore with the second division, we saw the British ensign waving on the breach which had been effected in the walls, and on arriving found that, notwithstanding the high tone assumed by our friend the *Killadar*, we had gained a bloodless victory at the expense of some five or six thousand pounds of powder and a proportionate number of thirty-two pound shot.

The *Killadar* and his *brave* comrades had deserted the garrison after the fourth or fifth round, and sought refuge in the crevices of the rocks, where a few of them were taken.

During the landing of the troops of the First Division, one gun was fired from the fort; the shot struck the water and bounded on, doing no further injury than splashing the boat's crew against which it had been directed. Doubtless, the garrison would have favoured us with many more specimens of their prowess in the art of gunnery, but, unfortunately, this gratification was placed beyond their attainment by the *obstinacy* and *incapacity* of their guns,—one of which had no carriage,—another (the one which had been fired that morning) had jumped from its carriage, which it had destroyed in its violent effort for freedom,—while the only remaining one, I believe, had evidently resisted every attempt to make it serviceable in the defence of the fortress, and had *positively declined* going off. This gun was also loaded to the muzzle, and the last time I saw it, months after the capture of the fort, it remained still a loaded gun, notwithstanding the unremitting exertions of many an idler who visited Minhora to discharge it.

The whole affair was, however, a pretty thing, or if I may be allowed to use the expression, a brilliant field day; and, in a *military sense*, it ought to have been permitted to remain such. The orders issued, however, rather overshot the mark, and tended to bring into ridicule the capture of the fort, which really was, from its important position as the principal sea-port of Scinde, and the effect of its fall on the *Ameers* of Scinde, a matter of much consequence.

The enemy, as if not to be out-done by us in their official report to the *Ameers* on the fall of the fort, stated that after a gallant and obstinate defence of two hours, they were at length compelled to yield to the irresistible attack of seven thousand British, backed by the guns of an immense fleet! One of the thirty-two pound shot was sent to Hyderabad that their Highnesses might judge of the extraordinary strength and means of the besiegers. The number of British who met a warrior's grave was not mentioned.

Having reported myself on landing, I proceeded to inspect the fort, and have a look at that portion of the garrison, amounting to about thirty, who had been made prisoners. Minhora, in size, was very inconsiderable; it had, however, been always supposed, from its commanding position, impregnable, and would possibly have defied the attempts of any native power to reduce it. One great obstacle to its making any lengthened defence would arise from the total want of water on the promontory on which it is built,—that and all other necessary articles for the use of the garrison being brought from Kurachee, a distance of at least two miles. In the garrison was found a magazine, well stocked with very indifferent powder and several piles of small round shot; it boasted of little or nothing else—and this small rectangular sea-defence was as deficient of architectural beauty as of prize money! I was much struck with the fine features of the defenders of this stronghold.

I have never seen handsomer or more athletic men.

The capture of Minhora appeared to have struck the greatest terror into the inhabitants of Kurachee. During the afternoon, the clouds of dust that rolled along the hills marked the progress of those who were deserting their city, fearful that it was soon to become the prey of an advancing army. We, however, remained close to Minhora, where we bivouacked for the night, our chief having sent Captain Gray and Lieutenant Jenkins to offer terms to the authorities of Kurachee, which were accepted.

The admiral and brigadier landed in the evening to inspect *the scene of their triumph*, after which they returned, accompanied by Colonel Powell, to enjoy a comfortable dinner, while we small fry amused ourselves planting picquets.

After this, those off duty contrived to pass the evening tolerably happy, having been furnished with a few bottles of wine and some hard biscuit by our gallant friends of the *Wellesley*. All fires having been put out in the ship, when she cleared for action, nothing could be cooked there; to compensate, as far as possible, for our disappointment in not getting our dinner as we had anticipated, the gentlemen of the ward-room sent us a live sheep on shore, which was delivered to us with most humorous solemnity by the middy who had been intrusted with the mission, and who enjoyed to the utmost our chagrin, or rather our dismay, in debating what we were to do with the animal, destitute as we were of every means of cooking it—even if we had understood the art of butchery sufficiently to have slain it.

By a fortunate coincidence our colonel had been provided by some kind friend with a cold duck; this, on going off to the *Wellesley*, he had placed in his haversack, intending it for his breakfast the next morning, and had hung it up in a small idol-house of which we had taken possession. Some sharp-nosed hungry *sub* accidentally found it out; it was too much for human nature to resist, especially considering that it was upwards of twelve hours since we had breakfasted; so down came the duck, which sufficed for one of the most delightful meals conceivable.

The colonel bore his loss with much equanimity, and although the transaction at the time did not call forth that approbation from him which the perpetrators thought it deserved, yet he often laughed at it heartily afterwards. As night advanced, we began to look out for as soft a stone as we could; Olpherts and myself secured a good berth in one of the guard-rooms near the gate of the fort. That I slept well, and that my friend was comfortable also, may be inferred from the fact that I did not awake till long after the sun had risen, when I found that Dick Olpherts had, by a piece of singular dexterity, most unintentionally of course, and unknown to me, appropriated my cloak to himself.

February the 3rd.—This morning I was indebted for breakfast to my friend Major Hibbert, who had succeeded in the morning in foraging to some advantage. We remained all day at Minhora,. it having been decided that the force should not proceed to Kurachee until the treaty had been ratified, which was to be done that day. About noon the authorities of Kurachee repaired on board the flag-ship, where, after an interchange of civilities, the terms of the treaty were agreed on; the prisoners of war were then released, their arms restored to them, and orders were issued to the troops to be in readiness to move on Kurachee the following morning.

In the evening we moved down to the beach under the fort, where we were to bivouac for the night; here we received a supply of ship's pork from the *Wellesley*, and also a quantity of pea soup,—which latter being brought ashore in an old rum-cask, had little on the score of improved flavour to recommend it. Thus ended the taking of the fort of Minhora on the high point of land at the mouth of the harbour of Kurachee.

Chapter 3

Proceed to Kurachee

About eleven a.m. of the 4th of February, the small boats of the fleet rendezvoused close to the beach under the fort of Minhora; and the business of embarking the troops having been completed, we proceeded, led by the admiral, to Kurachee.

The first appearance of the city was rather prepossessing, and those whose lot was likely to be cast in it for some time, looked with a degree of satisfaction and happy anticipation at being established in a quarter seemingly enjoying so many natural advantages, and possessing, from situation, so many requisites for a healthy station.

Being early in the year, everything bore a pleasing aspect, and in our imaginations we had transformed the distant forests of mangrove and prickly pear which greeted our eye, into extensive plains of cultivated land, intersected and varied by tracts of jungle, where the sportsman would find ample space for the indulgence of his favourite amusement;—in fact, that we were about to enter on a land of promise, where plenty reigned, and which, from its proximity to the sea, would ensure that rude health would be our never-failing attendant. Vain hope! our first landing showed how futile were all our expectations. Then the sad reality burst upon us, that our home for some time would be in the dreary sterility of a barren plain, scarcely diversified by the bleak, uninteresting, and unproductive hills around, whose dull monotonous brown was varied, but not relieved, by the stunted prickly-pear bushes with which they are studded. A further knowledge of the land proved to us, that we had indeed entered the "gloomy portal of a desolate and uninteresting country."

We had timed our arrival at Kurachee badly, as when we got there it was low water; and we deemed it judicious, with a due regard to comfort, to get ourselves carried for some distance through the mud on the shoulders of the Scindees. This was rather a tedious and unpleasant operation;—at length it was effected, unattended by any event of interest,—unless the usual proportion of accidents which, on such occasions, generally befall the more corpulent, deserve that character.

The dignitaries of Kurachee were ready to receive us, and, after the usual *salaaming* in such cases, the admiral, brigadier, and staff set off to visit the fort, and pay their respects to the Hakim. My boat with my two horses having arrived, I was enabled to mount in good style our *sea* and land chiefs—which of course was a more becoming and dignified manner of proceeding to the house of the Governor, than if they had been compelled to walk.

The town of Kurachee is exceedingly dirty, and the inhabitants generally are a most squalid-looking set of wretches. Its population, according to Lieutenant Postans, is about ten thousand; but other accounts estimate it at more than double this number. The great majority are Hindoos. The houses are generally mud-built and flat-roofed; on the top of them are wicker ventilators facing the sea, which perform the double duty of windsail and skylight. The streets are narrow and incommodious. The bazaar is covered over with matting, to prevent the rays of the sun penetrating, but which also precluding a free current of air, adds much to the *désagrémens* of those frequenting it. The remains of a mud-wall surround the citadel, where there are a few wretched guns;—altogether the defences are in a most dilapidated state, and, had we been obliged to attack, we should have found numerous very practicable breaches readymade.

The principal portion of the better description of houses are in the centre of the town, but there are no public buildings worthy of notice. The suburbs are extensive: in their vicinity are several tan-pits, the stench from which is most disgusting and overpowering. For the preparation of hides. Kurachee has great celebrity. A considerable trade is carried on between this port and Bombay, Dumaum, Mandavie, the Malabar Coast, Muscat, &c. The principal exports are fleece, wool, sharks' fins, dried fruits, dyes, leather, silk goods, &c.; and the principal imports sugar, spices, British cloths, grain, wood, brass, steel, tin, &c.

The creek which leads from the harbour is navigable for small boats only, and goods are usually conveyed to and from the larger vessels by means of flat-bottomed boats— an outlay of a few thousand *rupees* would, however, remedy this inconvenience.

The majority of the inhabitants appeared delighted at our arrival, and hailed our occupation of the city as if a brighter beam of happiness were about to dawn on them. The anticipation of a *free circulation of Bombay rupees* among them was not, I dare say, without its effect in ministering to their hopes of enjoyment for the future.

The visits of ceremony having been performed, the brigadier, along with the acting quartermaster-general and commanding officers of corps, went to reconnoitre the country, and fix on a place for the encampment of the troops. A suitable position having been determined on, the different corps marched up to their ground, and prepared to bivouac for the night.

Not having had our meals regularly for the last two or three days, and being withal tolerably hungry, I was much pleased to find that one of my servants, who had got to my ground before me, was already far advanced in the preparation for himself of a fish curry. I thought it but fair, having had no breakfast, and seeing not the most distant prospect of getting a dinner, that I should share the feast with my *slave*;—a friend coming up at the time, warmly applauded my design,—so we appropriated a portion of the mess, and freely verified the old adage, that "*hunger is the best sauce*." I never enjoyed a meal more; and the pleasure was heightened by the conviction, that however questionable might be the manner in which the refection was procured, there was more than sufficient to satisfy the cravings of all who partook of it,—the *artiste* himself included.

On the morning of the 5th, at daybreak, the force was paraded for fatigue duty, to land such part of the camp-equipage, &c., as had arrived by the Mandavie boats, which were now beginning to drop into port. This, from the nature of the landing, was a more difficult and tedious undertaking than we had anticipated; and the delays and difficulties were increased by the impossibility of procuring any baggage-cattle by which to carry our tents, &c., from the landing-place to the camp,—a distance of upwards of a mile. Our own camels had not yet arrived, nor could we expect them for some days, as they had gone round by Lukput from Mandavie. When evening closed in, and prevented our working any longer, we found that but a limited supply of our goods had been landed, and indeed that it would require several days before everything could be brought on shore.

Time accomplishes all things; and, after having been engaged for some days in the above duty, our camp at length assumed its usual appearance of comfort and regularity. Most conflicting reports reached us of the progress of the army, and, among others, that an action had been fought between Tatta and Hyderabad, in which our loss had been most severe, and our success most questionable. However, in this land, where certainly "*truth is stranger than fiction*," nothing could be relied on, and this report, like many others, turned out to be devoid of foundation. The generally received opinion seemed to be, that our force would be permanently stationed at Kurachee; but, to guard against all accidents, we resolved to keep up our baggage-cattle.

This was done at an enormous expense, for Kurachee, though it was represented as being more than usually well provided with supplies of every necessary description, we found to be utterly destitute of almost everything. Grain there was little of, forage there was none; both these essential articles had to be procured from Bombay and the Kattywar Coast: and the native merchants, knowing we were so entirely dependent on them for supplies, did not fail to dispose of their goods at an exorbitant profit. Water fit for use was only to be had from wells dug in the bed of a river, at a very great distance from the camp. There was nothing, however, as far as I could judge, to have prevented our pitching our camp near the river. One or two wells were sunk in the camp, but the water was extremely brackish, and quite unfit for use.

One fatigue-duty was hardly finished before it was necessary to commence another. Our camp was surrounded by a forest of low prickly-pear bushes, and for some days we were busily engaged in clearing a space in front, rear, and flanks. It was an easier undertaking than we had supposed,—the bushes, having but a slight tenure of the ground, gave way to the united exertions of a few men with drag ropes; others collected this Scindian shrub in heaps, which being fired, the work of their destruction was completed.

During the whole of February we were kept in a continual state of bustle and excitement; fresh troops and detachments were daily coming in, officers proceeding to join their regiments in advance, and a few to swell the crowd of *grumblers* here.

The flag-ship remained some time after the capture of the fort, and our *blue-coat* friends often visited us on shore. The only sight in the neighbourhood was the Mugger Talloa, or alligators' tank, distant seven or eight miles, to which we frequently went in small parties. Considering the very doubtful degree of friendship that subsisted between the Beloochees and ourselves, it is a matter of surprise, and should be one of thankfulness, that we were not attacked in the hills, on some of these excursions, and cut up to a man. The route to this place lay over an extensive plain, covered with large loose stones, intersected by numerous *nullahs*, and the dry bed of a river.

About four or five miles from the camp is a long range of hills, in one of which is a narrow pass; having cleared this, you get into a valley, which, although actually not much richer than that of Kurachee, has some remote claim to verdure. Proceeding along this valley for about a mile, the white dome of the shrine, rising from amidst a grove of beautiful date and other trees, bursts on the sight, forming one bright spot in the vast desert around. In the neighbourhood, scattered among the hills, are numerous and very perfect tombs, most elaborately and chastely carved in a sort of yellow sandstone. Close to the shrine is the Alligators' Tank, the great lion of the place, on the banks of which is one of the most beautiful trees I ever beheld—a magnificent tamarind, Under this we usually pitched our tent on occasions of picnic, or rather more frequently satisfied ourselves with the shade its noble branches afforded.

The tank in which the alligators are kept is a low marshy place. The number of these animals I should estimate at about eighty or one hundred; many of them are very large, and take them altogether they are very unprepossessing. The subjection in which they are kept by their keeper, an old priest or *Peer*, who lives at the shrine, is quite astonishing; immediately he called them, they assembled on the bank, where they remained till the carcass of a sheep or goat, which was generally presented by the visitors, was thrown among them. The celerity with which this donation was torn limb from limb, and then devoured, was quite remarkable. Where so many were to be fed, and so few could share, of course great exertions were made to secure a portion of the prey, the result of which was usually a contest between several of these horrible creatures, which generally ended by a sly looker-on walking off with the prize.

It is curious to see, feeding in the midst, unheeded and unmolested by the alligators, cows, donkeys, and goats of the neighbouring villages; and yet were one of those animals *thrown* among them it would be torn to pieces. It certainly seems as if they had not only a knowledge of, and respect for, the property of their own villages, but that they were perfectly aware of the presence of any strange animal; dogs which sometimes accompanied the picnic parties to this tank, were always watched by the alligators, and by them in numerous instances destroyed.

Times were now sad and changed for the poor "Muggers"—for instead of receiving the almost universal homage to which they had hitherto been accustomed, scarcely a week passed without a picnic to the tank, and the favourite amusement was throwing bowling-knots over their heads, pulling them ashore, running them up to the tops of trees,—in fact, offering them every indignity that tormenting ingenuity could devise: this, as might be expected, sadly interfered with the discipline of their keeper, making them heedless of his summons to repair to the bank when they saw a large concourse of spectators. The shrine, which is built on a rock close to the tank, is evidently a building of very recent date; there is no architectural beauty about it, and in this respect it contrasts disadvantageously with the tombs to which I have before referred.

Gushing from the rock underneath the shrine, is a beautifully clear hot spring, the temperature of which is about 96°: the water, although having a strong sulphurous smell, possesses no disagreeable taste or property. At about one mile and a half from this is another hot spring, the temperature of which rises to 120°; its qualities appear the same as those of the spring at the shrine. I was astonished to see several natives bathing in the latter without, apparently, suffering the slightest inconvenience from the heat; I put my hand in, but was unable to keep it there many minutes.

Of course both these springs are celebrated for the wonderful cures they perform; there is no bodily ailment for which they do not prove an almost certain remedy; and if used on a stated day, they act infallibly, not only in removing all diseases, but also in preventing their recurrence. The proper day I never could learn, so I did not derive the promised benefit from the charm.

The best of friends must part. The time for the departure of H.M.S. *Wellesley* at length arrived; we were sorry to bid *adieu* to its gallant officers, leaving a blank as they did in our society,—and that, too, in a place where all beside was desolation.

Our horses were the only things that gained by their departure, as they, poor beasts, had double work to do, being always put in requisition to enable our friends to see the alligators' tank before they sailed, and I hope for their sakes left these shores never to return.

When we had been encamped for a few days, we were visited one morning with the severest squall, accompanied by the heaviest rain I ever remember to have witnessed. We were all in the mess-tent at breakfast at the time, and in an incredibly short period the water was flowing through it like a river; the rain came through both flys of the tent, as if they had not been thicker than a lady's pocket-handkerchief;

and but for our exertions in holding on by poles, ropes, &c., our canvas walls must have fallen on us. When it had passed, and we had time to look about us, the appearance presented by the camp was ludicrously dismal. On all sides were to be seen fallen tents, masters and servants rushing indiscriminately about to recover books, papers, boots, shoes, &c., which were streaming through the camp. Such squalls we understood were not uncommon, so we took precautions in case of a repetition.

Shortly after this, we received intelligence of a most distressing event, involving the death of three officers, which had occurred with Sir John Keane's army. A party of officers had gone out shooting some distance from his Excellency's camp, then near Jurhk. Some of the party, however, tired of the amusement, had returned, leaving three officers of the Queen's Royals to pursue their sport. Shortly after, the jungle was observed to be on fire: no fears, however, at the time were entertained for the shooting party; but at length their absence from the camp caused the most fearful apprehensions, which, alas! were too well founded. A party of irregular horse was sent in search early the following morning, and after scouring the country, they at length came on the blackened corpses of the poor fellows.

It was supposed that the jungle had been fired by a party of native sportsmen, in order to drive the game out of cover, and that the unfortunate victims had not perceived their danger until they had become completely and hopelessly surrounded by the devouring element. Thus, by the most awful of deaths, were cut off in the springtime of life three fine young officers, one of them a nephew of my much esteemed friend Major Hibbert; adding another to the many painful and forcible proofs of the truth of that passage "*in the midst of life we are in death*."

The month of February had now drawn to a close. During its passage much of interest had occurred; the reports from our advance were conflicting, but those upon which we could place most reliance were satisfactory and cheering.

Chapter 4

Brigadier Valiant Proceeds to Tatta

Tatta having been suggested as an eligible site for the cantonment for the headquarters of the Scinde field-force, Brigadier Valiant, attended by some of the staff, proceeded to inspect that place, and judge of its fitness. From the inquiries he made as to the nature of the climate, he came to the conclusion that, however advantageous it might be in many respects as a station for troops, in point of healthiness, it would be worse than madness to establish it as a cantonment.

Our camels having arrived, it was found necessary to send them out some distance to forage. A guard furnished from the irregular horse attached to the force accompanied them, but it was unequal to the duty imposed on it. A party of Beloochees succeeded in carrying off several of our cattle: we were consequently obliged to increase our guard, and keep our camels nearer the camp.

Early in the month of March, we were roused from our monotonous and inactive life by the unwelcome appearance of cholera. There is an inexplicable something attendant on this dreadful complaint, whether arising from the painful and appalling suddenness of its nature, whereby, in a few short hours, the man of health becomes a lifeless corpse, or from the knowledge that it has hitherto baffled all the skill and talent of the most scientific and experienced of the medical profession, which strikes terror into the hearts of men who look calmly and resignedly on death in other shapes, and for a time prostrates the energies—nay, seems even to impair the faculties—of the strongest mind.

During the prevalence of this malady, our camp resembled in character what one would suppose of a city infected with the plague; there appeared to be a feeling of dread even in holding communication with one another, fearing to hear some fresh intelligence of the spread and havoc of this relentless scourge. The breeze blew fresh off the sea, and the sun shone bright and clear above us, but yet there was a heavy torpid oppression in the atmosphere which weighed down the spirits, crushed every effort for physical exertion, and extending its influence to the mind, blighted and withered as it rose every thought or impulse of enjoyment.

The gloom thrown over the camp by the ravages of cholera was diversified by the following melancholy event. On the morning of the 20th of March, a report was brought into camp that two officers had been murdered a short distance from it. On inquiry it was found that this report was correct to a most lamentable extent. Captain Hand, an officer of the 2nd Grenadiers, had gone out in the morning to take a walk; having reached the top of a lofty hill about a mile in front of the camp, which he had probably ascended for the purpose of obtaining a view of the country, he discovered in a dark ravine at its bottom, a number of men seated round a camp fire. Being an excellent linguist, and particularly fond of conversing with the natives, it is supposed that he mistook them for some of the gypsies of the country, and went down to talk with them. The party, who in all likelihood had secreted themselves with a view to making another attempt on our cattle when grazing, became alarmed in case he should return to camp and give notice of their being in the neighbourhood, and determined on murdering him.

As he approached, they rose; but he, nothing doubting, moved on. A few of the gang now advanced, and when close on him drew their swords and cut him down. Walpole Clarke, a lieutenant in the same regiment, who was on horseback, happening to see Hand in the distance, rode in the direction for the purpose of joining him. On turning the spur of the hill, he came on the party while they were perpetrating the foul deed.

Impelled by the generous idea that he could save the life of his friend, he dashed his horse in among the ruffians; but seeing that poor Hand's life had already been sacrificed, and that he must himself be soon overpowered by the fearful odds against him—the party amounting to about forty—

He turn'd, and well he'd need,
And dash'd the rowels in his steed.

He was destined, however, not to get off scathless, for a well-directed shot from a matchlock took effect on his thigh. Notwithstanding this, he was enabled to gallop into camp; but, weak from pain and loss of blood, fell from his horse opposite the quarter-guard of H. M. 40th Regiment, to whom he gave information of the sad event.

Immediately on the truth of the report being known in camp, the first idea—the foremost desire—was to take the murderers dead or alive. Acting blindly on the impulse of the moment, however, the best intentions were frustrated; for, instead of co-operating unanimously and on a fixed plan, officers quickly mounted their horses, and in small parties issued from the camp, scouring the country in all directions but the right one, as it afterwards proved.

Fortunate it was, that we did not fall in with the marauders, as few of our parties consisted of more than four or five, and consequently they could not have made much impression on a well-armed, and reckless body, numbering at least eight times that strength.

The Light Company of the 40th was ordered out, but too much time had elapsed since the commission of the murder. The local knowledge of the country possessed by the Beloochees likewise, and the facility and aptitude with which these savages can conceal their arms, and suddenly become *poor shepherds*, placed it beyond hope that they should be taken.

After having, in company with Major Forbes of the 2nd Grenadiers, and Magnay and Irwin of the 40th, traversed a considerable portion of the country, we fell in with Brigadier Valiant, who had come out from camp accompanied by some of his staff, and a party of irregular horse. We continued our search perseveringly, but finding it hopeless, determined on returning home.

Brigadier Valiant ordered me to take one *suwar*, and search for the light company, and order it into camp. This I proceeded to do; but I must confess, I have frequently felt happier when passing some most suspicious and cut-throat-looking ravines, than I did while engaged on this duty. The irregular horseman and myself, having none other to assist us in the event of coming suddenly on any hostile party,—and both our horses being knocked up from the day's work,—I question whether we could have made even a respectable *running fight*. I had, I may say, been in the saddle since four in the morning, at which time I had ridden down to the sea—a distance of three or four miles—to bathe, and had only returned to camp a few minutes ere the alarm was given, when I instantly remounted.

I was unsuccessful in my search for the light company, and hoping that they would reach the camp before me, I directed my steps thither, and arrived shortly after two p. m. Soon after, the company made its appearance, bringing with it a few prisoners, most suspicious-looking villains certainly, but as no proof could be adduced of their having belonged to the party of which we were in pursuit, they were discharged.

Meanwhile the cholera continued to rage: moving the camp and every alternative that could be suggested, were resorted to, but all in vain; Death whirled on in his devastating career. Victim followed victim to the grave, and among those who fell were the youngest and finest of our men.

In the list of those who were thus suddenly summoned to their last account, were Colonel Powell, late commanding the 40th regiment, and Mr. Magnay of the same corps,—the former an old officer who had participated in the glories of the Peninsula, under the immortal Wellington, and had afterwards served with distinction in America. He had, on the morning of the 21st, received intimation of his removal from the 40th to the 6th Regiment. Having sent for me, he delivered to me his farewell order to his old regiment, expressive of his regret at leaving a corps to which from long and pleasing associations he was so much attached. During this interview there was a settled gloom on the veteran soldier's manner, which told me plainly that sorrow at leaving his old corps was not the only saddening thought that pressed on him.

A presentiment (engendered by the contemplation of the melancholy events around him) that his mortal career was drawing to a close possessed his mind and imagination, and, exerting as ever a baneful influence in inciting disease, contributed to draw on his devoted head the stroke which he fain would have averted. In the afternoon he sent for Major Hibbert and myself, to request we would witness his signature to his last will; he spoke then, much and feelingly, of the pleasure he had experienced while in command of the 40th, and assured Major Hibbert, who had succeeded him in the command, of the deep interest he should ever take in the welfare of the corps. Meantime, the cholera was gradually but securely wreathing itself round him; he spoke of the future with the feeling of one who was assured that in this world there was no future for him; and in the air of abstraction that ever and anon stole over him, there was a something which seemed to say,—

I, ere long, that precipice must tread
Whence none return that leads unto the dead.

In the evening the symptoms of cholera became worse, and early the following morning he passed "*that bourne from which no traveller returns.*"

The same morning, Mr. Magnay and myself returned from parade, and afterwards breakfasted together; when this was over, I proceeded to the performance of my duties. About eleven, a.m., I was much shocked to hear that my young friend had been suddenly attacked with the prevalent complaint. Hoping that the report might be incorrect, I hastened over to his tent, where I found him lying on his couch. Not thinking, however,—especially as he appeared in excellent spirits,—that there was much wrong with him, I left him. In a few hours I heard that the symptoms had become most alarming; and on visiting him a second time, I found that his case was hopeless. Poor fellow! he was perfectly aware of the awful change awaiting him; he displayed the most unostentatious fortitude during his illness and severe sufferings: and who shall dare to blame him if, with a calm resignation to the will of the Lord and Giver of life, there should have mingled regret at departing from those pleasant places in which his youthful and happy lot had been cast?

On the evening of the 23rd, the mortal remains of Colonel Powell were consigned to the grave, and on the following afternoon the same last tribute of respect was paid to my poor friend Magnay.

During the 24th we again moved the camp, in the hope that we might shake off the cholera; and towards the end of the month it departed from us as suddenly as it had appeared.

A few nights after we had encamped on our new ground, firing was heard from the picquets on the left of the camp; the alarm being sounded, the whole force immediately turned out, and stood to their arms. Reports had been brought into camp during the day, that considerable parties of Beloochees had been seen moving about on the hills, some distance from camp, and it was thought not improbable that they might attempt a night-attack. After remaining some time under arms, nothing further occurred for which it was at all likely our services would be required, and the corps were dismissed and returned to their tents.

The sentries who fired stated that they had seen a large party approach their posts; that no reply being given to their challenge, they fired into them, and the party retired. We never could learn any further particulars,—probably it was a *ruse* to ascertain the degree of alertness in a British camp at night, in order that they might plan accordingly, either for a general attack, or for petty attempts on property. The only satisfactory part of the whole business was the celerity with which the troops turned out, and the quiet, soldier-like manner in which they fell into their places on the rendezvous of their respective regiments.

Chapter 5

Storm and Capture of Ghuznee

Early in the month of April, orders were received to commence preparations for hutting the men during the monsoon; and the brigadier was busily employed in fixing on a spot of ground suitable for cantonments. Of course there was much diversity of opinion as to the most eligible site; but at length one was decided on, occupying a considerable portion of our second encampment,—the front of the European cantonment facing the sea, the officers' quarters, or rather the compounds in which it was intended the officers' quarters should be built, being on a rising ground in rear of the men. For many reasons I did not coincide with the opinion of the judiciousness of this situation, and ventured to suggest that the front of cantonments should look inland, that the barracks should occupy the range of rising ground, and the officers' compounds be marked out on the low ground between them and the sea. I failed, however, in persuading "the powers that were," that my view was the correct one: there is, nevertheless, a degree of satisfaction in knowing that the plan of cantonments at Kurachee has lately been altered, and that the European barracks are now situated nearly, if not entirely, as I had proposed.

When everything had been settled so far, a new difficulty arose, as to where the wood, &c. were to be procured for the erection of the *pendalls.* The most stringent orders were issued, prohibiting any one, on any pretence whatsoever, from cutting down trees or even entering the *shikargahs* of the *ameers,*—the almost only places where wood suitable for our purposes could be obtained: the consequence was, timber had to be brought from a considerable distance, and our work progressed slowly. The hospitals were commenced first, but owing to the great scarcity of material, and the apparently numerous saints' days in the Scindian calendar, all of which were most religiously kept as holidays, our buildings certainly did not rise as if by magic.

The officers, receiving no allowance from Government for hutting themselves,—being assured, also, by the Scindians that the monsoon in this country was ever slight—and being quite uncertain as to how long they might remain in this place, came to the general determination to weather it in their tents, which resolution, with but few exceptions, was carried into effect.

One of the great sources of annoyance and preventive, or rather destroyer, of comfort in Scinde, was the dust, which was so penetrating, that no measures we could adopt were sufficient for its exclusion; so dense and continuous were those sand-clouds, that for hours together I have been unable to see the nearest tent, which was pitched at not more than ten or fifteen yards from me. The thermometer during the *dust season* always ranges high, and the excessive heat inducing what would be professionally termed a "*healthy* moisture from the articular pores," facilitates and encourages the adhesion of the dust to the face and form, adding neither to the comfort nor elegance of the person.

To make everything the more unbearable, all reports concurred in the certainty of the 40th being stationed here for at least another year; and not even the most sanguine of us could apply the flattering unction to his soul, that there was a probability of our escaping further torment. I have never known any place so generally disliked as Kurachee: I only trust, for the sake of those who may come after us, that it will improve. Assuredly, none of our associations with it were pleasing, and most were melancholy. As for myself I began to feel the influence of an unhealthy climate on my constitution, and was most desirous to re-establish my health by returning to—

——*The dear, small world of home,*
A tiny paradise, from which our wishes never roam.

But the difficulty of achieving this was great; the desire of revisiting England, and self-interest,—which dictated the propriety of my remaining, holding out as an inducement that resistless allurement, *promotion*,—struggled for the mastery; the latter asserted the superiority of its claim, and I can never be too thankful that I resolved to remain with my corps.

To soothe us in our distresses, our brigadier continued to buoy us up with the hope that a regiment would certainly be sent to Deesa towards the end of the year. There is a pleasure in looking on the bright side of things, even when you feel convinced that it amounts to a species of castle-building in the air; for, although it was difficult from the then position of European corps to divine whence one was to spring to occupy Deesa, yet there was a consolation in indulging the hope, that at no distant period we should have an opportunity of disposing of our *landed properties* in that part of the Indian empire.

April passed and was succeeded by May, but not to us the "*merry month of May*," for it brought no relief to vary the sameness of our existence, nor did it produce any improvement in the sanitary condition of the troops. Fever and ague, with dysentery, had succeeded cholera; and although not so appallingly sudden in their attacks nor so fatal in their consequences, they had become so general as to increase to an alarming extent the number of our sick: indeed, during six years that I had served with my regiment abroad, I had never known it so unhealthy.

We continued to receive satisfactory reports of the brilliant manner in which our advance was progressing: so astonished, in fact, were the Affghans with the rapidity of our movements, that it was confidently asserted that the Auckland policy would be carried out without a single shot being fired, except in the shape of royal salutes to commemorate our folly in restoring the long but conveniently neglected Shah Soojah to his empire.

While peace was thus talked of in Afghanistan, we were not without wars and rumours of war in other parts of India; Birmah, Nepaul, and the Punjaub (the state of our old and faithful ally!!) each in its turn was held out as a sort of land of promise, where England's young army was to emulate the deeds of its predecessor. Runjeet Singh, it was said, had departed this life, and a state of fearful anarchy in the selection of his successor would, it was anticipated, follow the brilliant and successful reigns of "one of the most extraordinary upstarts" recorded in history.

As the season advanced, the heat increased in an excessive degree. On the 25th of May I was confined to my tent by a slight attack of fever, brought on by the great power of the sun. A young brother officer, Mr. Irwin, came in the forenoon to visit me. I remarked that he had no other protection for his head than one of our very small forage-caps, and remonstrating with him for going about in the heat of the day so ill protected, I endeavoured to point out to him the great risk he ran. I little thought then the danger was so imminent; the intensity of the heat, aided by the thoughtless exposure I have mentioned, brought on apoplexy, which carried him off the same evening.

Brigadier Valiant having been appointed to the command of the garrison at Bombay, handed over the Scinde force to the next senior officer, Lieutenant-Colonel Spiller, and sailed from Minhora on the 2nd of June, for the purpose of commencing the duties of his new command.

The monsoon having now set in, all communication by sea with Kurachee was cut off for some time; and the little pleasure we drew from the arrival of ships, and the variety contributed by the fresh appearance of troops and new faces, was for a time debarred us.

Thrown on our own resources, cricket was revived, and a tolerably successful attempt to get up a few races being made, we were enabled in this way to occupy such time as was not devoted to our professional duties, or spent in more intellectual amusements.

The rains were certainly not heavy,—mere passing summer showers, compared to what I had seen in India, particularly in Bombay. They were, however, more than welcome, had they done no more than lay the dust. There is an old adage, that every one during his life is doomed to eat a peck of dust; should it be a matter of consequence to achieve in a very short period what we are supposed, under ordinary circumstances, to take a lifetime in performing, I would suggest a *séjour* at Kurachee for one *dust season.*

The *pendalls* were at length finished, and occupied by the troops. They were, however, not only badly constructed, being too low and narrow, but the manner in which they were placed was highly objectionable. Being desirous that they should take up as little space as possible, as well from a misapprehension that, by opposing their front to the prevailing breeze, too great a draught for comfort would be caused, they were built *end on* the breeze; the consequence of which was, that while at one end of this long narrow building there was a strong current of air, there was at the other nothing but suffocation. This led to an indulgence in an injurious, but, I must admit, most pardonable practice, by many of the men,—of leaving their barrack-rooms at night, and sleeping in the open air. Many measures were resorted to to prevent this, and induce the men to abstain from such an indiscretion, but still the evil continued; and certainly it is easy to understand the desire to escape from the stifling effects of a confined barrack-room in the tropics, to breathe a pure atmosphere, even should the present relief be attended with imminent risk.

To this practice is much of the sickness from which the men then suffered to be ascribed; for in no place have I ever experienced anything to equal the heaviness of the dews at Kurachee. In the morning the tents which had remained pitched were as wet outside as if they had been exposed to a heavy shower.

The idea of giving the men huts was of course to add to their comfort, and guard them against unnecessary exposure. I am inclined to think they would have been more healthy in their tents, had the precaution been taken to raise platforms on which to pitch them sufficiently high to guard against the possibility of the rain flowing inside, and having a drain for each tent to carry the water off clear of the camp. The temperature in tents is more even, and the ventilation more easy. Indeed, with regard to the latter part, the facilities are so great, that there is nothing to prevent the walls being taken down once or twice a week, or even oftener, if necessary. I conceive, by adopting this system, the troops would have better preserved their health than in the temporary buildings in which they were quartered at Kurachee, constructed as they were of green unseasoned wood and mud, which had not had time to dry before their occupation by the different regiments.

The principal actor in the murder of Captain Hand, Chaka Kalifa, had been apprehended, and this month we had the satisfaction of hanging the scoundrel on the spot where he had perpetrated his atrocious crime. He was an infatuated priest, more distinguished for his enormities than his virtues. The feeling throughout the country was, that we should not dare to put to death one holding his sacred office; and the astonishment at our carrying our threat into execution was increased considerably by our hanging him,—a mode of execution considered by the Mahommedans the most degrading and ignominious. Springing on the gibbet, Chaka coolly adjusted the rope round his neck, and, gazing calmly around him, seemed evidently to consider himself a martyr, who, by ridding the world of an unbeliever, had done God a service.

In August we learned that the advance army had been repaid for all the hardships it had undergone, by the glorious storm and capture of Ghuznee. Regret, we all did, that we had not participated in its perils and honours, and in the arduous operations connected therewith. Regret, however, was unavailing; and we lived in the hope that, ere long, an opportunity might be granted us of displaying our zeal and prowess in deeds of arms.

A few days brought us the Government order, with the dispatch of his Excellency Sir John Keane, giving the particulars of the storm and capture of Ghuznee. This latter document has frequently been challenged, on account of its extreme prolixity and verbosity; and the opening paragraph, at least,—however flattering it may be to those who shared in the exploit,—must appear overcharged, emanating, as it did, from one who, during a service of forty-five years in every quarter of the globe, had shared in the glories of some of the most eventful and most brilliant feats of arms of this or any other age.

The very sudden and extraordinary manner in which the fortress of Ghuznee had been captured, while it astonished and almost paralysed the Affghans, had dashed to the ground any reasonable hope that the reserve might have entertained of being actively employed, notwithstanding a report which was most industriously circulated, that a force was to set out immediately from Kurachee to attack Khelat, the stronghold of Meerab Khan.

Meanwhile the overflow of the Indus began to subside, and the waters gradually to disappear from the country near its banks, which had been inundated. The exhalation from the marshy plains producing, as is usual, fever of the most virulent description, fully verified the worse predictions of those who had been inimical to Tatta being fixed upon as a site for cantonments. The list of mortality among the troops which were stationed at this place was something fearful. The 22nd and 26th Regiments, Bombay N. I., were indeed completely *hors de combat*; scarcely a man of either of these regiments escaped the influence of the malady. Indeed, when the latter corps was brought (march it could not) to Kurachee from Tatta, whence it was absolutely necessary to withdraw it, it may, without exaggeration, be asserted, that the whole was in hospital, and so completely disorganized by sickness that it was evident a very large proportion of the men would never sufficiently recover to be enabled to continue their service as effective soldiers.

Chapter 6

Capture of Khelat

In September our communication by sea was re- opened, and fresh detachments of troops destined to serve in this fearful climate continued to pour in. Brigadier F. Farquharson arrived from Bombay, and relieved Lieutenant-Colonel Spiller from command of the Scinde force.

The great and exciting piece of intelligence received at this time, was the storm and capture, by the intrepid little band under General Willshire, of the fortress of Khelat, on the 13th of November,—one of the most dashing morning achievements ever performed, and certainly, for brilliancy of conception and the gallantry displayed in its execution, second to no event in the Affghan campaign.

The perils of this campaign as far as mortal foe was concerned, were now at an end, but many of those who had sustained its hardships and perils were destined never to return; cholera of a most malignant kind broke out at Sukkur, shortly after the return of the Bombay division, and caused severe loss, particularly in the lines of the 4th Light Dragoons, two of whose officers, Captain Ogle and Mr. Janvrin, fell victims.

Towards the end of the year numbers of the Affghanistan heroes made their appearance in camp, *en route* to Bombay: of course they were much *lionized*, and their varied accounts of the stirring events of the campaign were listened to with the liveliest pleasure and interest.

Early in February several of the officers of the Scinde force were ordered from Kurachee to Sukkur on that most unpleasant of all our duties—a court-martial. To render it still more disagreeable, the individual to be tried was an officer, and the charges against him were of a most serious character, affecting his reputation as a soldier in the most vital and vulnerable point.

The 2nd (Queen's Royals) marched into camp this month, and encamped some distance in rear of the lines of the 40th. I went out to meet the regiment, to welcome back my friend and brother-adjutant Simmons, and congratulate him on his recovery from the wounds he had received at Ghuznee and Khelat,—at both of which places he had been distinguished for his bold and gallant bearing. I had not seen the Queen's for upwards of six years, and was much struck with their fine steady soldier-like appearance. But for their *honourable rags*, they gave one the idea of a regiment fresh from the barrack-yard, rather than a corps returning from a long and arduous campaign.

By the arrival of my friend Lieutenant F. White from England, I was relieved from the duties of Adjutant, which I most unwillingly resigned.

On the 18th of February, his Excellency, now Lord Keane, arrived in camp. The following day he fixed upon for the presentation to the 40th Regiment of a handsome stand of colours, the gift of our late distinguished Colonel, General Sir James Kempt.

About four p. m., on the afternoon of the 19th, H. M. 40th Regiment being drawn up in line, received with the usual honours his Excellency Lord Keane, who came on the ground attended by Prince Hyder Khan (Dhost Mahommed Khan's son, who had been taken prisoner at Ghuznee), and a numerous staff.

After his Lordship had received the salute, he proceeded to the right of the line, moved down the front, and made a most minute inspection of the corps; then, passing along the rear, returned to his place in front. Upon this the grenadiers, which I had the honour to command, having advanced a few paces, wheeled to the left and marched along the front of the line, preceded by the band playing *the British Grenadiers*; on reaching the centre of the line they halted, and having opened their ranks received with presented arms the old colours, which were then conveyed by the guard of honour to the left of the line (the band playing as before), and there handed over, under a "general salute," to an escort formed a short distance in rear of the line. During the latter part of the ceremony, the remainder of the regiment formed three sides of a square, the bass drum was placed in the centre of the blank face, and the grenadiers which had returned formed in rear of the drum.

The new colours having been placed on the drum, his Lordship, attended by his staff and all the officers in camp—among whom was the hero of Khelat—and accompanied by a number of ladies, entered the square. The ceremony of consecrating the colours having been performed in a heartily impressive manner by our much-respected chaplain the Rev. Mr. Burnell, they were handed over to Lord Keane, the guard of honour presenting arms. His Lordship now addressed the regiment, taking a review of its past services, and dwelling particularly on the Peninsula, where he himself had witnessed the acquisition of its brightest laurels. He expressed a regret, in which we all most cordially joined, that he had not had us with him in the late campaign; and his conviction that we only wanted the opportunity of filling up the little space left in our colours, to add many more to the noble victories, with the names of which they were now so nearly covered. His Lordship, having concluded by complimenting the regiment on its fine, healthy, and *business-like* appearance, and expressing his hope that he would ere long meet it in that best of lands, "Old England," delivered the colours to Ensigns Russell and Vance, the senior Ensigns, the grenadiers again presenting arms.

Major Hibbert, commanding the 40th, then, in behalf of the regiment, tendered his best thanks to Lord Keane for the honour he had done the corps in presenting the colours, and the flattering allusions he had made to its past services, assuring his Lordship, that should the time come when the services of the 40th would be required in the field, that the young 40th would be actuated by the same spirit that had distinguished the "old and bold," in by-gone days. The gallant major also expressed his gratitude to the Rev. Mr. Burnell for the very eloquent and impressive manner in which he had performed the sacred ceremony of consecration.

The square was now reduced, and line re-formed; the ranks were opened, and the guard of honour proceeded, attended by the band and new colours, to the left of the line, filing along the front in slow time. When the Ensigns, with the colours, reached the centre, they moved into their places, on which a royal salute was fired from a battery of nine-pounders, that had been drawn up in front and at right-angles to the 40th, by a company of Bombay artillery, under Captain Brett, who had expressed a wish, and had obtained the sanction of the authorities, to pay this compliment to H. M. 40th.

The grenadiers having recovered their place in line, the whole regiment presented arms; ranks were then closed, and the battalion broke into open columns of divisions right in front, and marched past in review order. Thus ended the presentation of colours to H. M. 40th regiment,—a ceremony perhaps the most imposing, impressive, and interesting a soldier can witness.

I regret not being in possession of a copy of the addresses of his Lordship and the Rev. Mr. Burnell, and of the reply of Major Hibbert, the perusal of which would have conveyed to the reader, unversed in such matters, a far better idea of the impressive nature of the ceremony than can be derived from my imperfect description.

On the following day his Excellency embarked for Bombay, on board one of the Honourable Company's ships, which had been placed at his disposal by the Bombay Government. With his departure from Scinde may be said to have terminated the first Affghan campaign, and the first act connected with the extraordinary policy pursued towards that country. A peerage was awarded to the gallant chief of the army, and Government was profuse in bestowing honours on the persons who had distinguished themselves in the campaign. The public mind was intoxicated with our military successes, the steady perseverance of our troops, bearing down in their triumphant advance every obstacle which the energy and ingenuity of an enterprising enemy, or the treachery of fictitious friends, could suggest.

The extraordinary rapidity of their movements, and the dazzling splendour of their achievements, contributed for a time to conceal the iniquity, the impolicy, and the errors of our unholy aggression;—a popular monarch had been driven from his throne, and, in his stead, had been foisted on an unwilling people a detested and unprincipled tyrant. Our relations, diplomatic and hostile, had been greatly extended, while our power to maintain these relations with dignity had certainly not been increased, if indeed it were not weakened.

The progress of Shah Soojah through his capitals was marked, it was said, by the most joyous welcome of the inhabitants; but these acclamations, if neither constrained nor purchased, were as hollow, unmeaning, and evanescent as popular applause usually is; for the dull sullen murmurings of insurrection which already echoed through the land, gave evidence of the existence of a rooted feeling of disaffection in an insulted people,—prevented only by the presence of a foreign army from hurling from the throne one who had already been rejected as incapable of governing them.

A few days after the departure of Lord Keane, H. M. 17th Regiment, a wing of the 4th Light Dragoons, and a troop of Horse Artillery, marched into camp.

The Queen's, having, fortunately for us, been ordered to proceed to Deesa, embarked from Kurachee for Mandavie in country boats, and from thence marched to their new cantonment by the same route that the 40th had pursued in 1839. Our houses at Deesa were purchased by our friends of the Queen's, and we were once more men without property. The 17th Regiment marched a few days afterward for Bombay, concluding their perils by land and flood with a shipwreck. The steady exemplary conduct of this regiment, when the *Hannah*, in which they were, struck on a sand-bank off the Hujamree mouth of the Indus, and became a complete wreck, was worthy of universal admiration, and called forth the most marked approbation of Government.

Gradually the horse-artillery and dragoons disappeared, and Kurachee relapsed into its former uninteresting state. The weather becoming excessively hot, many of us procured leave, and went to Fort Minhora for the benefit of sea-bathing, and pure fresh air. Boating was the principal amusement, and much enjoyment was derived from the excellent fishing. Turtle we got in numbers; but they were either of an inferior quality, or we understood not the *cunning art* of properly preparing them for the table. While at Minhora, I received intimation that his Excellency the commander-in-chief in India had been pleased to reappoint me to the adjutancy of the regiment,—vacant by the resignation of my friend Ferdinand White. Accordingly I proceeded to Kurachee, and on the 1st of May received charge of the office, and recommenced the performance of its duties.

Chapter 7

State of Upper Scinde and Afghanistan

The month of May set in with a more than usual degree of heat, the thermometer rising in tent to about 120° in the middle of the day. Our sufferings here were, however, a mere trifle compared to those of the force stationed at Sukkur. The officers of the 40th, who had been absent on court-martial duty at that place, returned about this time, and described the heat there as positively terrific.

Upper Scinde was now in a state of insurrection, and indeed over the whole of Affghanistan the spirit of revolt was spreading. A most disastrous event occurred this month in Upper Cutchee. Lieutenant Walpole Clarke, of the 2nd Bombay Grenadiers, who had so narrowly escaped with his life in his gallant, but fruitless, attempt to save Captain Hand in March, 1839, had shortly after that melancholy occurrence been appointed to a corps of Scinde irregular cavalry. Early in May he left the Fort of Khan, in charge of an escort of camels, accompanied by a small body of infantry, and a detachment of his own corps. Having marched about twenty miles on his return to Sukkur, he directed a portion of the infantry,—with which his party had been strengthened, the more easily to enable him to get his escort clear of the passes,—to return to Khan, and ordered the remainder of his force to bivouac.

While in this position, he was attacked by an overwhelming body of the Beloochees. Leaving his cavalry to protect the camels, he placed himself at the head of the infantry, and advanced to meet the enemy. Long and stubbornly was the contest maintained; but at length the gallant commander fell, the infantry were cut up to a man, and the cavalry, overpowered by the increasing numbers of the Beloochees, were obliged to retreat, leaving the enemy masters of the field, and in possession of the camels, stores, &c. Elated with their success, the Beloochees started in pursuit of the small party returning to Khan, and having come up to them, fell on them, leaving not one to carry back the tale of this serious disaster.

During our long campaign in Scinde and Afghanistan, many a gallant soldier fell; but among the noble spirits that fled, there was not one more chivalrous and daring than Walpole Clarke.

Scinde meanwhile continued in a most disturbed condition; the whole of the Upper Province was in a state of insurrection, and Nusser Khan at the head of a large force of Beloochees was in the field. Early in July, a requisition was made by the political agent for H. M. 40th regiment, for service to Upper Scinde. The Brigadier at Kurachee, however, declined complying with this request to the full extent, as it would have left Kurachee almost entirely unprotected. It was therefore arranged that only one half should for the present be moved, and the right wing, under Captain Boscawen, was ordered to hold itself in readiness for this duty. On the 16th of July, two companies only, under Captain Stopford, embarked at Gizree Creek, for Gharra, *en route* to Tatta, sufficient boats to move the whole force not being procurable at that time. The heat to which this detachment was exposed, at the commencement of its march from Gharra to Tatta, was excessive; and several cases of apoplexy occurred, three of which, on the first day's march, proved fatal.

On the arrival of Captain Stopford's detachment at Tatta, it embarked on board the Company's steamers, and moved up the Indus to Sukkur. It being necessary to await the return of the steamers to Tatta, the remainder of the wing did not leave Kurachee till the 10th of August, on which day it embarked at Gizree Creek, following the same route as the detachment by which it had been preceded. I regretted much that the headquarter wing had not been sent, and much more that the wings had been detached,—always considering, as I do, the separation of a regiment a fair subject for regret; unfortunately, it is too often necessary and unavoidable.

On his arrival at Tatta, Captain Boscawen found that the steamers would not afford sufficient accommodation for the whole of the detachment; Captain Adamson was therefore directed to assume the command of such portion as it was found necessary to embark in the small river-boats. All at length reached their destination, and took up position at Sukkur. On the passage up the river, Captain Boscawen, at the request of the political agent at Hyderabad, inspected the

Luckee Pass, and found that the road which had been made by Lord Keane's army was now entirely washed away, and that the route the *corps d'armée* had followed was no longer practicable.

Towards the end of August occurred the disastrous defeat of Major Clibborn, at Nuffoosk,—in all its results a most painful and calamitous event, evidencing, as it did, gross ignorance of the country or a recklessness utterly indefensible in sending a detachment on a most difficult service, by a route almost impracticable,—not only imparting additional confidence to an already sufficiently active and determined enemy, but enriching them with our stores, arms, and ammunition, and tending to impress our native troops with an exaggerated opinion of the warlike qualities of the Beloochees.

Khelat had now fallen, and it became necessary that it should be retaken. Numerous were the reports as to the destinations of different corps; several of the regiments in this country which expected to return to India, found, from the state of affairs in Scinde, that the corps which had come for the purpose of relieving them, could now be viewed only as reinforcements. Fresh troops were pouring in from all quarters, and most extensive operations were anticipated. Dhost Mahommed had appeared in force in the north of Afghanistan, and had already gained considerable advantages; while in Upper Scinde, Nusser Khan, with his lawless hordes, was devastating that unhappy province.

The headquarters of H. M. 40th Regiment received orders early in September to be in readiness to march to Sukkur on the 15th of October. On the 8th of October, we were reinforced by a strong detachment of recruits amounting to about two hundred; and a few days after, Mr. Talbot of H. M. 13th Light Infantry, and a few men from that regiment, landed at Kurachee, and were attached to the 40th.

The only camels procurable, we obtained at Soomneamnee; they were of a most inferior description and unequal to carry much more than half the load usually placed on this animal. Notwithstanding this, no increase was made to the number of camels furnished; the consequence of which was that the men had to travel with very reduced kits, and were unable to take with them their bedding, which was put into store until an opportunity should offer for sending it after the regiment, when it was known where it would eventually be stationed. Among other annoyances, we experienced the greatest difficulty in getting camel-men, and the few we did procure were utter barbarians and in no way to be depended on.

By the 16th, all was declared ready for a start, and on the morning of the 18th of October, we marched from Kurachee *en route* for Larkhana,—where report said we were to be joined by General Brooks and some more troops,—thence to proceed through the Gundava Pass to Khelat. This pass it was arranged should be occupied by the 25th Bombay Regiment, which had moved up the country a short time before, under Colonel Marshall.

Our small force consisted of headquarter H. M. 40th Regiment, a company of European artillery without their guns, under Lieutenant Sealy, and a small detachment of H. M. 13th Light Infantry, under Ensign Talbot, the whole commanded by Major Hibbert of the 40th. The route as far as Sehwan having never been traversed by troops before, a greater degree of interest was attached to that comparatively unexplored part of the country, especially as our commander was required to make a report on its resources, and how far it would be practicable or advisable to send large detachments by this route for the future.

As our rear guard left cantonments, a Company's steamer entered the harbour, having on board H.M. 41st Regiment; this was an entirely accidental circumstance, but was not without its effect in giving the natives of the country a great opinion of our resources, and admirable arrangement. Our first march was to Doozan, a halting-place for Caffillas, a distance of about ten miles over an extensive, uncultivated, and uninteresting plain. The heat was most oppressive, and tended greatly to increase the number of our sick,—so great a portion of our men being recruits, not only uninured to the climate, but having only landed a few days before from on board ship, where they had been shut up four or five months on their passage from England. Owing to the badness of the camels, and the mal-arrangements of the commissariat, our equipage and stores did not come into camp until late in the afternoon; and when the latter did arrive, there was no fuel of any description to enable the men to set about their cooking,—rather a bad beginning for our march.

Considering that we were distant only ten miles from a cantonment that we had occupied for nearly two years, the fact of the total want of wood or any other fuel at this place, and the scarcity and excessive brackishness of the water, ought to have been known to the quartermaster-general's department. On the 19th we were compelled to halt, but having replaced some of the camels which had already given in, we resumed our march on the morning of the 20th to Peeprie. Owing to the intense heat, we deemed it expedient to convert our night into day, and determined on marching for the future every morning at two o'clock,—a system, by adopting which we were more likely to preserve the health of the men, but which was certainly a most tiresome and unprofitable manner of travelling.

The country through which we passed the second day was more rugged, and the long range of the Halla Mountains on our left contributed to improve its general appearance. We encountered a few *nullahs*, which would have presented considerable obstacles to the passage of guns, cavalry, &c., though a very little pioneering would have rendered them thoroughly practicable. Our encamping-ground was good and extensive, water excellent and abundant. No supplies, however, of any sort were to be procured. A short distance from our camp was a small hill-fort, nearly in ruins; there lived a few shepherds, and round it were some fine trees, but no traces of cultivation appeared.

Today, October 20, we heard that our right wing had likewise taken the field, and that they were in expectation of meeting the enemy on the 18th. The arrival of the overland mail brought us intelligence of the promotion of my friends Boscawen and White. The current rumour of the day was, that we should be obliged to move on and take the Gundava Pass, a service which it was intended should have been performed by Colonel Marshall, with the 25th Regiment. He, however, finding that his camels were failing him, had fallen back on Sehwan, whence embarking his men in river boats, he proceeded up the river to Sukkur.

On the 21st, we continued our march, entering the Gorban Pass, the country about which was very picturesque and grand, though barren; but the Pass itself was not one of any great strength, and could easily be turned. Our halting-ground today was on the banks of the dry bed of a river; the encamping ground was good and extensive, and water was procurable in large quantities and of very good quality, by digging in the bed of the river to a depth of one or two feet. The grazing for our baggage-cattle, too, was excellent, and no difficulty was experienced in procuring good forage for our horses. No supplies of grain were, however, obtainable; the country around was thoroughly uncultivated—there was not a trace of its being inhabited, no human being moving about, and not even cattle or sheep to be seen feeding on the hills to give an air of life to the scene around.

The weather had become rather cooler, but still it was most oppressive, and our young soldiers suffered much; our cattle, also, were now completely exhausted. The distance of this day's march was only about twelve miles, but several of our camels were unable to bring their loads into camp. The officer of the rearguard sent in to report that unless some of the camels which had already reached the camp, returned to assist in bringing up the baggage, he should be obliged to abandon a great portion of it. We were compelled, consequently, to send out our already over-worked cattle; and the rearguard today did not arrive in camp until about four p.m., having been nearly fourteen hours in traversing a distance of twelve miles, over a country not at all difficult for camels.

On the 22nd of October, we were forced to halt and rest our cattle. A dispatch was sent off to Major Outram, the political agent at Hyderabad, representing our crippled state, in the hope that he would be able to give us some assistance. On the 23rd we marched to Trak, about sixteen miles, the country still continuing to display the same desolate, rugged, uncultivated, and uninhabited character it had presented since the commencement of our march. An extensive Mahomedan burying-ground, close to our camp, alone gave evidence that the country was, or once had been, peopled.

Our misfortunes increased as we went on, and the last blow seemed now to have been struck at the efficiency of our camels. Quantities of oleander bushes flourished in the neighbourhood of the camp, and many of our cattle fed eagerly on them: unfortunately for us, this shrub turned out a most powerful poison; several of our camels died from eating it, and many were rendered for a long time incapable of service.

Water was rather scarce at Trak, but what we did get was of excellent quality. Notwithstanding our crippled state, we struggled on to Dummuj on the 24th, a distance of about ten miles. We had anticipated that a considerable quantity of our baggage would be left behind, and were agreeably surprised to find that the greater part of it reached the camp, although it was certainly late before it all came in. Two of my camels died from the effects of poison; owing, however, to the kindness of my friend Thomas Nelson, who had charge of the commissariat, my kit all came up on one of his spare camels. Dummuj was the first village we had seen since leaving Kurachee: it was composed of a few miserable huts, built of matting; there was no cultivation about the place; the inhabitants were shepherds, but on our approach had driven their flocks some distance into the hills, having probably formed no very high estimate of our character for honesty.

We could not procure supplies of any kind here; there were two *banyan*-shops, but they contained only sufficient to satisfy the wants of the villagers. Shortly after we had encamped, the chief man of the village, accompanied by several others, visited us: the former was one of the finest old men I ever saw; his beautifully regular features and splendid white beard gave him a most patriarchal and venerable appearance. He was not without vanity, and to judge from the satisfaction he evinced in regarding himself in a small looking-glass, presented to him by Major Hibbert, it was evident he was fully aware that he had no slight claims to be considered handsome. The old gentleman was particularly civil, and sent us a present of some new milk and fresh eggs, both of which were very acceptable. Water was scarce, there being only one well; it was consequently a tedious operation—watering our baggage and other cattle.

Here I was fortunate in being able to hire two camels to replace those I had lost. I could not persuade the owner to go further than Sehwan; but even this piece of good fortune was more than I had expected, having made up my mind that I should be obliged to leave behind me the grain which, from suspicion of the poverty of the country, I had luckily taken the precaution to bring with me for my horses. On the 25th we continued our march to Marraie, another small village similar to that of Dummuj.

Having been unable to procure any supplies since leaving Kurachee, our stores were beginning to get very low. On approaching our ground, I was rather amused to see our commissary driving before him a large herd of milch cows. His request to the villagers for sheep had been most pertinaciously refused, and he had adopted this system to frighten them into a compliance with his demands. There was a marked difference in the bearing towards us of the lords of the soil here, and that of our friends at Dummuj. The former were most anxious to get us out of their vicinity on any terms; and even went so far as to say, that there was only one very small well near the village, from which it would be impossible to supply the wants of all our force, adding a suggestion that we should continue our march for about three miles further, where we should obtain a plentiful supply.

We had already marched upwards of sixteen miles, and did not feel inclined to extend our morning's walk, and moreover we were not at all disposed to take for gospel all that we were told in this country. A little searching proved that we were correct in our surmises; for, at a short distance from the village, we observed several spots where the earth had apparently been lately disturbed, and on continuing our scrutiny, found three or four wells which had been carefully filled up with sand and bushes. After a little working with fatigue parties the wells were cleared, and afforded us as much water as we required. We made special report of the insolence of the villagers to the political agent, with a view to his laying it before the *ameers*, and no doubt the chief man of Marraie received the thanks of their Highnesses for his friendly conduct to their allies.

On the 26th, we resumed our march to Dooba, and continued advancing every day until the 30th, when we came to another village, Choula. From this Major Hibbert and Mr. Nelson went on in advance to Sehwan, in order to make arrangements to facilitate our moving on as quickly as possible to Larkhana.

In the evening a few of our young men went out to ride, and succeeded in losing their way; it was very late before they returned to camp. I confess I was becoming most anxious about them, knowing well the very questionable terms of affection on which we were with the natives.

On the 31st we marched into Sehwan, our baggage-cattle quite exhausted, notwithstanding it had occupied us fourteen days in accomplishing a march of about one hundred and forty miles. The country through which we passed was certainly trying for the cattle; the supply of forage, generally speaking, was limited and bad; in most places the water was not only scarce, but difficult to be got at;—frequently, doubtless, many of the numerous cattle in our train were but scantily supplied with this vital necessary, and often probably not at all,—added to which, at several of the halting-places it was exceedingly brackish.

The country between Kurachee and Sehwan is altogether uncultivated,—in many places, indeed, incapable of cultivation, and, with the exception of Dummuj and Marraie, uninhabited. Supplies of the most common description are unprocurable; and any force marching through this territory in its present state, would be dependent entirely on its own resources.

CHAPTER 8

Defeat of Dhost Mahommed

The approach to Sehwan was through a grove of beautiful tamarind and palm trees, near which, and on the south side of the city, our encampment was situated.

The city is built on a rising ground, on the banks of the River Arul, and is distant about two or three miles from the mighty and classic Indus, of which we got our first view on October the 31st. Sehwan is larger than Kurachee, but, from the deserted appearance of many quarters of the town, I should say it did not possess so large a population: the greater majority of the inhabitants I saw appeared to be Hindoos.

In its neighbourhood are numerous very fine mosques and tombs, and within the city is a remarkably splendid *musjid*, erected in honour of the celebrated Mahommedan saint, Lai Shah Beg.

The object, however, of greatest note here is the old Castle of Sehwan, which, although now in ruins, is sufficiently perfect to attest its former strength. The inspection of this extensive and venerable pile, with its still numerous arches, cells, and passages, compensates fully for the time and trouble it requires; calling up, as it does, a host of associations connected with the progress of Alexander the Great through this country, to which his deeds have added an imperishable interest.

This castle is generally conjectured to be coeval with the time of Alexander the Great; indeed, the following extract from such an authority as Burnes goes far to confirm this supposition:—

> The old castle of Sehwan, the erection of which is attributed to Alexander the Great, is perhaps the only veritable relict of the age of the Greeks which can be traced in Scinde; and coins have lately been found in it, which, when submitted to the

careful inspection of Mr. Princep, will probably attest its high antiquity. It is built on a mound of earth, nearly eighty feet in height, fifteen hundred long, and eight hundred broad, intersected by subterraneous passages.

While at Sehwan, we received letters from our right wing, mentioning that the force under Major Boscawen, of which it formed part, had been slightly engaged near Cunda, in Upper Scinde, on the 18th of October, when they had cut up a number of the enemy, sustaining little or no loss themselves.

Subsequently, in consequence of Dadur being threatened by Nusser Khan, Major Boscawen with his small detachment moved on that place, and reached it on the morning of the 30th of October. Unfortunately, on its arrival, the *Political* had not correct information of the movements of the Khan, (no very unusual circumstance,) and had but little idea that his Highness was close upon him. Never dreaming that their services would be required, the men were dismissed, and were busily engaged in pitching their tents, when, to the surprise and disgust of all, intelligence was brought in that Nusser Khan, with a large force, was actually encamped within one or two miles of the fort, and had been there some days. Orders were instantly given for the troops to fall in, and advance on the enemy. It was, however, too late; for his Highness, now apprised of the proximity of this detachment, which, it would appear, had come on him as unexpectedly as the news of his Highness being so near had on the *Political*, had commenced his retreat, and, long before Major Boscawen could get near his camp, had fled. The gallant major and his little band were thus deprived of a very excellent chance of securing his Highness, and effectually crushing any further attempt at disturbance in the country.

A few camels, tents, &c., fell into our hands; but the regret at having lost this opportunity of bringing the young chief to action was heightened when, on entering his camp, our troops found the mangled body of Lieutenant Loveday. This young officer had been political agent at Khelat; on its fall he was taken prisoner, and, during his captivity, was treated with the greatest barbarity. When Nusser Khan went on any of his expeditions, Loveday was invariably taken with him, being carried about in a *kajavah*, (a sort of chair, placed like a pannier on either side of a camel,) to which he was chained, exposed to the burning heat of the climate, and almost entirely divested of clothing. When he was found, his head was nearly severed from the trunk, which was yet warm, and the galling chain had struck into, and grated on, his weak and emaciated body. Poor fellow! it was hard to die, when imagination must have been whispering hopes of future enjoyment, and a speedy restoration to his friends and countrymen,—and yet death must have been a release.

Continual marching is most wearisome; we were therefore not at all sorry to find that it required a few days to make arrangements for our future movements, and that we should thus have an opportunity of resting ourselves, and remodelling our kits to meet the capabilities of our baggage-cattle. Finding it impossible to get any addition to our camels, it was determined that the company of artillery under Lieutenant Sealy should embark here, and move up the river to Larkhana, taking with them the heavy baggage,—the remainder of the detachment crossing the Arul close to Sehwan, and moving direct on Larkhana.

The stream here is sluggish, but rather deep, and the bottom is composed of slippery and tenacious mud; the breadth of the stream, at this time, was from thirty to forty yards. To guard against delay, and prevent as much as possible any injury befalling the camels, an attempt was made by a few of the *scientific* men of the force, among whom I include myself, to construct a bridge of boats. I am constrained to admit that we failed in our laudable exertions for the good of the service; but at the same time, in justice to myself and fellow-labourers, I must remark that, had the promises of procuring boats made by our native agent, who had come from Hyderabad, been fulfilled, not only would our endeavours have been crowned with success, but the passage of the River Arul would have occupied about one-fourth of the time it did, and many a camel which was rendered unserviceable by sticking in the mud, slipping, and straining itself in its attempts at extrication, would have been preserved. They are most helpless animals in deep water;—it is, I believe, a fact in natural history, that they cannot swim; and when the stream is deep, and the bed muddy and slippery, as was the case in this instance, they become perfectly paralysed by terror, and with difficulty can be induced to move. Several of our camels occupied nearly a whole day and night in crossing the Arul.

The best method of getting camels across a river when boats cannot be procured, and which we adopted at length with success, is by tying their legs together and floating them over on their sides.

On the 6th of November, the artillery embarked and proceeded *en route* to Larkhana, and on the same evening all our cattle and baggage were on the left bank of the Arul; on the 7th we halted to recruit the camels, after their exertions in fording the river; and on the morning of the 8th we again resumed our march, moving on Tartee, a distance of about nine or ten miles.

Here we encamped on the banks of a beautiful and extensive lake, very prettily, though not finely, wooded. There was a boat on it, into which some of our party got, in the hope of having some wild-fowl shooting, but they were not repaid for their trouble, not even seeing any.

The country through which we now passed was most extensively cultivated, affording a pleasing contrast to the wild barren hills we had left behind. The finest crops of Kirbee I have ever seen, were in the fields around Tartee, and our horses and cattle revelled in the delightful change afforded them.

From our camels being so much less heavily laden, we were enabled to move along more quickly than we could at the commencement of our march,—added to which, water was always to be obtained in abundance, and we had now the means of feeding the camels in a manner that enabled them to perform their work. The only difficulty now experienced was on account of the many irrigation canals over which we had to pass; the bridges being narrow and few, our baggage was much delayed.

The detention was greatly increased, and the difficulties much augmented by our servants and the camel-drivers, who, in their obstinate anxiety to get quickly on, persisted in crowding and pushing one another. Not the least provoking part of this emulation to get first over the bridges was, that camels, loads and all, were often precipitated into the canal, where, of course, everything became well saturated with mud and water, or more frequently altogether lost.

Our line of march was most tortuous; frequently we moved for miles along the banks of the mighty Indus, then entering a dense forest of *baubul* and mangrove, would leave the river, and lose sight of it altogether for some days.

The natives at the different villages through which we passed, were very civil and obliging; the country, as we neared Larkhana, was neither so rich, nor so well and extensively cultivated, as in the neighbourhood of Sehwan. With the exception of the lake at Tartee, and the variety afforded by occasional glimpses of the Indus, there is nothing beautiful or interesting in the march from Sehwan, the country generally being flat and monotonous.

On the 16th we marched into Larkhana.[1] Here we were delighted to find awaiting us a fresh supply of camels, which had been sent out from Sukkur, in consequence of our representation of the wretched plight in which we were. The general at Sukkur was very anxious for our arrival: the accounts from the north were represented as most unsatisfactory; and Nusser Khan, who was still at large, kept our troops continually employed and moving about.

The commissariat having to make a few arrangements connected with the camels, it was decided that we should halt here until the arrival of Lieutenant Sealy, with his company of artillery, and the heavy baggage.

Larkhana is a fine eastern town, cleaner than any I have seen in Scinde,—indeed, I might say in India. Its extent and population seemed greater than that of Sehwan. Previous to encamping we crossed the great Larkhana Canal, the bed of which is very deep and wide; during our stay here it was perfectly dry Near our camp were some singularly fine palm-trees, and in the vicinity several extensive and very well arranged gardens and orchards, containing numerous mango, plantain, orange and lime trees, &c. This, however, was not the fruit season, so we did not benefit to the full extent from the gardens. The walls of the fort are of mud, and appeared in tolerably good repair. In the city was a fine mosque, near which, in a large cage made of staves driven into the ground, covered over with a slight roofing of matting, was a magnificent tigress, to which the natives attached the attribute of immortality. This wild tenant of the forest appeared perfectly satisfied with its position,—indeed, if it had been anxious to visit the depths of the jungles, one good leap would, I should think, have razed its rickety prison with the ground.

On the evening of the 19th Lieutenant Sealy, with his detachment, made his appearance; and having on the 21st, again set out on our travels, we reached Sukkur on the morning of the 25th. The country between Larkhana and Sukkur, is not so rich or well cultivated as that near the Arul; on its left bank, there is also a greater extent of jungle. We found, however, supplies of grain, forage, &c., in sufficient quan-

1. "Beyond Sehwan is the large town of Larkhana, containing about five thousand inhabitants, the capital of one of the most fertile districts in Sindh, being that watered by the Indus, and the large branch called the Narrah, before mentioned: it throws off below Sukkur. Larkhana, like most of the towns in Sindh, presents a miserable and dilapidated appearance, though it bears evident marks of having been at one time a place of considerable size and importance; a large canal from the river affords means of water communication during the floods."—*Postans's Sindh.*

tities for a much larger force than ours, and at a very moderate rate. The natives were civil, with the exception of those at one village, who were unwilling to provide us with anything; indeed, one old scoundrel ordered some of us out of the village, threatening, in case of refusal, to send Dhost Mahommed after us. From this we inferred, that accounts must have reached them of further successes on the part of this unfortunate, dishonoured, and most ill-used prince.

Captain Delhoste, quartermaster-general, came out on the morning of the 25th to meet our force, and direct us to our position in camp at Sukkur: from him we learned the very unexpected intelligence of the defeat of Dhost Mahommed by Brigadier Dennie at Bamean, and his subsequent surrender to the envoy at Cabul. These events had, of course, dispelled for the present all our hopes of active employment in Afghanistan; for the now blasted fortunes of our fallen but noble enemy, and the fact of his being a prisoner would, it was asserted, be the means of restoring peace to Affghanistan,—"of tranquillizing the spirit of insurrection which was rife in various parts of the country, and of effectually destroying all influence Dhost Mahommed might have hoped to create; and—by establishing Shah Soojah securely on the throne, and insuring the extensive exercise of his power,—of removing all the encouragement afforded to dangerous intrigues, by the division of Affghanistan into weak and disunited chiefships."[2]

The defeat of the *Dhost* was as fortunate as it was unlocked for. It was then regarded as one of the most auspicious events which had happened since the commencement of our unjustifiable hostilities in Affghanistan.

Defeat, disaster, and disgrace were impending and seemed inevitable; but by the surrender of the *Dhost*, and the circumstances leading to it, these misfortunes had been averted, and India resounded with acclamations and rejoicings; and yet the evils and calamities by which, at no very distant period, we were to be overwhelmed, had only been postponed.

Since our departure from Sehwan our men had become most sickly, owing entirely to the almost complete want of bedding, and our being obliged frequently to encamp near the Indus on ground which had been but a few weeks before inundated by that river, and which, of course, was still damp and unwholesome. We lost several of our men on the march from Sehwan, and, on entering Sukkur had a large proportion in hospital.

2. Affghan Papers.

Chapter 9

Desert March

On our arrival at Sukkur, (see note below), we found it filled with troops. We occupied the same ground on which our right wing had encamped during their stay here. It was the best and coolest about Sukkur, and prettily situated on the banks of the river opposite the curious old fort of Bukkur. The day after our arrival I had the honour of paying my respects to the General commanding the forces.

> *Note*:—In the centre of the stream, nearly opposite Rori, is the celebrated fort of Bukkur, and on the western bank Sukkur, now designated 'Victoria on the Indus'. The latter is the site of a British cantonment, and being situated on an elevated spot overlooking and commanding the passage of the stream, is in every way advantageous for the purpose required; these are important points in Sindh, and on the river,—whose scenery, by the way, at this particular part assumes the most picturesque appearance.
>
> There are few finer views in the world, perhaps, than that of the mighty Indus at this part of its course. The eastern bank is clothed with beautiful gardens (celebrated by Persian poets as those of Buburlú) of date, acacia, pomegranate, and other trees. These extend for many miles down the stream. The old fort of Bukkur, round which the river rushes with immense velocity, is situated on a high rocky island, evidently disengaged from both banks by the action of the stream which, formerly, took a more eastern direction at this part of its course; for the ruins of the old Hindu capital, still to be seen, are ten miles to the eastward of Bukkur, yet that city was situated on the Indus, and the old bed of the river is distinctly to be traced.

Opposite Sukkur is the old town of Rori, built high and overhanging the stream; it was formerly a place of great size and commercial importance, but now reduced by the rapacity of the Khyrpúr *Amirs*. On the small hills and islands near Rori are some very beautiful tombs of Mahommedan saints, one of which is said to be so sacred to everything Sindhian; that the fish of the river, particularly the *palah*, pay respect to it, by never turning their tails when receding from it! Sukkur, Rori, and Bukkur are esteemed very sacred by the Mahommedans: they had formerly large colleges and establishments of *Sujuds* and holy men, whose minarets and tombs still contribute to add to the picturesque appearance of this part of Sindh.

A pretty building occupied as the residence of the British authority, is erected on the western bank. This is also the headquarters of our steamers and flotilla on the Indus; the British sailor here mixes in the groups of swarthy Sindhians, Parsi traders, Punjaubis, Biliechis and Hindustanis. Our position has infused a degree of animation and bustle into the place, which is very un-Sindhian; a large force is stationed, and it is proposed to erect barracks and other accommodation for European troops. The large military bazaar at Sukkur is a very busied and varied scene: the poor traders of the country here seek an asylum from oppression and extortion not to be found elsewhere; and if matters in Sindh had remained on their old footing, we might, by simple invitation, have attracted the bulk of the trade of the upper country to this particular spot.—*(Postans's Sindh)*.

The grand military event of the day was the defeat, by Colonel Marshall, of Nusser Khan, at Kotra. Our victory on this occasion seemed to have been most decisive, and had evidently completely blasted any hopes the young *khan* and his party might have ever entertained of being able to grapple with a British force. His followers had dispersed, and throughout the country the feeling seemed to be, that His Highness's cause was now hopelessly lost. The dispatch of Colonel Marshall, in which the operations at Kotra are detailed, is written in that comprehensive but prolix style which, unfortunately for the utility, beauty, and elegant simplicity for which these documents were wont to be distinguished, has of late years become so fashionable.

"The Clibborn Commission" had just finished its sittings when we arrived, and all were anxious to learn the result of its deliberations. We were greatly astonished, however, at the appearance of the document in the public journals long before Government could have had time to peruse it, much less to deliver an opinion. Whether it be regarded as containing matter totally irrelevant to the subject under inquiry,—by which an unworthy and vindictive feeling was gratified in a most unbecoming animadversion on the acts of a distinguished officer who had long ceased to have any connection with India or Indian affairs,—or viewed as having appeared before the public in the unauthorised and premature manner in which it did—and by which the sanctioner of such *dénouement* was guilty of a gross breach of faith,—it must be considered one of the most extraordinary and censurable productions that ever emanated from a military court.

My time at Sukkur was completely occupied during our halt in perfecting in the drill those recruits who had joined us shortly before leaving Kurachee, and for whose *exercise* there had been so little opportunity since they had been at the headquarters of the regiment. The numerous brigade field-days which we had, and on which occasions old and young soldiers had to join the ranks, rather interfered with the *pipeclay instructions.*

Extensive military operations were talked of at this time, and Herat was significantly mentioned by those who professed to be in the secret, as the field on which we were to gather fresh laurels. A few examples were to be made in Upper Scinde before advancing, so as effectually to quench any spark of power or hope that might yet remain to Nusser Khan, and by preventing the possibility of his reassembling an army, to induce him to throw himself on the mercy of the British, a step which I believe he would gladly have taken, had he not been apprehensive that he would follow Dhost Mahommed as a prisoner to India.

During the month of December our force was augmented by the arrival of a wing of H. M. 41st regiment, and a portion of our old Deesa friends, the 3rd Cavalry.

On the morning of the 2nd of January, 1841, we marched from Sukkur,—*no one*, I believe, having the most remote idea of our destination. Our force consisted of two troops of horse artillery, a battery of nine-pounders, two wings of cavalry, H. M. 40th, a wing of H. M. 41st, 20th, and 21st Bombay N. I., and a host of irregular horse. Our first stage was to Jufferabad, a distance of eight or nine miles. I had never before marched with so large a force, and was much struck, as everyone must be, who witnesses it, with the far extending—almost interminable line of baggage by which an Indian army is followed. The country near our halting-place was generally open, but our quartermaster-general preferred pitching us in the midst of an adjoining jungle,—a new theory in the art of castrametation, suggested probably by someone for the purpose of concealing us from the enemy, and thereby adding to the mystery and secrecy in which our actions and movements at this time were veiled. On the 30th of January we halted, and on the morning of the 4th made another march of about eight miles to Abdoo, where we encamped. On the 5th another halt, and on the 6th, having again moved, we reached Shikarpoor,[1] thus, in five days, accomplishing a march of twenty-seven miles over a level country,—a sure method possibly, certainly a slow one, of coming up with the enemies of whom we were supposed to be in search.

Shikarpoor is one of the principal towns in Upper Scinde. Like the others we had visited in the north and south of this province, it struck me as being very meagrely peopled in proportion to its size; many parts of the town, indeed, were quite uninhabited. Here I had the pleasure of renewing my acquaintance with Mrs. Postans who has contributed so much to our enjoyment by her talented and interesting work on Western India.

During our stay, we occasionally went out to participate in the amusement of hawking,—a sport which I believe is much indulged in by the richer classes of this country. I cannot say it is a branch of venery into the spirit of which I can thoroughly enter. However, I

---

1. Shikarpúr, the great mart of Sindh, and the city of greatest commercial importance beyond the Indus, from its extensive banking influence over the whole of Central Asia, as well as other countries, is situated about twenty-four miles N.W. from the river at Sukkur, on the high road to Candahar, by the great pass of the Bolan. We had a large establishment and a considerable force here so long as our armies were beyond the Affghan passes; but on their withdrawal, the necessity no longer appearing to exist, we abandoned Shikarpúr. Its position will always give it a direct influence on the trade of the Indus and countries beyond. It shares with Multan the title of one of the gates of Khorassan, and contains 22,000 inhabitants, according to an accurate census taken by the Author. It is walled in, but is in a very dirty and dilapidated state; and the large bazaar, for which it is famous, is half-a-mile in extent, and the walls make a circuit of nearly three miles. A rich country extends for about twenty miles, and then all is a mere desert: and the extent of Sindh is here defined by the territories of the Kilat chief and his predatory subjects. Subzulkót, the last remaining place of any moment, is about sixty miles above Rori, on the same side of the river; the town is a fort of a moderate size, but the lands in the vicinity are valuable for their great productiveness, particularly in cotton. The Daodpútra country here commences.—*Postans's, Sindh.*

never had seen it at home; and the specimen we had in Scinde may possibly have been of a very inferior description, if not a burlesque on this ancient sport, which has still so many votaries.

The wing of H. M. 41st regiment, and part of the artillery which had accompanied us from Sukkur, were directed to return to that station, owing, it was supposed, to some change in the intentions of Government as to the nature and extent of the operations to be carried on by this force,—influenced probably by the disturbed state of affairs in the Punjaub.

Our encampment was some distance from Shikarpoor. Here we halted until the 15th, when we commenced moving off in small detachments, on different days, and by different routes, a step rendered absolutely necessary by the great scarcity of water on the routes by which we were to march in order to gain the other side of the desert.

The infantry, under Brigadier Valiant, having separated from headquarters, moved across the desert to Bushoorie, *via* Sultankajote, Janadeera, and Rozan; at each of these places we experienced a very great scarcity of good water for ourselves, and had much difficulty in obtaining even a limited supply of brackish water for our cattle. On the morning of the 18th, we had arrived at Rozan, having still a long march of nearly thirty miles across the desert before us. Our brigadier determined on making it during the night.

Accordingly, after an early dinner, we set out at five p.m. About half-way across the desert we came up to some splendid fires which our quartermaster, who had gone on in advance, had lighted; near them we halted for about two hours; and, having produced the contents of haversacks, canteens, &c., we turned to, and enjoyed ourselves quite *à la picnic*. After this rest we proceeded merrily on our march, reaching Bushoorie about four in the morning of the 19th, and then learned that we should have arranged better had we postponed our departure from Rozan for a couple of hours, as in that case we should have been enabled to reach our destination as day broke, and been saved the discomfort of groping about in the dark, not knowing how or where to pitch our camp.

At Bushoorie we found water as scarce and bad as at the side of the desert. On the 20th we continued our march on Mungal-ka-shere, where we arrived on the morning of the 30th. Here we were directed to halt, until some arrangements with the neighbouring tribes with which the Politicals were engaged had been completed.

The country between Sukkur and Mungal-ka-shere, is singularly monotonous. It is generally uncultivated; but I conceive this is to be attributable more to the total want of security for property, especially in the immediate vicinity of the hills, than to the poverty of the soil. The inhabitants, generally speaking, are a wretched, spiritless, and oppressed race; till and sow the ground they may, but they are never certain of reaping the fruits of their labour.

As a proof of the appalling state of poverty to which they are reduced, and the degrading extremities to which they are driven, numbers of men, women, and children were daily to be seen eagerly picking from the dung of our cattle the undigested particles of grain, which, when cleaned, they used as food for themselves!

On our line of march we saw numerous ruined villages, several of which had evidently been recently plundered and destroyed, the walls still continuing to smoulder. How thankful should the contemplation of the state of a country like this make those whose lot is cast in a happier land! What a contrast is presented by the happy homes of England—aye, even by the vilest hovels of poverty in a Christian land, to those countries where war with all its terrible and desolating attendants is ever raging!

During our stay here, numerous petty thefts were committed by the villagers. I must do the Scindians the justice to say, that they are the most expert appropriators of the goods of other people I have ever known.

In the vicinity of the camp were numbers of wild hog: we made several attempts to have some sport with them, but were generally unsuccessful in inducing the "old grey boar" to break cover. One day we had some excellent fun with a fine old tusker, although not in the most legitimate manner of sporting. On the right of our camp, was a very deep *nullah.* One morning a splendid boar was foolish enough to wend his way along it; being seen by some of our men, a view *holloa* was given, and quick as thought the unfortunate brute was surrounded by an immense mob. Hearing the noise, I rushed out of my tent, and found the enraged but devoted animal charging and upsetting his tormentors in all directions. At length, with the assistance of a friendly bayonet, he was dispatched; and, strange to say, without his having inflicted a scratch on any one of his enemies.

A Tent lascar, coming up at this time to assist in the fray, drew a sword which he had with him and inflicted a severe gash on the loins of the prostrate boar. A regular *John Bull*, who happened to be stationed near him, and who doubtless was fearful lest the carcass should now be spoiled for the table, most unceremoniously, and much to the astonishment of the lascar, rewarded him for his officiousness by sending him sprawling on the ground; reminding me much of a most amusing incident which had occurred while hunting in Guzerat, some years previous, and which I cannot resist taking the opportunity of mentioning here.

A number of *griffins* had made their first appearance as hog-hunters, on one occasion, not far from Deesa; a fine boar was soon started, and, after a beautiful run, he fell by the unerring spear of an old and experienced sportsman. The *griffs*, however, being most anxious to blood their first spears, galloped up and as they dashed past the fallen animal, plunged their weapons into his carcass. An old and esteemed friend of mine, who with his strong attachment to the pleasures of the chase combined a lively regard for the good things of this life, unable any longer to stand the repeated attacks on the unoffending pork, at length exclaimed, "For heaven's sake, stop these griffins; they will spoil the chops!"

About the end of January an order was issued for the right wing of the 40th to proceed to Mungal-ka-shere, there to join the headquarters; and early in February I was overjoyed to find once more with me the many old and valued friends belonging to that wing.

It was, however, a source of much regret to us all to witness the acute sufferings of this portion of the corps owing to the great prevalence among them of a most dreadful ulcer, commonly called the Scinde boil. The whole of the troops which had been for any length of time stationed in Upper Scinde, were attacked with more or less severity by these painful and disgusting sores, which were attributed to the peculiar and very unwholesome properties of the water in this part of the province. There was scarcely an officer or man in the whole wing who was not labouring under their loathsome influence; it was, however, so far fortunate that the general health of the wing did not appear to be much, if at all, affected by them.

After the junction of our right wing, some capital steeple-chases were got up; and, for those who had time to indulge their tastes in that way, there was abundance of excellent shooting.

Attempts were repeatedly renewed, but always unsuccessfully, to have a boar-hunt; it was almost impossible to get these animals out of cover, and, when on one or two occasions they did break, it was only to shew that they were there, and double back again.

Chapter 10

Defeat of our Troops

A neighbouring tribe having declined to pay tribute to our puppet Shah Soojah, a small force under Colonel Wilson of the Bombay cavalry was directed to proceed early in February to their stronghold Kujjuk, in the Seebee country, for the purpose of forcing them into a compliance with the demand upon them.[1]

The Kujjuks, Punnees of the Caukur tribe, nothing daunted by the appearance of a British force, still refused to accede to our terms; it therefore became necessary to attack their town. The artillery, accordingly, were placed in position near the fort, and an attempt was made to breach; but the guns making little or no impression on the mud-walls, it was determined to take the place by assault. At this time Colonel Wilson, when with the guns, was severely wounded by a matchlock ball, and was taken off the field. A storming party was formed, and an effort made to carry the gate; this was, however, unsuccessful, and our troops were driven back with severe loss. Their leader, Lieutenant Franklin, 2nd Grenadiers, was killed, and Lieutenant R. Shaw, of the commissariat department, who had volunteered his services, was severely wounded.

Another essay was determined on, and Lieutenant Creed, of the Horse Artillery, with thirty volunteers from among the men of his troop, led this second attack. Gallantly the Europeans rushed to the onset, carrying all before them, and gaining possession of the gate. The

1. Seewee is entered by a traveller from Daudur, in the course of his first march to the northward. It is a flat, dry plain of hardened clay, but in some places its natural defects are relieved by streams from the hills, and round the town of Seewee, at least, is highly cultivated. The Punnees still form part of the Affghan nation, and are under a governor appointed by the king.— *Elphinstones Account of the Kingdom of Caubul,* vol. ii.

besieged, however, seeing that the assault was not supported, returned to the charge, and, overwhelming the troops with their superior numbers, drove them from the fort, with the loss of the intrepid Creed, arid ten of his gallant followers.

For the character of the native soldiery I entertain the greatest admiration, and often have I witnessed their gallant bearing in the field;—I trust, therefore, that I shall not be accused of uttering anything approaching to disrespect, or in any way derogatory to the fair fame of those who were engaged in what has been described as a most unequal contest at Kujjuk, if I state my conviction that, had a few European infantry been at the storm of that small fort, we should not have had to record a disastrous defeat.

After the repulse of Lieutenant Creed, no further attempt was made to carry the fort; and Captain Rawlings, of the Grenadiers, on whom the command devolved when Colonel Wilson was wounded, having, as he *supposed*, closely invested the place, a dispatch, announcing the disaster, was sent to General Brooks, which reached our camp at Mungal-ka-shere about one p.m., on the 21st of March.

Orders were immediately issued for the troop of Horse Artillery under Captain Leeson, H. M. 40th, and the 21st Bombay N. I., to be in readiness to march that evening on Seebee, a distance of about forty miles. Expedition, of course, being a great object, the General commanded that as small a quantity of baggage as possible should accompany each regiment. We therefore took only a limited number of tents, and supplies for five or six days,—General Brooks intimating his intention to return to Mungal-ka-shere within that time: and, leaving the remainder of our kits, and most of our tents, in charge of the *depôt*, which was ordered to remain behind, we marched from camp about four p.m.

The general, with the artillery, moved on at a quicker pace than the infantry, and reached Mettrie, about half way, some hours before us.

The guides with whom we had been furnished either did not, or would not, know the road, and we were led about by them in the dark in a most unsatisfactory manner, over *nullahs* and through jungles. Indeed, I know not when we might have reached our destination, had not General Brooks, suspecting, from the length of time that we were out, that we had lost our way, fired a gun and burned a few blue-lights, by which we were enabled to find a road to his encampment. As it was, in some of the ravines during the darkness of the night we lost four companies of the 21st regiment, which did not reach Mettrie until several hours after the remainder of the infantry.

On coming up to the general, we ascertained that he had received a second dispatch from Seebee, intimating that during the previous night the enemy, anticipating the arrival of reinforcements, had evacuated the fort, and escaped into the neighbouring hills: desirous, however, of judging for himself of the nature and extent of the opposition offered, by which our men had been so signally discomfited, he pushed on with the artillery to Seebee, directing the infantry to bivouac for the remainder of the night at Mettrie, and follow him the next morning.

About four o'clock p. m. of the 22nd of February the infantry, under Brigadier Valiant, resumed their march on Kujjuk. At about eight o'clock the sky became suddenly overcast, portending an approaching storm; the wind moaned mournfully through the jungle forest, and—

What at first was called a gust, the same
Hath now a storm's—anon a tempest's name.

I had never before seen such a storm come on so quickly and so unexpectedly, nor has it ever been my fortune to witness anything so sublimely yet so gloomily dark as was this night: the rain poured down in torrents, the growling of the deep-toned thunder was echoed back, again and again, by the distant hills, and the frequent but momentary flashing of the brilliant lightning contrasted strangely and hideously with the dismal blackness around.

Our guide, apparently paralysed by this sudden and appalling conflict of the elements, declared his unconsciousness of the localities of the country, and his inability to proceed further till daylight; we had no other alternative, therefore, but to remain where we were, as quietly and comfortably as circumstances would admit. The rain at first soaked readily into the earth—but the earth soon becoming satiated, the water remained where it fell, and speedily formed an immense pool, extending like a lake over this level country; and long ere the morning star appeared, "*to tell the dawning day is drawing near,*" the greater portion of the brigade were standing up to their knees in water, with their feet well cased in six or eight inches of most tenacious mud. When we had time to scrutinize ourselves and our neighbours, we presented a most ludicrous appearance,—the only consolation remaining to us, if we may credit Rochefoucauld's axiom, being derived from the fact that we all were alike!

Continuing our walk, about six o'clock a. m. of the 24th, we made the best of our way to Seebee, struggling as if through a river .nearly the whole way. The ground pointed out to us for encamping—the only available piece in the whole neighbourhood— was a perfect lake; but, with the assistance of the pioneers' tools, we soon took off the surface-water, though we should have been none the worse had a few of the gentlemen-farmers of England been present with their complete draining-apparatus, to relieve us of the rain with which the ground was so completely saturated.

Immediately after parading and inspecting the men for duty, I galloped off to my friends of the 3rd Cavalry, got a comfortable breakfast, and was dressed out by my brother-adjutant, Forbes. Many of our tents did not come up that day, and several never reached Seebee at all. Camels never can travel in muddy or slippery countries, and many of these poor brutes slipped with their loads, fell, and in many cases split up. The loss to the public in camels alone in this one night's march was between three and four hundred.

Accompanied by some of my brother officers, I went off after breakfast to inspect the town of Kujjuk, situated close to the Murree Hills in the Seebee district. It is a small oblong fort, and at the time of its attack by our troops, did not possess any extraordinary degree of strength; the walls, which were of mud, were high, but in many places much dilapidated. At one time there had evidently been a deep ditch extending completely round the defences; but only on the front, where our troops attacked, and on the left flank, was there any water in it.

On the right and rear faces the ditch was perfectly dry, and indeed, in some places, quite filled up. In some places, also, there were several practicable breaches, and close to one of them on the rear, growing almost out of the wall, was a large tree, which would have assisted materially in enabling the attacking party to gain admission, had their assault been made on that point. It would appear that the commander, who directed the operations, had gone out of his way to find difficulties; and in fixing on the gateway as the point of attack, he had certainly succeeded in choosing that part generally best defended.

The phraseology usually adopted when a commander fails in an Indian expedition is, that he fell into the common error of having too great a contempt for his enemy. In the present instance, it may with more truth be said, that the error consisted in acting in opposition to every principle of common sense; for the most cursory view of the fort and its defences ought to have satisfied even the most obtuse of *would-be-generals* of the propriety and expediency of taking advantage of the breaches already made;—of the practicability of this course, some idea may be formed from the fact of my having seen an officer ride over one of these ruined parts of the wall, without any undue exertion, or even attempt at leaping on the part of his horse. A small tower on the right, and within a few paces of the wall, completely commanded the front of the fort and the gateway on which our attacks were made; this, however, was never occupied, or even attempted to be occupied by our troops.

The gateway itself was perfectly open, and leading straight from it was a short but narrow street, terminating in a large open square, which may be said to be the centre of the town. On the right and left of the gates were long narrow lanes running parallel to the wall, and which were commanded by the tower to which I have before alluded. In these lanes the enemy made their stand, and by rushing down on the flanks of the attacking party as they entered, overpowered and drove them back.

Chapter 11

Destruction of Kujjuk

The fort had been taken possession of by our troops on its evacuation by the enemy, and on our arrival a small detachment was quartered in it. As we entered it, was presented one of those very repugnant spectacles which unfortunately, in similar cases, are but too common. Camp-followers were straggling about intent on plunder; the most wilful and iniquitous demolition of property took place; sheep, cattle, &c., were wantonly and heedlessly destroyed, notwithstanding the exertions of the Provost Marshal and his myrmidons. A committee was appointed for the management of the prize-property,—it having been decided by the general that everything taken at Kujjuk should be disposed of for the benefit of the troops—pending, of course, the sanction of Her Majesty.

When we had been at Kujjuk about a week, Colonel Wilson died of his wounds, and was buried near to those who had fallen at the assault on the place, and close to the spot where he had received his death-wound. He was a young active soldier, and bore the reputation of being one of the best, if not *the best*, cavalry officer in the Bombay army.

On the day following his funeral, the auction of prize-property commenced. Impelled by curiosity, I went down to see what there was to tempt the purchaser. Truly, a heterogeneous mass of goods. Grain, *ghee*-flour, &c., even down to incomplete portions of wearing-apparel of the women, all were offered for sale. I felt that our character was tarnished by the whole transaction, and the very recollection of this undignified proceeding still calls a blush of shame to my cheek.

The villagers who had been driven to the hills, could plainly see the destruction of their property. A few short days before, the rich plains were adorned with most luxurious crops—now, all was desolation. In the fields, where the fruits of their labour were springing up, roved a host of cattle spreading ruin far and wide. Many of these poor wretches, who, driven to despair by the cravings of hunger, had stolen clown to the fort under cover of the darkness of night, in the hope of being able to carry off something for themselves and friends, were detected and shot by the sentries.

The fort had been gutted of everything valuable; and, the sale of prize-property being now over, it was given up for two days to the camp-followers for plunder; after which, fatigue parties from the different corps commenced, under the superintendence of the engineer, the destruction of the defences, and, when this work was completed by springing a few mines, the troops were withdrawn, and the houses fired.

The smiling cots no more appeared,—
Or dimly seen, where darkly reared
Their mould'ring walls, whose falling, heard
By watching swains, told them interred
Was every hope,—their home!

There is something attaching to the wanton destruction of property, and more especially to the desolation of the fair fruits of the earth, which is particularly revolting. There are times when the stern necessities of war require the commission of acts which humanity cannot but view with abhorrence; but I do not admit that these necessities existed at Kujjuk. The dignity and honour of the British name are ever best upheld by the practice of generosity and magnanimity, and it is idle to suppose that such conduct is not appreciated, or that it is always put down to the score of fear. There is a wide difference between the concession which has too often disgraced our policy, and humane forbearance after victory, the practice of which has never failed to call forth admiration and do honour to our national character; and certainly, in the present case, the practice of that forbearance,—the exercise of that generosity,—if not imperative, would have done more towards pacifying this country and securing for ourselves the respect and affection of its people, than did the inexorable course of rapine, savouring strongly of the acts of lawless plunderers, which we pursued,—a species of brutal revenge we are so ready to condemn in others, but the sincere detestation of which we can only show by the ennobling contrast of our own conduct.

During my stay here, while walking through the camp, I met some of the wounded Horse Artillery who had volunteered with poor Creed. Having entered into conversation with them, I made some inquiries as to the numbers by which they were opposed, and the nature of the weapons used by the besieged. With regard to the first, they represented the strength of the Kujjuks actually engaged in close combat with the European storming-party as vastly superior to the latter; and with reference to the weapons, those generally used were the sword and shield of the country. This elicited the remark from one of the soldiers—the truth of which appeared to be admitted by the rest,—that if the thirty men who had attacked with Lieutenant Creed had had musket and bayonet, instead of the light dragoon sword, with which they entered the fort, they would not have been driven back. This, I think, may safely be taken as an example of the general estimation in which the musket and bayonet are held by the greater portion of the British Army, and proves the existence of one point of great importance, *viz.*—the firm and implicit confidence reposed in those weapons alike by English, Scotch, and Irish.

The intention of the general to march to Mungal-ka-shere was completely frustrated by the inclemency of the weather; for, instead of our being able to return to that camp, the rain had fallen in such quantities as to render the country perfectly impassable; we were consequently weather-bound at Kujjuk until the morning of the 16th, when we directed our steps on Dadur,—whither our depot, with the tents, baggage, &c., which we had left behind us, was ordered to proceed.

Our first march was to Koranna: here we encamped near the ground on which we had passed such an uncomfortable hydropathic night on the 22nd of February. The country on the line of march, more especially near our encampment, was strewed with the bodies of the dead camels which had been sacrificed that night; and the effluvia from their decaying carcasses did anything but add to the *agrémens* of the neighbourhood. On the 17th we marched to Mettrie; the river here, the bed of which was perfectly dry when we passed in February, was now a fine stream, and the water at the ford where we crossed was nearly up to our middles. On the 18th we halted, and on the 19th reached Dadur. A battery of nine-pounders inarched into the camp the same day, and here we received intelligence that H. M. 41st were again ordered to advance, and that a battery of eighteen-pounders was being prepared at Sukkur by order of the Bombay government,—which, with a host of other troops, was also to come on;—in fact, everything gave evidence of the intention of our rulers to be *at something*, and Herat was still looked upon as the devoted city against which we were to proceed.

The commissariat having as usual numerous arrangements to make, and the Political, Mr. Ross Bell, with his immense retinue of camels, amounting to about five hundred or six hundred, (a much larger number than is necessary to serve a European regiment,) being anxious to get through the pass before the troops, we were ordered to halt here some days.

The camp at Mungal-ka-shere had not escaped the storm on the 22nd of February, and we found that our kits, &c., which we had left behind, had in no way been improved by the action of the rain. Three of my camels, for which I had paid a large sum in Lower Scinde, had, from the wet and cold, been rendered perfectly incapable of work, and I was glad to dispose of them all for the small sum of fifty *rupees*. The public camels had suffered to a great extent also, and considerable difficulty was experienced in replacing them,—a circumstance which naturally calls forth the inquiry, why so large a number were apportioned to the political agent, when such a scarcity existed?

By paying a heavy price, I was enabled to replace the camels I had been compelled to dispose of, and had the mortification to see one of them, a very splendid-looking animal, die suddenly, and in the most unexpected manner, on the following day, without leaving me the satisfaction of having got one day's work out of him.

Dadur is a small fortified town, and, like the rest in this country, mud-built. Situated as it is in a basin formed of barren hills and mountains, it is not difficult to form an idea of the dreadful heat of its climate in the summer months. The country in the neighbourhood is very unproductive, and intersected with numerous water-courses and deep ravines.

The heat was beginning to be most oppressive, and we were not sorry to turn our backs on this station, which we did on the morning of the 26th of March. After marching four or five miles, we entered the Bolan Pass, with which I confess I was disappointed,—its general appearance and strength falling very far short of what I had conceived of them from the descriptions of those by whom we had been preceded. Our first halting-place was Cundya, about thirteen miles from Dadur. The road is principally through the bed of the Bolan River, which, from its serpentine course, we had to ford no less than eighteen times in one day; and, from the loose jungle over which we had to move, the marching was not only exceedingly fatiguing, but very destructive to shoe-leather. Our encampment was close under a precipitous range of rugged hills. On the right of the camp flowed the Bolan River, and on the other side of it was an extensive plain, on which I should certainly have preferred encamping, had it been for no other reason than to save the troops wading through the river the first thing next morning. However, we must take it for granted that our quartermaster-general was right, and that it is highly refreshing to get one's feet cooled at the commencement of a long march.

We had been assured that it was impossible to drive our tent-pegs into the ground in the Pass, so we adopted the recommendation given us of tying our tent-ropes to large stones. Before morning we found out that it would have been more satisfactory to ourselves if we had, at least, endeavoured to pitch our tents in the legitimate manner; for towards the middle of the night a booming noise was heard, instantly followed by a most violent gust of wind, which, rushing through the hills with renewed and increasing fury, in an instant after levelled our tents with the ground. The occupants, who had struggled out, stood like spectres, gazing on the absurd scene which this mishap had caused; while those who had not been enabled to extricate themselves in time from under their canvas-dwellings were calling lustily for help. The wind blew during the remainder of the night with unabated force, rendering every attempt to re-pitch our tents futile, and increasing our discomfort by the clouds of sand and dust which it raised. The wisest course left us to pursue, and which was generally adopted, was to get hold of our clothes, dress ourselves, and remain until the beating of "the general" summoned us to prepare for advancing.

Our next stage was to Kirta, a distance of nine or ten miles. Today (March 27) we crossed the river eight times, the nature of the road being much the same as yesterday. The scenery as we advanced was much grander, and the pass much stronger. The wind had not at all lulled; and we found it quite impossible to pitch our camp unless in some few places where a slight shelter was afforded by a neighbouring hill. On the 28th we marched on Beebee Nanee: the ascent now was very perceptible, and we began to feel an improvement in the temperature.

We crossed the river once. The road on this march was rougher and more fatiguing than any we had yet travelled. The pass becomes much wider and the country more open in the neighbourhood of Beebee Nanee. On the 29th we marched to Abigoom. The river flowed through our encampment today; the country again became more confined and rugged. Here a few of our cattle either strayed or were carried off; a company was sent in pursuit, with orders that, in the event of the latter being the case, not one of the plunderers should be spared. The lost cattle were found a few miles from the camp, among the hills, mingling with the herds of some of the tribes. The herdsmen appeared in considerable numbers, and, like the rest of the inhabitants of this country, they were well-armed; our troops attacked them according to the orders of the general. The remembrance of such a disgusting style of service, however, can recall no feelings of pleasure to those who had the misfortune to be employed in it.

Some distance from Beebee Nanee are to be seen a few graves, in which rest the remains of a number of travellers, who some years before had been attacked and murdered by the Beloochees.

On the 30th we reached Sir-i-Bolan, a distance of about eight miles. The water gushing out from an aperture in the rock is the source of the Bolan River. Here the pass becomes very narrow and very beautiful. On the 31st we advanced to Dust-ta-be-Dowlet, or the Valley without Wealth. For about four or five miles our march was through a narrow and tortuous defile of great strength, varying from fifteen to twenty yards in breadth, with perpendicular rocks on either side, towering to the height of about two hundred feet. The heights were crowned by the light companies today, previous to our entering the defile—the first *precautionary* measure we had adopted since entering the pass. After marching about ten miles, we made a very abrupt ascent of about one hundred yards, clearing the pass, and entering upon an extensive valley. One of the officers in the rearguard today shot a remarkably fine *doomba*—a species of wild sheep which are to be found in great numbers on the hills.

During our march through the pass the infantry had never once been required to assist the guns—a duty which I had fully anticipated, from the description of the pass, we should often have had to perform. One of the great difficulties, if not the greatest, connected with this pass—and it certainly is a most serious one—is the total want of forage in it, and the consequent necessity for encumbering an army with additional baggage, in the shape of indispensable supplies of grain and other provisions for men and cattle. On the 1st of April we made a long march over a very extensive plain to Sir-i-ab; and on the 2nd, continuing our route, we reached Quettah.

CHAPTER 12

Quettah

On arrival at Quettah, we learned that if it ever had been the intention of Government to send an expedition to Herat, such intention was now completely abandoned. The heavy battery which was preparing at Sukkur had been countermanded; but the 2nd brigade, under Brigadier England, was directed to advance, and was now moving through the Pass. This part of the force, it was said, was to proceed to Candahar, while we of the 1st brigade were to remain stationary at Quettah. There was certainly nothing prepossessing in our promised station, and we would all have willingly gone on in the hope of finding a better.

Quettah, the capital of Shawl, is a small insignificant fortified town, with a high mound in the centre, dignified by the name of citadel, to which our troops were obliged to retire, on the occasion of Nusser Khan threatening our cantonment there. It is situated in a valley, nearly surrounded by the mountains of the Tukatoo and Bolan range. The general appearance of the country was singularly uninviting; nor could I see any traces of the richness which has been attributed to the *Fertile Valley of Shawl*,—as it has been called by some authors. A few very small and irregularly-fortified villages, generally built close to the hills, were studded about; and the orchards, which in some favoured spot added a grace to the scenery, and a few other isolated patches of cultivation, tended only to exhibit more forcibly the general barrenness of the land. All supplies of grain were either procured from the plains below the passes, or brought from the country about Candahar.

The forage we procured for our horses was really execrable: it was dangerous giving it to them, from there being a small weed indigenous to the soil which is a certain poison, and which springs up in great profusion in the crops of lucerne. Several of our horses died from the effects of eating it. For our camels there was, however, a tolerable supply of southernwood, in which they seemed to delight. At this season of the year the climate of Quettah was exceedingly cold and wintry—the surrounding hills were covered with snow, and violent hail-storms, attended with thunder and lightning, were frequent.

Our encampment was some distance from the town; the ground was covered with loose shingle, but, when cleared of the numerous scorpions with which it was infested, was on the whole good. To the south-west of the town were a few good houses, built by the officers who had been some time here; there were also comfortable barracks for the native troops.

The 2nd brigade followed us here in a few days, and after a short halt were moved off to Moostung. A detachment of Skinner's Horse, which had left Dadur about a week or ten days after the 2nd brigade, met with a most extraordinary but terrific opposition in the pass. They had entered the narrow defile when a loud rushing noise was heard, and immediately after an immense volume of water was seen vehemently torrent down the pass: the troopers immediately wheeled about, and charged back towards the more open part of the defile, in the hope of escaping the destruction which seemed all but inevitable. The stream, swollen by the late rains, had burst its bounds, and rushing down the narrow gorge with irresistible force, carried all before it. To those who gained the height and escaped the overwhelming fury of the current, was left the appalling spectacle of their less fortunate comrades being whirled past them to certain death by the impetuous torrent. The loss of life and property in proportion to the strength of the party on this occasion was very great.

During the month of April, the only subject of interest to this part of the Indian army was Herat,—the usual number of conflicting reports regarding our relations there,—and the different causes assigned for the sudden departure from that city of Major Tod.

April continued a cold disagreeable month; but early in May, the transition to excessive heat was most sudden, and it was attended with many evils. Quettah, which had been looked upon as really healthy, was not long in showing how utterly mistaken was this idea. Dysentery and fever of the worst description broke out with the greatest virulence among the unfortunate troops, who had been—

Sent in this foul clime to languish.

The hospitals were filled to overflowing; and, to make matters worse, the hospitals, owing to the very culpable mismanagement of the commissariat at Dadur, were scantily supplied with the necessary medicines,—even of quinine, so essential in cases of fever, there was always a scarcity, even often a deficiency. That the supplies left at Dadur for the use of the army should not have been forwarded with regularity, cannot, however, be a matter of wonder to those who witnessed the "admired disorder" in which the stores were lying about there, when our force marched through.

An expedition against a refractory chief, Fuzil Khan, composed of troops furnished from Quettah and Moostung, under command of Colonel Soppit, set out on the 3rd of May. A forced march of upwards of forty miles was made during the night of the 4th of May to Nooskee—the fort of the chief, with the intention of making a *chuppao* (night-attack) and taking him. The expedition however failed; on his arrival at Nooskee, the Colonel found that the bird had flown to the desert. Unwilling, however, to let slip the slightest chance of securing him, the cavalry and two companies of H.M. 41st—the latter mounted on camels—went off in pursuit: but they too failed in their object; and all that this force seemed to have succeeded in was the contraction of a dysentery even more than usually virulent, and from which few who were attacked with it ever recovered.

Meanwhile Nusser Khan still kept roaming through the country, wishful, it was said, of coming in, but prevented from doing so by his party. All was quiet in this district, but to the north—particularly in the neighbourhood of Candahar—there were disturbances. Our troops were continually employed in attempting to collect the tribute for Shah Soojah—an object in which they very rarely succeeded; and even when their efforts were crowned with success, it was achieved at an expense to ourselves far outstripping in amount the sum which we tried to recover. Verily, our occupation and manner of conducting operations in this country seemed to indicate that our treasury was inexhaustible.

Close to the town was an extensive plain of fine turf, where was formed an excellent race-course, on which, during the time of our *séjour* here, we contrived to vary the monotony of our existence by getting up some cocktail races; indeed, in the exercise of all manly sports, a great degree of emulation was excited among the members of the two presidencies, Bengal and Bombay, stationed here.

Major-general Brooks and Brigadier Valiant having been removed from their respective commands by order of the Bombay Government,

Brigadier England assumed command of the headquarters of the force at Quettah about June. An extract from a letter from Government was published at this time, declaring that no part of the property taken at Kujjuk could be considered prize, it having been found in a town belonging to a friendly power, which it had been found necessary to *occupy* as a temporary measure. The money realized by the sale of these things was returned; a reparation was made for the property destroyed, and a sum of money was placed at the disposal of the Kujjuks to enable them to rebuild their fort.

On what had our attack on this town been grounded? Was it through error, misconception, or mistake, that it had been stormed, that part of its defenders had been slain, the rest hounded from their homes, and that we ourselves had sustained a loss of three officers and a number of men? Questions such as these cannot indeed be agreeable to those through whose folly, ignorance, or incapacity such a sacrifice of human life and British reputation was consummated.

Fever and dysentery continued during the months of May, June, July, August, and September, with unabated fury: the number of deaths during that time was immense. Within a very few days Mr. Ross Bell, the political agent, Captain Jones of the 20th, Mr. Cureton of the 21st, Lieutenant Valiant of the 40th, and a great proportion of men were carried off. Hardly a morning or evening passed that one or more funeral parties were not required. Poor Henry Valiant! in him we all regretted the loss of as kind, warm-hearted, generous a fellow as ever lived.

That frequent resource which in cases of fever is oftentimes beneficial, a change of ground, was again essayed, but we derived little or no advantage therefrom; the whole of this valley appeared equally unhealthy, and nothing we could do short of turning our backs on Shawl, was likely to contribute to our good. So alarming were the accounts of the dreadful state to which the troops here and at Moostung were reduced by sickness, that special reports were called for by Government from the medical men.

Surgeon M'Andrew of the 40th, who, though suffering severely from bad health, had, *unassisted*, performed—with a zeal, cheerfulness, and disregard of self, which claim, and have obtained for him, the undying gratitude of his regiment—the entire medical duties ever since its departure from Kurachee, spoke of Quettah as the most unhealthy place in which he had ever been stationed during a service of upwards of thirty years in many parts of the globe, the island of Walcheren not even excepted.

A horrible murder was committed by a gang of one of the Bolan tribes, in the pass, early in September: the unfortunate victim was Mrs. Smith, wife of Mr. Smith, a conductor in the Bombay Commissariat, and perhaps one of the decidedly most efficient men in that department. She was on her way to join her husband, and had employed a native escort to take her clear of the pass. The cowardly scoundrels seeing a few Beloochees coming down the hill, turned and ran, leaving their unfortunate charge to the relentless hands of the barbarians, by whom this defenceless woman was cut down, notwithstanding the very romantic tales one hears of the almost superstitious horror with which they view the murder of a woman.

Nusseer Khan had now come in, and Major Outram, who had been appointed to conduct the duties of political agent in Scinde as successor to Mr. Ross Bell, arrived here early in September. The greater part of the beginning of this month was employed in brigade field-days and similar amusements for the benefit of our young friend and ally, Nusseer Khan, (an interesting-looking, but not a handsome youth,) who appeared delighted with the evolutions of the troops, and seemed more than charmed with the Horse Artillery and the extraordinary rapidity of their movements. He certainly saw this branch of the service to great advantage. I cannot conceive anything finer, in every military sense of the word, than the troops of Bombay Horse Artillery with which I have been fortunate enough at different periods of my service to be quartered.

Scinde now assumed a very peaceable complexion; and as everything in the north was declared pacific, it appeared settled that the 40th at least were to return to India; we were therefore not a little surprised towards the end of September to receive an order to be prepared to march on Candahar, where it was intended we should winter.

In common with the rest of my brother-officers, I had this month to regret the withdrawal from our corps and the service (to both of which he was an ornament) of our much-respected comrade, Major Boscawen. Anxious, on account of impaired health and other circumstances, to proceed to England, but being unable to obtain leave,—notwithstanding the assurance on all sides that this country was now in a state of perfect tranquillity,—he at length determined on retiring altogether from the army; and on the 27th of September he took his departure, carrying with him the best wishes of every individual in the corps, and leaving us to regret the loss of a highly esteemed and sincere friend.

Chapter 13

March from Quettah

Captain Blood's company of artillery (four guns) which was ordered to accompany the 40th regiment to Candahar, having arrived from Moostung, and everything being declared ready for a start, we struck our tents on the morning of the 6th of October; and gladly bidding adieu to Quettah, where so many of those who entered this country with us had found a grave, we proceeded to Candahar.

Our first march was into the Pesheen Valley, which we entered through the small pass of Kooshlac, in the Tuckatoo range of mountains, dividing this valley from that of Shawl. We took the precaution to occupy the pass with our light company until the guns and camels had moved through—a step always prudent, if not quite necessary, in a country where there are marauders frequently lurking about, ready to take advantage of any oversight by which they may be enabled to plunder the passing traveller.

The first few miles of our march was a gradual ascent over a tolerably level plain. As we neared the pass, at a distance of five or six miles from Quettah, the country became intersected by numerous ravines, which considerably retarded the progress of our guns and wagons,—particularly the latter, which were drawn by bullocks;—excellent animals for draught, generally, but not at all suited to a shingly country, similar to that which we passed over in today's march.

In the Kooshlac Pass, which does not extend above half a mile, there is no difficulty to overcome: the descent, however, is rather precipitous, especially by the path to the left, along which the infantry moved; the road for the guns to the right, and which is cut out of the side of the hill, is also steep and narrow, overhanging on one side a precipice. Over this steep, owing to some fracture in the drag-chain, one of the guns rolled, carrying with it the wheelers and driver, (the leaders fortunately had been taken out): Everyone, of course, concluded that there must be an end of gun and all that accompanied it; but first the driver getting up and shaking himself, and then the horses following his example, showed that they had not suffered much by preferring this short way to the bottom; and on further examination, it was found that neither gun nor carriage had sustained any serious damage.

Having cleared the pass, we continued our march a few miles, and encamped close to the village of Kooshlac. Immediately the hills hid Quettah from our view, there seemed to be a depression removed from our spirits. The valley in which we had now entered appeared more cheerful, and the inhabitants struck us as being of a more energetic and light-hearted disposition than those of the district we had just left. Our encamping-ground was good, we had excellent grazing for our cattle, and were enabled to obtain some trifling supplies of forage and grain.

On the 7th we continued our march to Hyderzye over a flat and uninteresting country, intersected by numerous ravines, which presented some trifling obstacles to the passage of the guns; at several, the assistance of the infantry, with the drag-ropes, was required. We were also a good deal delayed in working the guns over a river, the bed of which was composed of deep and adhesive mud. Our encampment was near the village of Hyderzye, which, like all other villages in this country, was small, irregular, mud-built, and fortified.

On the 8th we resumed our march to Hykulzie, over a particularly easy country, and encamped some distance from the town on fine open ground. Supplies of grain, &c., although in small quantities, were brought into camp by the natives from the neighbouring villages, a few of which we saw studded about the plain. On the 9th we halted,—several of the officers rode toward Hykulzie. The country, in the immediate vicinity, was much intersected by *nullahs*; and one of the largest villages, about four miles from camp, was quite deserted, and almost in ruins. Hykulzie, and its neighbourhood, have obtained a degree of notoriety from having been the scene of the repulse, by Mahommed Zadeek, of General England's force, in March 1842.

Today we received our letters by the overland mail, the more welcome from being unexpected.

On the 10th we marched to Syed Rokun Kagote, a distance of between seven or eight miles,—road, until near camp, very good and level; then, however, we were obstructed by a most formidable ravine, extending for a great distance, and with highly precipitous banks. There were the remains of a road which had evidently been constructed at some former period for guns, but which had now been almost completely washed away. We were consequently much delayed, but at length succeeded in getting everything over in safety, and halted near the small village on good, open, and extensive encamping-ground.

On the 11th we marched to Arumbee, a distance of seven miles, crossed a small branch of the River Lahe, and encamped on its right bank. Near us a number of natives had pitched their tents, and shortly after our arrival visited us, bringing with them, for sale, quantities of beautiful grapes, apricots, &c.

On the 12th of October, we marched to Killa Abdoolah, six miles and a half, and encamped near a small fort, situated close to the range of the Kojuk Mountains, the northern boundary to the Pesheen Valley. According to Mr. Elphinstone, the Valley of Shawl excels in fertility that of Pesheen; but, from what I observed in the neighbourhood of Quettah, and on our march to this place, I must beg to differ from so high an authority.

Our next march, through the Kojuk Pass, being a very difficult one, it was deemed expedient to get as many of our camels as possible across the mountain before the troops should enter the defile. Captain White, with the light and No. 7 company, was directed to take charge of the heavy baggage, and proceed with it, under his escort, to our next halting-ground, Chummum, in the country of the Atchikzyes, one of the Douranee clans. He accordingly started on this service about two in the afternoon of the 13th.

Today (13th) the two officers stationed with the detachment of *sepoys*, at Killa Abdoolah, dined with us; glad to avail themselves of the opportunity, so seldom afforded them on their outpost duty, of mixing with their fellow-countrymen.

On the 14th we started at three a. m., and having entered the defile in the mountain, reached the bottom of the grand ascent about half past six. There being no opposition to our march, we thought it best to conduct everything systematically, and with a due regard to comfort. So having piled arms, and unyoked horses and bullocks from the guns and wagons, fires were lighted, and preparations commenced for breakfast previous to entering on the arduous task of dragging the guns up the hill,—a duty which, from the extreme slipperiness, narrowness, and many windings of the road preventing the horses being of service, devolved entirely on the men. While the *tea* was preparing

I ascended the hill, and was gratified with a most magnificent view of the surrounding country. The bold rugged mountains, which were beautifully wooded, extending on either side as far as the eye could reach, presented a picture sublimely grand, and the white tents of the small portion of our force which had preceded us the day before, pitched at the foot of the hills, in the valley below, added a pleasing and graceful interest to the scene.

The road, which on entering the pass was good and wide enough to admit troops and camels, had at this place where we halted become narrower. There were two paths to the top of the mountain; the one to the left being easier for guns, the other was open for the passage of the few camels which accompanied us.

The ceremony of breakfast being now finished, and a strong guard placed over the arms and knapsacks, the remainder of the force was formed into fatigue parties, and at eight o'clock commenced working up the guns. The length of the ascent was nearly half a mile; it occupied about fifty minutes in getting the first gun on the table-land at the top. The rest of the nine-pounders and the five wagons soon followed, and by twelve o'clock all had reached the summit. Having corrected the meridian and refreshed ourselves with a short rest, we resumed our labour, which was not yet half finished. The descent on the northern side of the mountains was very precipitous, and at the commencement of the narrow road, in which were two exceedingly sharp and awkward turnings, proved a much more serious operation than the ascent, being rendered more dangerous and difficult of passage from the steep precipice on its left.

However, to work we went with the utmost prudence and caution; wheels were locked, and strong parties of men with drag-ropes attached to each gun, to regulate and impede its progress down the hill. We were just beginning to congratulate ourselves on having accomplished the labours of the day without any mishap, save the loss of a few camels that had fallen over the crags and been dashed to pieces, when, much to our regret, we found that the drag-chain had been taken too soon off the last gun, which thus gaining additional velocity, became unmanageable, knocked an artillery-man down, and, passing over his foot, lamed him for life. A light wagon, the private property of our commandant of artillery, also got free of the drag-chain, and rolling over the precipice, was, with all it contained, almost completely destroyed; the fragments were, however, picked up and brought into camp.

The horses and bullocks were now put into the guns and wagons, and the men having resumed their arms, and the parties from the heights being withdrawn, we continued our march, reaching camp about half-past six, tolerably fagged with our day's work—the most fatiguing we had yet had.

The distance from Killa Abdoolah to Chummum is eleven miles and a half, and the time we occupied in traversing it unopposed was upwards of fifteen hours.

Finding water at Chummum in greater quantities than we expected, Major Hibbert determined on halting the following day. It was intended that our next march should be on Puttonah Killa;; but learning during the 15th, that water there was excessively scarce as well as bad, our route was altered to Kalzie, a distance of upwards of thirty miles.

The artillery, escorted by two companies, left camp about five p. m. on the 15th, and the infantry marched the same night at eleven, and moving over a desert plain, reached Kalzie about ten the following morning, encamping near a large pool of brackish water.

We had now two hundred men in hospital, and our cattle were completely exhausted from the severity of the march across the Kojuk, the limited supplies of forage at Chummun , and the general scarcity and badness of the water.

Our *bheesties* assured us that the brackish pool was the only place in the neighbourhood from which to procure water. After a little inquiry, however, we ascertained that about three-quarters of a mile off, near the hills, there was an excellent stream; and having assured ourselves of this fact and that the water was of good quality, it was determined that the detachment should halt until the 18th; we then again resumed our march on Mile-i-Munda,—the road good, the country as we neared Candahar becoming more rugged and beautiful. Numbers of the Candaharees came out to meet us here, bringing supplies of delicious grapes, pomegranates, &c. On the 19th, we marched to Tukta Poole, on the banks of the Doree River, where we encamped. The country between this and Kojuk is exceedingly barren; considerable difficulty was experienced at almost every halting-place in getting water, and that which we did procure was generally brackish.

On the 20th we marched to Deh-i-Hadjie, a distance of fourteen miles. The country was still rocky and barren. It being uncertain whether the road hence to Candahar laid down in the route furnished us by the quartermaster-general, could at this season be practicable,

Lieutenant T. Nelson, who was staff-officer to the force, and myself, were directed to move on in advance to Candahar, for the double purpose of reporting on the road and of taking over the barracks in which our regiment was to be quartered, so as to admit of the men occupying them on arrival. In pursuance of orders, we accordingly set off late in the afternoon, with a small escort of "Skinner's Horse," bivouacking when night closed in near a small village; and the following morning early we proceeded on our journey to the late Douranee capital.

A few miles from our encampment we met two *suwars*, who were going out with letters to our camp. By them, Nelson received a letter from Captain Ripley, fort-adjutant at Candahar, conveying intelligence of disturbances in the north, and the disasters which had attended some of our operations there. The illusion that Affghanistan was in a state of tranquillity and perfectly satisfied with the existing rule, was now at an end. The events above referred to were but a prelude to the storm of strife and blood which was impending.

The dark cloud of rebellion was gathering unheeded, yet not unseen; and though forewarned of the danger that was hanging over their self-devoted heads, no measures were taken, no precautions adopted by those at the head of affairs in Affghanistan, to stem the fury of a torrent which in its headlong course was to carry destruction to a British army, and attach a disgrace to our arms unprecedented and unequalled in the annals of British history.

On the morning of the 21st, we reached Candahar and proceeded to the house of Captain Ripley, with whom we breakfasted. Having found the country between Deh-i-Hadjie and Candahar perfectly impracticable, on account of its general inundation for the purposes of agriculture, and experienced much difficulty in riding through it ourselves, a guide was dispatched to our small force with a view of bringing them by a different route. After breakfast we called on Colonel MacLaren, commanding the garrison in the absence of General Nott,—who was moving through the districts in the neighbourhood collecting tribute, and then proceeded to inspect the barracks which we were to occupy.

They had been built originally for native troops, but to us who had, for three years, been accustomed to canvas, they appeared a sort of palace. They were situated to the north-west of Candahar, between the city and the Baboowalla Pass; there were three distinct sets of barracks for the men, built in line, having a space of two hundred or three hundred yards between each. The square on the right was handed over to us for the 40th: on its right, and about two hundred yards to the rear, was the hospital,—a rectangular comfortable-looking building, enclosing a small square. In the rear of the hospital about two hundred and fifty yards, and to the right, were the barracks for the officers of the corps occupying the right barrack,—this was a long narrow building containing thirty-two rooms, exclusive of mess-room. It was not, however, completed on our arrival.

On the left, and on the same line, with a space of two hundred or three hundred yards between, was a similar range of buildings, also unfinished, for the officers of the corps occupying the barracks on the left. The general magazine for the cantonment was in line with the hospital, and in rear of the centre barracks. The barracks were built of mud and brick like the houses generally, wood being scarce, indeed almost unprocurable in sufficient strength for such a purpose. The roofs were all arched; their conical shape presented a curious appearance very much resembling enormous beehives. There were no defensive communications between the detached squares and buildings; on the right they were flanked at the distance of about one hundred yards by a deep water-cut, two or three ruined villages, and some burying-grounds. In front there was a parade-ground, circumscribed, however, by deep and rugged hills, which, rising abruptly about two hundred yards in front of the men's barracks, divided the Candahar Valley from that of the Urghundaub. On the left flank were innumerable water-courses, ravines, and gardens; and on the rear, between cantonments and the city, was an extensive plain.

From the above imperfect description it will be remarked that the cantonments at Candahar not only extended over a large tract of country, but were badly planned, and difficult, if not incapable, of defence.

On the 21st we had the pleasure of dining with the 16th regiment Bengal N. I., one of the officers of which, Mr. Burnett, I had known in former days, when he was adjutant of the Joudpore legion. After walking about, we returned to our tent, which had been pitched near the cantonments, to dress for dinner; when we were surprised to see at it a guard of *sepoys*. On inquiry, the *naique* told us they had been sent there by order of the Colonel Sahib. At dinner we took an opportunity of thanking him for this very great, and as we thought, superfluous mark of attention; he assured us, however, that such precautions were quite necessary in this country. At night, when we rose to depart, we were still more astonished to find that our kind friends not only insisted on our taking swords with us, (we had not brought our own) but would not let us move without an orderly. They remarked that we were most imprudent in going about unarmed in the manner in which they observed we did:—after-events proved that there was discretion in their advice.

On the 22nd we dined with the 43rd Bengal N. I., the officers of which, like those of the 16th, were delighted to see us, not only from hospitable feelings, but, as the arrival of the 40th was to be the signal for their return to India. Little did we think that night, that in a few months we were to perform under the illustrious Nott a series of operations which have won for this distinguished and lamented officer the gratitude and admiration of his country.

On the 23rd, H. M. 40th and Blood's nine-pounder battery, marched into Candahar, Nelson and myself riding out to meet them. From them we learned that the road by which they had been brought that morning, was the worst they had yet encountered—a network of ravines and water-courses, and, in many places, inundated; in fact, the staff appeared to have had very little knowledge of the surrounding country.

Ukrum Khan, a celebrated rebel chief, was this morning to be blown away from a gun. Our detachment was ordered to march through the town to cantonments, as in case there should be any *émeute*, it was wished that the execution should take place while we were in the city. On arrival at the gate by which we were to enter, it was found that the bridge leading to it over a deep water- course was not wide enough to admit of the guns going over,—a fact which we thought might have been known to some of those staff-officers who for several years had been stationed at Candahar: the guns were therefore taken direct to cantonments.

While marching through the city, the report of a gun was heard, which told that the career of Ukrum Mahommed Khan had closed. Judging from the apparent indifference of the populace, one would suppose that such executions were of frequent occurrence.

Candahar[1] is a large city, built in the midst of a plain, and sur-

1. The city of Candahar is large and populous. Heraut and Candahar are the only cities in the Douranee country, and, except Furree, probably the only places which ever merit the name of a town. The ancient city is sometimes said to have been founded by Lohrasp, a Persian king, who flourished in times of very remote antiquity, and to whom also the founding of Heraut is attributed. It is asserted by others, with far greater probability, to have been built by Sewnder Goolkurjlyne; that is, by Alexander the Great. The traditions of the Persians (continued next page),

rounded by high mud walls that form an irregular pentagon: a deep dry ditch environs the wall. The streets are very narrow but regularly built. In the heart of the town, where the four principal streets meet, is a large dome called the Charsoo, from a hook in the centre of which the bodies of criminals who have been executed are exposed.

There is a citadel inside, which comprises the palace and other public buildings; in front of this is a large square. There is nothing of architectural beauty in the palace, or indeed in any building in Candahar, if we except the tomb erected to the memory of Ahmed Shah, the founder of the Douranee Empire,—a large octagonal structure with a handsome, lofty, and elegantly-painted dome.

"It is held," writes Mr. Elphinstone, "in high estimation by the Douranees, and is an asylum against all enemies, even the king not venturing to touch a man who has taken refuge there."

The valley of Candahar is rich and highly cultivated, but is of little extent, being surrounded and circumscribed by mountain and desert.

The day after our arrival had been fixed on for a race, open to all horses—the prize being a sword given by his Highness Prince Timour Shah. *We* of the Bombay force had received no warning of this event, and had not put our horses in training; notwithstanding which, and the Bengallees having had plenty of time for preparation, we entered some of our nags, and a *Duck*[2] horse proved victorious.

Captain Haldane, with two *rissallahs* of Skinner's, followed us from

---

here agree with the conjectures of European geographers, who fix on this site for one of the cities called Alexandria.

The ancient city stood till the reign of the Ghiljies, when Shah Hussian founded a new city, under the name of Hussianabad. Nadir Shah attempted again to alter the site of the town, and built Nadirabad; at last, Ahmed Shah founded the present city (1753 or 1754), to which he gave the name of Ahmed Shauhee, and the title of *Astrufool Beloud*, or the noblest of cities: by that name and title it is still mentioned in public papers, and in the language of the Court; but the old name of Candahar still prevails among the people, though it has lost its rhyming addition of Daurool Kurrar, or the abode of quiet. Ahmed Shah himself marked out the limits of the present city, and laid down the regular plan, which is still so remarkable in its execution: he surrounded it with a wall, and proposed to have added a ditch; but the Dooraunees are said to have objected to his fortifications, and to have declared that their ditch was the Chemin of Bistaun (a meadow near Bistaun, in the most western part of Persian Khorassan). Candahar was the capital of the Douranee Empire in Ahmed Shah's time, but Timur changed the seat of government to Caubul.—*Elphinstones Account, of the Kingdom of Caubul*, vol. ii.

2. "Duck," a pet name for the Bombay Presidency—Bengal being distinguished as "*Qui hi*," and Madras as "*Mulls*."

Quettah and brought up with him a portion of the heavy baggage, which, for want of camels, we had been obliged to leave behind.

General Nott having returned to garrison, arrangements were commenced to enable the brigade, consisting of the 16th, 42nd, and 43rd Bengal N. I., to return to India; they had pitched their camp some distance from the walls, when the continual alarming reports from the north decided the general in detaining them for some days.

Dispatches were a few days after received from the Envoy, requiring the services of this brigade at Cabul, should they not have passed the Kojuk Mountains; they were immediately ordered to advance on that city, and left Candahar about the beginning of November, under the command of Colonel MacLaren, the senior officer. After having advanced till within four marches of Ghuznee, the Commander of this brigade determined on retracing his steps to Candahar,—the advanced season of the year and the inclemency of the weather, rendering it in his opinion impossible to proceed. Of course, as in all similar cases, there were many who disagreed with the colonel as to the propriety and expediency of this step, and many were the conjectures indulged in as to the effect his persisting in moving on would have had, and how far matters at Cabul would have been influenced thereby.

One thing is beyond a doubt, that had he advanced, and the defeat of his brigade been added to the number of reverses we at this time encountered, the small force left at Candahar—although I consider it superior to anything that was ever brought against us—would have been placed in a different position from that we were enabled to assume during the winter of 1841 and 1842 by the return of Colonel MacLaren's brigade,—as, in such an event, all our acts must have been entirely and essentially defensive.

I had often heard of the vast superiority in appearance of the Bengal *Sepoys* over those of the other Presidencies; and when I saw them paraded I was certainly in no way disappointed. Of the splendid regiments stationed with us at Candahar, *viz.*—the 2nd, 16th, 38th, 42nd, and 43rd regiments of Bengal N. I., it would have been difficult to say which had the superiority. I think, however, that without being accused of making any invidious distinction, I may particularize the 16th as being the finest infantry regiment I have ever seen.

On our first arrival here we had some capital shooting, and several of our sportsmen were very successful in their attacks on woodcock, numbers of this bird, but of rather a smaller size than those indigenous to England, being found in the orchards: there was also excellent fishing in the Urghendaub. But both these amusements were now put a stop to; the most distressing and desponding accounts from Cabul continued to reach us, and the natives of this part of Affghanistan were beginning to assume a very different manner toward us. A few matchlock balls came unpleasantly near the heads of some of our Nimrods, and at length communication on every side was cut off, and we were placed in a complete state of blockade, and could not even walk through the city without being well armed.

An insurrection being expected in the city, we were, during the greater part of the month of December, obliged to furnish a company of Europeans to keep guard over the guns, all of which had been brought thither.

Chapter 14
Disaffection of the Affghans

The disturbed state of the country having determined General Nott to detain Colonel MacLaren's brigade at Candahar, the troops were disposed of in the following manner:—The whole of the artillery, 38th, 42nd, and 43rd regiments of Bengal N. I., two regiments of Shah's infantry, and Skinner's Horse, remained in garrison, under the immediate command of General Nott; H. M. 40th, the 2nd and 16th regiments of Bengal N. I., and a regiment of Shah's cavalry, under Colonel MacLaren, occupied cantonments.

The extent of the dislike to the presence of the *Feringhees* in their country was daily becoming more evident among the Affghans; and there were but few who doubted the existence of a general and well-organised plan of operations throughout the whole country,—a plan having for its object the expulsion of the British from Affghanistan—and which, if not originating with, was certainly acquiesced in and encouraged by, Shah Soojah, who, now considering himself secure on the throne, had become tired of the restraint which our presence imposed upon him.

The details of the disasters at Cabul are familiar to everyone—the bitter remembrance of them can never be effaced from the hearts of Englishmen. In reflecting upon them, or on the events which preceded them, there is not one bright spot to which it is possible to refer. The fact that these disasters were not brought about by the mutiny, defection, or other misconduct of our soldiers, may indeed be some consolation; but it heightens the regret that troops, possessing those noble qualifications of soldiers which the devoted army of Cabul evinced to the last, should have been sacrificed by mismanagement, or have become the victims of an infatuation, the monstrous excess of which it is hardly possible adequately to conceive.

There are no terms harsh enough to express our intense abhorrence of the foul massacre of the Cabul army, nor can anything extenuate the perfidious conduct of the Affghans; but in condemning, however justly, the actions of others, we must also consider how far we may have drawn on ourselves the dreadful calamities left us to deplore. Does the review of the past in Affghanistan justify us in maintaining that our conduct there was without reproach? Had all our arrangements and engagements with the natives of that country been strictly and inviolably observed? Was there no breach of faith, no disregard of promises, to cause doubts of our integrity, or of our intentions, should fortuitous events have placed the army, which was afterwards destroyed, in a position where might would have empowered, if a sense of right would not have justified, our non-observance of those obligations?

I fear to these questions no satisfactory answer can be given: it therefore becomes an additional source of humiliation, that we *cannot* assert that our actions were irreproachable. It must ever be borne in mind, that the rights of the Affghans, as a nation, had been causelessly assailed,—their feelings wantonly insulted; that they felt degraded by our *surveillance,* and were anxious to throw off our yoke. They had grounds for the indulgence of revengeful passions; and had their cause not been stained by the commission of those acts of *treachery, by which our disasters were completed,* they must have claimed the admiration which would have been due to a people combating to the death for their assaulted freedom.

On the evening of Christmas-day, 1841, we were disturbed while at dinner by the firing from the piquets on the left of cantonments. The alarm was sounded, and officers immediately repaired to the barrack-square, where their men had fallen-in. What an easy matter, it then most forcibly struck us, would it have been for a few horsemen to have come down, under cover of the darkness, and cut up the officers, as they moved along the level plain, between their own quarters and those of the men!

The troops, being paraded, were marched out and formed on the plain in rear of cantonments. On inquiry, we ascertained that the firing was in consequence of an attempt having been made by a few Affghans to cut down some of the picquets; and as it appeared that no further annoyance might be anticipated, we were directed to return to our barracks—not, however, without having elicited a remark from the general, that it would perhaps have been more prudent had our chief allowed the troops to remain in the barrack-squares until it was known whether their services would be required—and if so, when; instead of abandoning the barracks, hospital, &c., to the charge of only a very small and insufficient guard. After dismissing the men, we returned to our Christmas dinner, the enjoyment of which was not heightened by this untimely interruption.

On the morning of the 27th we were suddenly disturbed in cantonments by a considerable uproar in the city, and the noise of our guns moving about. We fully anticipated being called on, conceiving that the spirit of insurrection, which doubtless had extended itself there, was about to break forth. The cause of the turmoil was soon explained, by the horrifying relation of perhaps one of the most cowardly transactions on the part of the Affghans that have ever disgraced that nation. A corps of *Jan Baz* (a sort of irregular cavalry in the service of the Shah, officered from the Indian army), commanded by Lieutenant Golding, had been ordered to proceed on duty to Ghirisk. They had, it seems, shown some disaffection on the orders being communicated; but after explanations, their objections appeared to be removed, and all was settled that they were to march *en route* for their destination on the morning of the 27th,—Lieutenant Patterson, an officer in the Political Department, being ordered to accompany them.

On the 26th Mr. Golding dined in cantonments. On returning to his camp, which was close under the walls of Candahar, he entered his tent, followed by about twenty of his men. They almost immediately attacked him sword in hand; upon which he rushed for his pistols, but found the charges had been drawn by his assailants during his absence, he then seized his sword, in the hope of being able to defend himself until assistance should arrive; but of this means of defence he had also been deprived, for the villains, with a precaution suggested by cowardice of the most revolting nature, had tied the sword to the scabbard—thus preventing their victim from defending himself, or inflicting any injury on his assailants. All hope was now at an end, and he fell under the repeated blows of his relentless, dastardly, and demoniacal assassins. Mr. Patterson, drawn by the noise to the tent of his friend, was also attacked, dreadfully mutilated, and left for dead. He was, however, afterwards carried into garrison by his servants.

Mr. Golding I had not the pleasure of knowing further than by report. Had kindness and attention to the wants of his men sufficed to have secured for him their affections, he ought to have possessed those of his corps in an eminent degree.

The miscreants, immediately after the perpetration of the crime, absconded, carrying off a considerable sum, which they were to have taken to Ghirisk for political purposes. It had for some time been agreed among the different *Jan Baz* corps that their officers were to be murdered a conspiracy which unfortunately, both here and to the north, had been carried into effect—a circumstance which goes far to prove that the insurrection in Afghanistan had been long and expertly organised. The intention was that Golding should not have been murdered until the corps had made one march from Candahar. What could have induced them to alter their resolution it is difficult to comprehend.

A troop of horse-artillery, with some of the Shah's cavalry, under Captain Leeson, were ordered off early in the morning after the *Jan Baz*. The former were, however, recalled; but Leeson with his troopers moved on, and after a smart ride came upon the greater portion of the objects of their search, the remainder having moved off by another direction with the treasure. On seeing Leeson advance they drew up on the plain, and as he approached met his charge resolutely. A spirited contest ensued; but the enemy were routed, leaving about sixty or eighty on the field, among whom was the principal instigator of the murder, an officer in the corps. His head was brought in and hung up in the Charsoo. At the request, however, of the Prince, the Political had it taken down, it being repugnant to the feelings of the true Moslems to see the head of a believer exposed, whose only offence, in their eyes, was ridding the world of a "dog of an *infidel*."

Two days after Golding's murder, Prince Sufter Jhung, son of Shah Soojah, and a worthy member of an ungrateful and treacherous brood, decamped from garrison, and joined Actar Mahommed Khan, a *Ghilzie* chief, who was assembling a large army for our winter's entertainment.

We now began to experience great difficulty in obtaining supplies; many patrols of the enemy were moving about the country, threatening the villagers with death and destruction should they in any way assist us; foraging parties were sent out two and three times a-week, on which occasions they had always a brush with the enemy's patrols, and invariably sustained a loss. On the 11th of January, 1842, information was brought in that the Prince and Actar Mahommed were advancing on Candahar, and our general determined that he would meet them half way. Our temporary doors and windows were therefore unscrewed, and the sick in cantonments, with all the baggage there, were ordered into garrison—a step which, from the straggling and indefensible nature of our barracks, to which I have before alluded, was rendered necessary on every occasion that we had to move out.

On the morning of the 12th of January the following force, the command of which was assumed by General Nott, rendezvoused at cantonments:—Blood's company of artillery (four nine-pounders); two troops of Shah's horse-artillery (six six-pounders each), under Captain Anderson; a regiment of Shah's cavalry, under Captain Leeson; two *rissallahs* of Skinner's Horse, under Captain Haldane; H.M. 40th, 2nd, 16th, and 38th; one wing of the 43rd Bengal N. I., and the 3rd regiment of Shah's infantry.

H.M. 40th, 2nd, and 16th regiments formed the right column, under Colonel MacLaren, and were directed to advance to the Urghundaub Valley, through the Baboowalla Pass (a narrow gorge between two hills of no great extent). The remainder of the force moved round the hills to the left, a distance of three or four miles. The pass, notwithstanding its being only about two miles from Candahar, and on the direct road to a luxuriantly cultivated and thickly inhabited valley, was quite impracticable for guns or cavalry, although a very few hours' labour would have rendered it completely otherwise.

Our light companies were thrown out as we approached the pass, but no opposition was here offered to us, although from the number of small parties of the enemy in sight, we fully expected its occupation to be disputed: they, however, as we advanced, retired on their main body, which on clearing the pass we could see drawn up about four miles on the opposite side of the river, presenting from its number and their many gay and floating banners a very imposing appearance. On either side of the Urghundaub River extend for miles numerous picturesquely-situated villages, connected with each other by rich luxuriant orchards, the latter generally surrounded by high mud walls; none of these villages on the left bank were, however, occupied by the enemy.

General Nott, who had accompanied our brigade, determined on moving down the river, effecting a junction with the rest of his force, and crossing at a ford about two miles below the pass to proceed at once to the attack, divining our object, the enemy marched in the same direction, and took up a very strong position at Killa Shuk, a fortified village built on a considerable eminence, and situated immediately opposite the ford. This village formed the centre of their position, and their right and left rested on extensive orchards, the mud walls surrounding which had been loopholed. In front of their position, between the river and fort, was a complete swamp, and in their rear an extensive plain.

About a quarter past ten, we commenced fording the river, and in a short time had all crossed, no further opposition being offered than a few shots fired by some of the enemy's skirmishers at a very long range. The two brigades of infantry were formed in columns *en masse* at quarter distance,—a troop of horse-artillery being on the right, the remainder of the guns and cavalry on the left.

Before commencing operations, it was communicated that a reward of five thousand *rupees* would be given for the head of Actar Mahommed Khan. Previous to our crossing the river, the skirmishers of the enemy had taken possession of the numerous water-courses which intersected the marsh between the rival armies. From them an incessant but ill-directed fire was maintained on our columns. Our guns were now opened on the main body, and our light companies proceeded to dispute the possession of the water-courses with the enemy; owing, however, to some misconception, they were recalled,—a step which was greeted with a yell of triumph from our opponents, who began to think that we had already had *enough*. A slight, spiritless, and ineffectual attempt was at this time made on our right flank, but was speedily repulsed.

Our skirmishers being again thrown out, the infantry columns were directed to advance, (one regiment being left with the guns,) and proceeding slowly and steadily through the swamp up to our knees in mud, we neared the enemy's position, who welcomed us with a heavy, but fortunately for us exceedingly ineffectual fire. Their line began to waver as we approached, and when at length the bayonets were brought to the charge, and the British cheer struck upon their astonished ears, they fell back, broke, and retreated in complete disorder across the plain. Our cavalry had now to make a wide *détour* to, avoid the swamp, and we did not derive the advantage which we should have enjoyed, had they been well placed. The enemy continued their retrograde movement, but at length rallied and re-formed in the plain. Long, however, before the infantry could get within musket-shot of them, they resumed their retreat in good order; our cavalry and one of the troops of horse-artillery which had now come up, were sent in pursuit, and overtaking them, cut up numbers of the infantry, who were abandoned to their fate by the *suwars*.

Our force engaged this day was three thousand five hundred, that of the enemy was estimated at eighteen or twenty thousand. Our loss was slight, six or eight officers wounded, and a few men killed and wounded; that of the enemy was said to have been very great, which I can easily imagine our artillery, which was beautifully served, having had such dense masses on which to play.

Prince Sufter Jhung and Actar Mahommed Khan commanded in person; the latter rode about enveloped in a shroud, expressing to his followers his determination to die in the field rather than yield. However, he seemed to have heard that discretion is valour's better part, and that

He who fights and runs away,
Will live to fight another day,

So it was with these chiefs. The *Killadar* of Killa Shuk being asked what induced him to join the enemy, answered, "My Prince and my chief called me to the field, and I could not refuse; they were, however, the first to run away, and I believe the Kaffers are running yet!"

Finding our pursuit of this broken and dispersed enemy to be labour in vain, we directed our steps on Candahar, and crossed the Urghundaub considerably lower down than we had in the morning, and at a place which, for its depth, and the rapidity of the stream, had little claim indeed to the name of ford: after some difficulty, however, we managed to get across, and had just time to re-form, when a large body of horsemen appeared in our front. We concluded that the sports of the day were not yet over, and prepared for another brush. The leader of this fresh force, Mirza Ahmed, a quondam ally, persuaded our Political that his disposition towards us was most friendly, and that he had only come out to assist us; consequently we were not allowed to slip at him. As a proof of the sincerity of his regard, he and his men joined the enemy on the following morning.

Continuing our march, we reached cantonments late in the evening, and from our kits being shut up in garrison, had the satisfaction of bivouacking in our wet clothes during the remainder of a cold freezing night.

Thus ended the "Battle of Urghundaub," the *first success after our recent disasters at Cabul*, although that honour has been awarded to another distinguished force, the Governor-general having, in a notification dated Benares the 22nd of April 1842, communicating the defeat of Akbar Khan by the "illustrious garrison at Jellalabad," congratulated the army on the return of victory to its ranks.

The success at Candahar on the 12th of January was most complete, and in its results most important. The victory having been obtained over a force so immensely superior to that which was opposed to it by the British, most effectually damped the spirit of our enemies in this part of the country, and destroyed the prestige prevailing that with the disasters of Cabul the glory of our arms had departed,

Next morning we learned that Mirza Ahmed had been moving about all the preceding day in the vicinity of Candahar,—doubtless with the laudable intention of cutting up our force on their retreat after defeat, which was looked upon as certain; or of assisting our enemies in the event of a revolt in the city, which was expected to have taken place on the town's being partially abandoned.

A dispatch detailing the events of the 12th was forwarded to Government, but no notification proclaimed them to the world. The exploits of "that army which was for so long a time neglected," were then unnoticed, if not disregarded.

About this time General Nott received instructions from Cabul to evacuate Candahar, and hand it over to the Affghans,—a measure from which his gallant spirit revolted, as compliance with this order must have affected our national reputation,—striking at the foundation of our power in India, and involving the abandonment of our small and gallant band at Kelat-i-Gilzie.

Our opponents, although for the time broken and disheartened, had not abandoned their cause; small parties kept moving about, pursuing most successfully the system of intimidation towards the villagers. The duties of foraging were very harassing, and the success attending them usually but slight; our cattle were beginning to die from sheer want; the cavalry horses were failing and becoming totally unequal to perform the duties required of mounted troops; the sheep and cattle which were procurable for the men, appeared as if in the last stage of consumption—the carcasses of the former, when denuded of their skins, bearing more resemblance to stable-lanterns than food for fighting men; while the only flour we could obtain for making bread, was at least one-third honest desert-sand to two-thirds of flour.

Added to all this, fuel was difficult to be got even in sufficient quantities for the purposes of cooking, much less to enable anyone,—even the sick in hospital,—to have the indulgence of a fire during a season of the year when the cold was equal to, if not more intense than the severest we had experienced in our fatherland, and felt the more from the total want of proper doors and windows in our unfurnished quarters. Nor did all the *désagrémens* of our position end here; towards the end of the month the enemy, encouraged by the accounts of our reverses to the north, had again united; rumours of an intended attack on our cantonments were brought in, the plan of operations being to assail the isolated quarters of the officers first,—an event which to our general surprise had not already taken place. Greater precautions were now adopted to meet the emergencies threatened: Blood's company with their guns was sent out to cantonments; one-third of the force was kept accoutred day and night; the picquet at the officers' quarters was strengthened; and on those days which were most frequent, when one of the numerous spies came in bringing *positive* information of an attack during the night, all hands were kept ready, and the officers assembled and remained during the night at the men's barracks. Such was the state of affairs at Candahar in January 1842, and such it continued during the whole winter, and until the arrival of General England in May.

No direct attack was ever made on cantonments, but the object in harassing our men was sufficiently gained by the enemy frequently coming down in small parties at night, shouting and firing a few shots, the result of which was usually the turnout of the whole cantonment brigade—a disgusting, annoying style of service, and the advantage derived by our displaying such an excess of alertness very questionable.

Chapter 15

Desperate Night Attack on Candahar

Shortly after the events of the Urghundaub, arrangements were made among some of the sporting community to get up a steeple-chase. An excellent piece of ground for this breakneck amusement was selected close to the walls of Candahar, and numerous horses were entered. The eventful day dawned at length, and the horses with their riders assembled at the starting-post. Among the steeds entered was one belonging to Mr. Terry, of the Bombay Artillery, the same on which, towards the end of last month, after all communication had been cut off with Quettah, he had gallantly and by himself pushed his way from Killa Abdoolah to join his company, which was at Candahar. His horse was a small chesnut Arab, and on this occasion was ridden by Mr. Eagar of the 40th.

Among the knowing ones it was looked upon almost as an absurdity,—this horse starting for a steeplechase over a stiff country, where there were so many larger and more powerful horses—many of them celebrated fencers—to oppose him; however, nothing daunted, Terry brought him to the barrier, the signal was given and away the field started. The first fence brought to a halt all but the *little Bombay pony*, as the chesnut was rather contemptuously called,—he cleared it, but galloping on, fell with his rider at the second wall; this enabled some of the others to come upon him, but horse and rider getting on their legs again, the latter sprang into the saddle, continued his course, and after a smart contest brought the little Arab in victorious. Thus, in this second struggle between the two presidencies for the superiority in horse flesh, a *Duck* horse again carried off the laurel.

To wile away the time, we constructed a fives-court at one end of the officers' barracks, and in this game, from constant practice, we became, we flattered ourselves, great adepts: it was our daily amusement, and regularly every afternoon large parties of officers were to be seen engaged in the play, while their movements were invariably watched by the enemy's scouts, a number of whom always occupied the Baboowalla Pass.

Prince Sufter Jhung and Actar Mahommed Khan, with other influential chiefs, had meanwhile assembled a considerable force, and had established their headquarters at Panjwy, a large village on the banks of the Turnuk, distant between thirty and forty miles.

Our General determined on moving out to attack them, and the troops to accompany him on this service received orders to hold themselves in readiness to march on the morning of the 4th of February. Light marching order, in its strictest sense, was to be observed; and the troops received intimation that no tents would be allowed either to officers or men.

On the 3rd the rain came down in torrents, which induced our chief to postpone his meditated expedition for some days. On the morning of the 4th, the ground appeared covered several inches deep with snow, upon which the General determined to abandon for the present all intention of moving any portion of his force from garrison.

For many years we had been sojourning in a land of sunny clime; it is impossible to convey an idea of the sensations with which this white vestment of the ground was regarded. How many pleasing reminiscences did it not recall! How many thoughts of home and those happy days when—

Releas'd from school, 'twas ours to wage,
How keenly! bloodless war,
Tossing the balls in mimic rage
That left a gorgeous star:
While doublets dark were powder'd o'er,
Till darkness none could find;
And valorous chiefs had wounds before,
And caitiff churls behind.

The snow! the snow! it brings to mind
A thousand happy things,
And but one sad one—'tis to find
Too sure that Time hath wings!
Oh, ever sweet is sight or sound
That tells of long ago;

And we gazed around with thoughts profound
Upon the falling snow.
—*Delta, Blackwood's Magazine.*

I am not ashamed to confess that we turned out in the morning, enjoyed a regular pitched battle of snowballs, and relished it with a zest not surpassed in similar contests of by-gone days.

Fortunately for us, the enemy had as great a dislike to expose themselves to the influence of this severe weather as we had; and during the month of February, which continued most inclement, we were permitted to rest in quiet, our foraging parties even meeting with little obstruction or annoyance, nevertheless getting few supplies for their trouble.

We had all fondly hoped that the climate of Candahar, which with justice has been represented as most salubrious, would have been the means of restoring our regiment to perfect health, and diminishing the arduous duties of Dr. MacAndrew, who was still not only unassisted, but had, in addition to the medical duties of his own regiment, to perform those of the company of artillery under Captain Blood. The constitutions of many of our men had, however, been undermined in the pestilential region of Quettah, and were unable to withstand the mordant effects of the cold to which we were now exposed. The principal disease from which we suffered was "*pneumonia*," an inflammatory affection of the lungs; from this we lost a great many men.

The supply of medicines, which ought to have been forwarded from Dadur to Quettah, and which should have come on with the regiment here, did not even arrive at the latter station in time to accompany the stores which left that camp, sometime after our departure, in charge of Captain Haldane. From this cause *we were entirely destitute of all medicines during the whole winter at Candahar, and until the arrival of supplies with General England's force in May* 1842. The native medicines were almost useless; therefore, when considering the sufferings of the troops from sickness, it is easy to conceive how unsatisfactory, if not hopeless, was the performance of medical duties where such small means were at the disposal of the surgeons to arrest the ravages of dysentery and fever, now becoming alarmingly prevalent.

February passed on with little to interest us; no communications from India, Cabul, or elsewhere, save by native report, ever reached us. The greater portion of our heavy baggage was unavoidably left at Quettah, and therewith the very small library which we had hitherto succeeded in carrying with us. We were thus deprived of the enjoyment which its possession afforded, and from the almost total want of books, and the impossibility of indulging in outdoor amusement at any distance from our barracks, we were reduced to a state of the most disagreeable and involuntary idleness it is possible to conceive, and even derived a sort of morbid pleasure from listening to the numerous conflicting and disastrous rumours which ever and anon reached our force.

The weather having again become fine, orders were issued to the troops that had been named to accompany the General in February, to prepare to move on the morning of the 7th of March to attack the enemy's headquarters, which were still at Panjwy. The former orders relative to tents and other heavy baggage being left behind, were renewed.

On the 4th, a *cossid* having succeeded in bringing a few letters from Quettah, I received notification of my promotion. I handed over to my friend T. Nelson the office of adjutant, whose duties, in consequence of bad health, (from which I had long been suffering,) I should have been unable, with a proper regard for the interests of the service, much longer to have continued. There was a satisfaction in learning of my advancement, increased by the knowledge that my successor was not surpassed by any adjutant in the service for zeal and ability, and equalled by few in *esprit de corps*.

On the 5th occurred two cases of cholera, both of which proved fatal; the one victim, Lieutenant Armstrong, the other a sergeant in the 40th, Poor Armstrong! he had been looking forward with ardent pleasure to the expedition on which we were about to set out; and little did any of us think that one of our last duties, before leaving Candahar at this time, would be to consign to his last resting-place our merry, warm-hearted, generous Irish comrade.

On the morning of the 7th, General Nott marched from Candahar with the following troops: Skinner's horse, Shah's cavalry, two troops of Shah's artillery, six six-pounders, Captain Blood's company, four nine-pounders, H. M. 40th regiment, 16th, 38th, 42nd, six companies of the 43rd, and a wing of the Shah's 2nd regiment,—amounting in all to about four thousand fighting men.

After we had proceeded about six miles to the south-west of Candahar, a strong body of the enemy's cavalry appeared under the hills on the right flank. Three hundred of our cavalry, with two guns, were moved out, the enemy retiring, however, as they advanced.

Continuing our march, we came to a small village, named Salianna, distant from Candahar about eight or ten miles, some distance from which we took up our ground, our bivouac forming a hollow square, the few baggage-cattle we had with us being in the centre. In the afternoon, Lieutenant A. Nelson, of the 40th, our commissary, went with a small detachment to the village, which he found deserted; in it were, however, supplies of grain and *bhoosa* (chopped straw) and dried lucerne. These he was beginning to appropriate for the force, when of a sudden a large body of cavalry appeared on a hill about a mile distant, where they took post; from this a strong party detached itself, and proceeded towards the village.

Nelson fortunately kept a sharp lookout, and was enabled to beat his retreat in time. In the evening, about two hundred horsemen came down to reconnoitre our camp; an attempt was made to mask a couple of guns, but it failed, and the enemy retired on their main body, which then moved off. We experienced no annoyance during the night. The march of today was only about ten miles. As a proof of the state of inefficiency to which our cavalry were reduced, numbers of the horses actually fell down from sheer exhaustion, and several had to be shot, being unable to proceed.

During the whole winter at Candahar, and in the subsequent operations on the advance to Cabul, the want of cavalry both in point of numbers and efficiency, was much and severely felt. I mean to cast no imputation on the men composing the corps we had; on the contrary, the spirit was in them, and they must indeed have been worse than cowards had they hesitated in following their gallant leaders; but it is an indisputable fact, that their horses were generally vastly inferior in size, strength, and condition to those of the Affghans, and that generally the enemy, who are no contemptible cavalry, had the advantage of them in numbers.

But to return from this digression. At daybreak on the morning of the 8th the troops were under arms, and, marching along the valley, left the Urghundaub some distance on our right. Having proceeded a few miles, a body of about five thousand cavalry, with a few infantry, were seen to our left; they had taken up a position near some villages among the hills. Our columns now wheeled to the left, deployed, and advanced. The artillery, opening a heavy fire on the enemy's line, when within about one thousand yards, made them beat a retreat, and deprived the infantry of every chance of getting near them. The Affghans continued to retire, and we to pursue, the guns keeping up a brisk fire, and doing considerable execution among the heavy *goles* of horse. The ground across which we advanced was everywhere intersected by large deep water-courses, over which the infantry with difficulty scrambled. As to the artillery they did get over them, but *how* was a sort of miracle.

For three hours and a half, we were kept advancing in line over this broken country. The infantry never fired a shot, and but a few ineffectual rounds were discharged from the enemy's skirmishers;—in fact, it was quite an "artillery affair," although one or two opportunities for the cavalry did offer, but of which, from the condition of the horses, we could not take advantage. The practice of the nine-pounders today, under direction of Captain Blood, called forth the admiration of everyone, and received the marked approbation of the General. The enemy having retired across the Turnuk, it was not deemed expedient to follow them. We moved on Punjwy, which we reached late in the afternoon, and found deserted. Here we took up ground for the night, which we were allowed to pass unmolested.

9th March.—Under arms again at daylight; and directing our movements on Lakanee—a large village to which it was reported the enemy had changed his headquarters—passed near an extensive range of barren, rugged, but not very high hills, known as the Koi Kyber or Small Kyber.

These we found occupied by the enemy in great numbers. On our approach, we were received by a volley from their matchlocks, but aim seemed to be no object, as no one was hit. The light companies of H.M. 40th and the 16th regiments under Captain F. White of the 40th, were directed to ascend the hills and drive the enemy from them; this duty was performed in gallant style. A similar service was effected with equal spirit on another hill by the grenadiers of the 40th, under Lieutenant Wakefield. The enemy now fled along the hills. Large bodies, principally of infantry, were seen moving towards the north, but from the numerous canals and swamps which intervened we could not get at them.

Today, a youth who had been fighting manfully against us was taken prisoner in the hills by some of our light company, and was brought before the general, who ordered him to be released. He was so overwhelmed with this very unexpected mercy, so different from what he would have experienced at the hands of his own countrymen, that he expressed a wish to prove his gratitude, and offered to carry a dispatch to Quettah. He was entrusted with a document, carried it safely to Quettah, and returned with an answer; and, during the remainder of our sojourn at Candahar, we continued to employ him most usefully in a similar manner.

After clearing the hills, the whole of the enemy's cavalry were seen drawn up in our front; their right was resting on a range of high ground, the line extending across the plain until their left rested on a ruined fort built on a high-scarped mound. This was occupied by infantry, large bodies of which were formed on the left of the cavalry. As was always the case, immense numbers of banners were displayed; among the rest, the black standard of Tezeen, and the red one of the *Jan Baz*, were prominent. It was hoped that they would now stand; the artillery were kept quiet, as the general wished, if possible, to get the infantry close up to our opponents; but we soon saw that fighting was not their game: *they were at present playing a much deeper one in drawing us away from Candahar.*

As we approached they retired, and continuing to increase their distance from us, crossed the river, when, as we afterwards learned, they marched on Candahar, having been preceded by the infantry we saw in the morning. The force now bivouacked close to two large villages, which, having been strongholds or points of rendezvous for the enemy, were burned. Information was brought in this evening, that it was the intention of Sufter Jhung to attack us during the night. About twelve we heard a little firing of matchlocks near camp, and a few balls whistled over our heads. The *ruse* succeeded; Sufter Jhung and Actar Mahommed, unsuspected, moved towards Candahar, and the additional object of harassing the force by turning it out having been effected, we were subjected to no further annoyance.

10th. Again ready at daybreak for a move; advanced to the banks of the river Turnuk; finding the main body of the enemy had crossed, we returned to Punjwy. A small body of cavalry, commanded, I believe, by Meerza Ahmed, who was kept out to employ and deceive us, molested our rear for a short time; they were, however, driven back by Aga Khan, a Persian refugee prince, who, with about two hundred followers, had accompanied our force from Candahar, and rendered our rearguard some very valuable assistance.

As we approached Punjwy, our quartermasters, with their escort, cantered on to take up ground; we soon, however, saw them return at a pace in which few of them usually indulged, but which was satisfactorily accounted for by their being pursued by a superior force of the enemy, that had unexpectedly come upon them.

On the 11th we marched, at our usual hour, in direction of Candahar; on our route we received intelligence, that a most determined attack on that city, the night previous, had been gallantly repulsed by the garrison left under Colonel Lane. At ten o'clock we halted for half an hour, and had breakfast, after which we continued our march over a disagreeable broken country till about seven in the evening, the rain pouring on us without intermission the whole day. Our rearguard, during the early part of the forenoon, was much annoyed by a body of cavalry, amounting to nearly a thousand men; on approaching Candahar, however, the latter drew off. After halting near old Candahar, we became acutely sensible of the claims of hunger, and, impatient of the inertness that was observed to distinguish the actions of our messman, began to call loudly for dinner.

At length the truth would out; for, anticipating that we were to go into Candahar, where he could have obtained some supplies, he had neglected to provide anything, and all that could be procured for our hungry mess were a few bones—actual undisguised bones!—we had often heard that there is more sustenance in bones than in meat, but we never expected to have been obliged to test the practical truth of the assertion. Soaked with rain, and irritated by a disappointment of so serious a nature, it will easily be credited that we were far from presenting a picture of the sweetest amiability.

On the 12th we marched into Candahar, when the regiments moved to their respective quarters. The following particulars of the attack on the city were communicated to us:—

Early on the 10th, large bodies of the enemy began to assemble near Candahar, occupying the gardens in the vicinity, and the cantonments also; during the day their numbers increased, and it was evident that their object was to attack the city. All the gates were shut and everything was deemed secure. After sunset a villager, professing to have come from a great distance, but who must have been well aware that the regulations of the garrison allowed no one to enter after that hour, came to the Herat gate, which was commanded by Lieutenant Cooke, 2nd regiment Bengal N. I., and requested permission to take in a donkey-load of faggots he had with him; this of course was refused, upon which the villager said he would leave the wood till the next morning, and, throwing it down against the gate, he departed. Nothing was then suspected; but about eight o'clock, a party of the enemy stole up unobserved, and, pouring oil and *ghee* over the faggots, set them on fire, and the flame quickly communicated itself to the gate which burned like tinder.

The stratagem having proved successful, a most spirited attack was made on the gate: but the measures of the commissary-general, were as admirably devised; seeing the danger, he threw open the stores, and, procuring all the assistance he could, succeeded just in time in forming a barricade on the gateway of the bags of flour taken from thence. The enemy rushed boldly on, the barricade was gained, but they were driven back; again and again they renewed the assault, but the destructive fire kept up by the gallant defenders at length prevailed, and the Affghans retired discomfited over a rampart formed by the bodies of their own countrymen.

It is curious to observe how very often the success or defeat of our plans depends on events in themselves most insignificant—how often the slightest accidental circumstance operates momentously on our destinies. To use a common phrase, our possession of Candahar on the night of the 10th hung by a thread.

The enemy's plan was to have fired all the gates at once, and made a simultaneous attack on them; and that this was not carried into effect, was certainly the result of a most fortunate accident.

Mr. Philips, quartermaster of the 40th, who had been left behind sick, was entrusted with the charge of the citadel gate: before fastening it for the evening, something fortunately induced him to look outside, and on opening it, he saw two or three faggots laid against it; immediately, it occurred to him that they could have been placed there for no good purpose, and he brought them inside. But for this, the gate of which he had charge, would in all probability have been fired, and an equally spirited attack made on it as on the Herat-gate, in which event I cannot doubt for a moment that the city of Candahar would have fallen, and the enemy become possessed of all our stores and ammunition, two eighteen-pounders, &c.

Fortune favours the brave, and the fickle lady did, in this instance, much favour our gallant general. It is difficult to conjecture what would have been the result had we lost Candahar, or what steps would have been pursued by General Nott with regard to the movements or operations of his force. It is perhaps not assuming too much to say, that the loss of this city would have endangered the safety of our Indian empire. The consequence to that portion of the Candahar force which was left in garrison, must have been certain destruction. Those troops which were out with the general were without tents, without supplies, and with a very limited number of rounds of ammunition; it would have been vain therefore to have attempted, with the small means we could command, the recapture of the city, and the only alternative left us would have been to retire over a difficult country to Quettah, which if we had reached—a doubtful thing—we should, with the force there, in all probability have been *compelled* to continue our retreat on Scinde,—a disaffected country, rejoicing in our disasters, ready to rise against us, and which we must have entered a disheartened, and virtually conquered army.

That General Nott committed a military error in marching from Candahar, and leaving so small a force for its defence, and that he was most palpably out-manoeuvred and out-generalled by allowing himself to be drawn away to so great a distance from that garrison, no one will deny. It will however be admitted, that the state of our cattle from scarcity of forage, and the difficulty we experienced in obtaining supplies, rendered it imperative that the country should be shewn that it was always in our power to send out a force sufficiently large to drive before it any army which the insurgents could assemble; so that, our superiority being proved, the villagers, impressed with a conviction of our strength, should be induced to bring supplies into garrison. A brigade of three regiments, with some guns and cavalry, would have been quite equal to this, and decidedly no greater force should have left Candahar, to be absent for any time.

It is vain to say that the best proof of the correctness of General Nott's operations was, that victory crowned them. It was indeed a singular piece of good fortune that success did attend them; but the risk he ran was too great; the stake,—the honour of our country, and the integrity of our eastern empire,—was too intensely important to be so lightly hazarded. He had certainly, previous to moving from Candahar, almost completely emptied the town of its inhabitants; he had deprived those who were permitted to remain of their arms,—wise precautions surely; but still, had the enemy not been divided in their counsels, (a misunderstanding having on the night of the attack on Candahar occurred among the chiefs,) had they not been foiled,—by the accidental but fortunate circumstance of Mr. Philips looking outside the citadel gate, and removing the faggots he found there,—in their design to fire the citadel gate,—neither the promptitude, energy, and prudence of the commissary-general, nor the distinguished gallantry of the small garrison under Colonel Lane, would have sufficed to withstand the force of a fearless, simultaneous, and well-organized attack on the different gates.

"*All's well that ends well!*" It is ever easy to find faults, especially after events have occurred, and when we have had time to study and reflect on what might have been the consequences. Candahar was still ours. The gallant and memorable defence by which it had been preserved, while it shed a glory on the brave guardians to whose keeping it had been intrusted, added another to the continued successes obtained by the Candahar army, during and since the occurrence of our disasters at Cabul.

The "*amusements*," during the rest of the month, were slightly varied by what were termed *moral-effect marches*. These consisted in the cantonment brigade being taken out occasionally under our commandant, Colonel MaClaren, who marched us to some neighbouring villages, generally near Baboowalla. The intention of this piece of diplomacy and generalship on the part of our brigadier, was to induce the villagers to bring in supplies. I never could find out, however, that we derived much benefit from these plausible displays of the "*pomp and circumstance of war.*"

Chapter 16

Fall of Ghuznee

The fortunate result of the attack on Candahar was the means of subduing, but not conquering, the spirit of animosity and perseverance in the rebel chiefs. The infantry dispersed and returned to their villages, but the cavalry still kept the field, moving about in strong parties, effectually cutting off all communication, and preventing our obtaining any supplies except in the immediate neighbourhood of the city, where now they were well nigh exhausted.

The town of Candahar presented now a widely different spectacle from what it did on our first arrival;—then the bazaars were so crowded that it was with difficulty a passage could be effected through the dense throng of human beings, speaking various languages and attired in the costumes of many nations,—then all was bustle, industry, and activity; now, the shops were partially closed, a few stragglers wandered listlessly through the streets, and among all classes there appeared to exist a sort of reciprocated feeling of suspicion and distrust.

The sacred name of religion was called to the aid of the insurgents, the superstitions of the natives were worked upon, men lurked about in the streets eagerly watching for an opportunity to fall upon the enemies of their cause, attempts were made almost daily to cut down the unwary Europeans,—those making such endeavours conceiving themselves more than honoured and rewarded by dying in their efforts to promote the interests of their faith.

Several of the 40th were severely wounded in the very streets of Candahar, and no one could safely move even a few paces from barracks, much less through the city, without being well armed.

A striking case of the perversity of human nature and the love of acting in opposition to the orders of superiors, which met with a quick and fearful punishment, occurred about this time. Four young soldiers of the 40th went unarmed a considerable distance from camp after breakfast; at dinner parade they were absent, and during the afternoon continued so; at length some villagers came in and reported that the bodies of four Europeans were lying a few miles from camp. They had, it appeared, been seen by one of the enemy's patrols, who, coming upon them, found it of course an easy matter to overpower them. They were sacrificed to their own folly; their heads, which were severed from their bodies, were carried as trophies to the enemy's camp, where those fortunate enough in securing such a prize, were rewarded at the rate of ten *rupees* for each, (the value I presume set upon a private soldier's life),—and they were sent through the country, represented as having belonged to some of the *Feringhee sirdars*, and as proofs of a victory which had been gained by the Affghans.

On one occasion, during the month of March, I observed a knot of men standing a short distance from the officers' barracks in cantonments, and soon after, I saw a man taken to hospital who had received a severe sabre cut from an Affghan. Meeting a son of Erin, I asked him the cause of the excitement, when he replied, "O, sir, one of these fellows has just cut down a lad of ours, and we have been tapping the villain on the head with our sticks till he was dead," and sure enough when I did go up to where the soldiers were, I found lying in the road a dead Affghan, one of the finest specimens of mankind I ever looked upon.

Fives-playing by day, and turning out by night, continued to be the employments of this month: the latter, however, rather received a check; for, on one of the grand *positive-information* nights, when the guns had been run out at the different barrack-gates, and pointed towards the approaches to them, a very lynx-eyed alarmist vowed that he could distinctly see the glimmer of numbers of the lighted matches of the matchlock-men in one of the ruined villages on the right of cantonments. We all strained our eyes, but there was hardly one who could persuade himself that there was anything visible save the bare walls. I was thoroughly convinced in my own mind that there was no one about, and readily consented to prove the fact by riding off with Major Hibbert and our adjutant, Nelson, to the occupied village, where we found that the dreaded force had not even the substantiability of "men o'buckram."

After this night the positive information either did not arrive so often, or was not so readily believed.

The arrival of Lord Ellenborough had long been looked forward to with the greatest anxiety: that event had at length taken place, 'and daily we anticipated receiving some intelligence from which we might form an idea of the line of policy his Excellency would pursue for the redemption of our national honour. The worse than want of all information which might enable Lord Ellenborough, on his arrival in India, to form an opinion of the actual extent of our disasters, the correct position of our troops in Afghanistan, and the means at the disposal of our generals there to carry out such operations as he should think conducive to the interests of the empire,—is well known, notwithstanding the unworthy endeavours to throw a shade over every act of his Lordship's government, and to deprive him of the laurels he won so nobly; and to this cause must be attributed the delays and seeming indecision which at first marked his counsels.

Among the first acts of his Lordship's administration was the placing in the hands of the General Officers in Afghanistan the chief political power. Of the wisdom of this bold step the strongest proof that can be adduced is, the new and better spirit which distinguished our operations after the power of acting for themselves had been conferred on the Generals. No longer were the proceedings of these distinguished men cramped by the interference of juniors who, however talented, however conscientious, however well versed in the history of the country, and in a knowledge of its language, were frequently too deficient in experience to understand aright the responsibility of, or to wield circumspectly, the power which their false position gave them.

On the 23rd of March the enemy began again to assemble about eighteen miles from Candahar, on the right bank of the Urgundaub. On the 24th, their camp was formed at a short distance from Killa Shuk. During that day some negotiations were entered into, having for their object the estrangement of Prince Sufter Jhung from the rebels; in this, however, we failed. A *Jan Baz* chief had the impudence to say, that if he was presented with one *lac* of *rupees*, he would either dismiss his men, or move off with them to Cabul,—a modest request indeed for men who had already in cold blood murdered several of our officers, and one of whose victims (Lieutenant Paterson) was at the very moment actually dying of the injuries he had sustained at their hands in December last! This demand the general, although *politically* urged to do so, of course declined complying with.

On the 25th, Colonel Wymer moved out with three regiments of infantry, four hundred cavalry, and a troop of horse-artillery, into the

Urgundaub Valley, for the purpose of procuring supplies, and grazing the baggage-cattle. Shortly after entering the vale, about two thousand of the enemy's cavalry were observed to cross the river, with the evident intent to attack and carry off the camels. These beasts were now quickly got together, and guarded on all sides as well as circumstances would admit. Several charges were made by the enemy, numbers of whom even penetrated into the hollow square among the cattle, where they were shot or bayoneted.

About two p. m., the firing from the six-pounders with Colonel Wymer was distinctly heard at Candahar, and as it continued for some time, the general at length moved out with H. M. 40th and 2nd N. I., four nine-pounders, and the rest of the cavalry. As we cleared the Pass, a most beautiful spectacle presented itself;—the sun gleamed brightly on a forest of sabres, and the whole valley glittered "with the pomp of war." The three regiments of infantry, forming a hollow square, were drawn up in the plain, in which was a host of camels; the troop of artillery under Lieutenant Turner was playing beautifully on the *goles* of the enemy's horse; and just as General Nott with the reinforcements came in sight, Lieutenant Chamberlain of the Bengal Service, an officer in the Shah's cavalry, who at the head of a small party had charged the enemy, was driven back, and emerging from a cloud of dust, formed in rear of the infantry, with the loss of a few men killed, himself and many of his party wounded,—but not without having given very satisfactory proofs of his powers as a swordsman, albeit his treacherous weapon had broken in his hand.

A large party of the enemy's cavalry and infantry were formed near some villages close to the river; against these the General opposed the fresh troops. The light company of the 40th, under Captain White, was ordered out in advance, and I was directed with my own company to support it. However, as we approached the village and had almost fancied ourselves in possession of a most tempting green standard that fluttered in the breeze, we were recalled and moved to join Colonel Wymer's force, on which the enemy had made another spirited attack that was as gallantly repulsed; and on our approach our opponents retired towards the river, which they crossed on our continuing the pursuit.

Late in the afternoon I heard that Lieutenant Paterson had expired. The wounds received in his leg were so bad, that the surgeons recommended amputation; this he opposed, hoping his limb might be preserved,—but at length seeing that this was "hoping against hope," he consented to the operation. It was then, however, of no avail, and he died two days after it had been performed, adding another to the already too many noble spirits sacrificed to our occupation of Affghanistan.

At length, the sanguinary sports of the day were over,—the sun sunk slowly, and with glorious splendour, in the crimson west, and the bright evening-star rose calmly over the dread scene of death and carnage. Exhausted with fatigue, Colonel Wymer's brigade prepared to bivouac, and the general with his reinforcements returned to cantonments.

Early in the following morning, General Nott again moved out to the Urgundaub Valley, with the same force as the day before; the enemy's camp was still on the opposite side of the river, but at about eight o'clock it broke up, and the numerous bodies composing it dispersed and moved off in different directions. The general returned to Candahar with the small force that had accompanied him, Colonel Wymer being left out to graze the cattle, which, from the dispersion of our opponents, he was now able to effect unmolested.

It being reported that one of the chiefs, Jalloo Khan, had, after the defeat at Baboowalla, gone off towards the Kojuk with a considerable force to intercept General England, who was soon expected, Colonel Wymer's brigade was recalled on the 29th of March, and directed to proceed to Deh-i-Hadjee, on the road to Quettah, there to wait further instructions.

Reports of the fall of Ghuznee, and of the massacre of our troops there, reached us during this month. We fain hoped that they were as unfounded as some we had seen in the papers relative to disasters which were said to have occurred to ourselves, but at length the poignant truth forced itself upon us, and we learned with sorrow and shame, that the cup of our adversity was not yet filled.

"*True it is, misfortunes never come singly.*" Scarce had the rumour of the fall of Ghuznee reached our ears, when information was brought into Candahar, that our troops to the south had met with a most severe check,—that they had been driven back,—and that they had lost one at least of the superior officers. This was indeed gloomy news for us who had been looking forward daily to the arrival of General England with treasure, ammunition, and supplies of various sorts, of all of which we were now in extreme want. But we were not kept long in suspense,—the dispatch of General England to General Nott confirmed the worst accounts we had heard,—our troops had been defeated—had been compelled to retreat—and the general was busy entrenching his position at Quettah. Captain May of the light company of the 41st regiment, was killed; Major Apthorpe, an officer of high reputation in the Honourable Company's Service, and who commanded the Bombay Light Battalion at Hykulzie, was mortally wounded, and died two days after the defeat. Several other officers were wounded, and a large proportion of men killed and wounded.

An event so disastrous, occurring at such a time, was well calculated to throw a gloom over our prospects, and engender a feeling of despondency as to the result of our many and complicated calamities. Fortunately, in General Nott there was a man at the head of affairs formed for the emergencies of the times: the only thought that actuated him was a desire to maintain the character of his country—to wipe off the stains that had tarnished our arms; and in this one sacred hope, every other consideration was absorbed. His dauntless spirit appeared to gain additional strength as the difficulties and dangers surrounding him increased: and seeing at once the perils which would beset our cause—the very ruin which would involve us—if the severity of the present blow should tend to damp the ardour or moderate the exertions on which so much depended the success of the darling project of his heart—the advance on Cabul,—he sent off a dispatch to General England, *peremptorily* ordering him to leave his entrenchments and move at once on Candahar; and to guard against the possibility of any second mishap, he arranged that a brigade under Colonel Wymer should proceed towards Quettah, to co-operate with General England, and facilitate the passage of the Quettah force over the Kojuck mountains.

As an offset to our disasters, on the 7th of April occurred the defeat, by the gallant Sale and his intrepid band, at Jellalabad, of Akbar Khan—an event which infused a spirit of hope and energy into our Indian councils, and which, joined to the long list of successes that had crowned the British arms at Candahar, diffused a joy throughout the empire, in the conviction that in the hands of Nott and Sale the honour of England would be asserted, retrieved, and maintained.

The day for General England's departure from Quettah being determined on, Colonel Wymer, with a strong brigade of infantry, some guns and cavalry, moved towards the end of April to the Kojuck Pass; and on the 2nd of May, having crowned the heights on the north of that range of mountains, General England, who had just been successful in defeating the enemy at the same place where he had met with so severe a reverse in March, effected a junction with the Candahar brigade. On the 9th of May, we had the pleasure of welcoming this force, who brought with it letters, for forwarding which from Quettah no opportunity had offered since November last,—supplies of treasure and hospital comforts,—our stock of which was completely exhausted,—and ammunition, of which we were also beginning to experience a scarcity. Added to all this, there was a host of old and valued friends, particularly among the officers of the 3rd Bombay Cavalry (old Deesa comrades), from whom we had much to learn of their doings since we had last met, and of course much to communicate of ourselves. The few camels brought up by this force were not the least valuable acquisition to our means, and the prospect of being soon able to procure an additional supply, and thereby empowered to act on a more extended scale, was a source of much gratification.

Among those who accompanied General England's force from Quettah was one of those most enterprising of all enterprising natives, the *Parsees*, bringing with him a few of the good things of this life, and by whose means we were enabled, although in a *very* moderate way as to *quantity* and *quality*, and at a very exorbitant price, to renew our acquaintance with generous wine, a thing unknown of late months in our messes, where the hydropathic system had been most rigidly although most involuntarily observed.

The chaplain, Mr. Allen, who accompanied General England's division, breakfasted with us on the morning of the arrival of the Quettah force, It was many months since we had seen one of his sacred calling, and the appearance among us in that distant and barbarous land of a clergyman of the Church of England, attached a degree of civilization to us, which, from long absence from polite circles, many of us had almost begun to think had departed. Mr. Allen has written a pleasing and beautiful narrative of the incidents which took place on his route to join the Candahar division, and during the eventful operations of that force, in all of which he participated. For the more than kindly feelings he has expressed towards my cherished corps, I tender him my best and warmest thanks; and can assure my reverend friend that these feelings of esteem are reciprocated by the regiment in the society of whose officers his lot was for a long time cast, and that his name is associated with some of the most pleasing recollections of our Affghan life.

Tidings reached us of the death of Shah Soojah, our puppet king. He was a prince possessed of but few, if any, virtues, and of a character deformed by the most horrible vices and disgusting sensualities. Long practised in the arts of treachery and duplicity, he at length fell a victim to their snares, and by the hand of an assassin was suddenly removed from a world where he had ever failed to inspire esteem or respect, and which he left at last unregretted.

A few days after General England's arrival, orders were issued for the following force under Colonel Wymer to hold itself in readiness to proceed to the relief of Kelat-i-Gilzie, the small garrison of which had so nobly held their ground during the winter:—H. M. 40th, 16th, and 38th Bengal N. I., 3rd Bombay Cavalry, troop of Bombay artillery, and company of Bombay European artillery with nine-pounders.

On the morning of the 19th we marched from Candahar, the remaining troops, which had been provided with quarters in garrison, having moved in previous to our departure and occupied them. Our first march was to Abdoolah Khareez, near which is a small insignificant fort; the road good, but the country almost as soon as leaving Candahar becoming desolate and sterile. To the right and left of our route was a dead flat, bounded by arid hills devoid of all vegetation. Water, which was procurable from a Kareez, was good, but not very plentiful.

On the 20th, continued our march twelve miles to Killa Azeem; road excellent, over a level and barren plain.

21st. Entered the valley of the Turnuk, in the country of the *Ghilzies*, and having marched about seventeen miles, encamped on the right bank of the river at Killa Akhoond. The valley is exceedingly narrow, and highly cultivated. Close to the river were growing most luxuriant crops, in the midst of which we encamped, and, necessity knowing no law, were compelled to let our cattle feed on the standing corn. The country in the immediate neighbourhood of the cultivated parts produced not a blade of any vegetation, and no villagers entered our camp with supplies. Received information today that the *Ghilzies* were assembling an immense force to oppose us a few marches a-head.

On the 22nd, marched to Sher-i-Suffa, twelve miles; road undulating, narrow, intersected by ravines, and passing for the first few miles through a narrow defile, the base of which was washed by the river. Delayed sometime today in making the road practicable for our guns. Some short distance from camp was a curious old fort, lately deserted. Encampment still on the banks of the Turnuk, in which there was excellent fishing.

23rd. To Teer-un-daz, ten miles over a very good road; pitched near the Turnuk, and still among the corn-fields. Near our camp was a large obelisk that marks the spot to which Ahmed Shah propelled an arrow from his bow, from the top of a neighbouring hill;—hence the name of the place, which signifies the "flight of an arrow." The distance from the hill to the obelisk is considerable, and proves that Ahmed Shah could have been inferior to none of his countrymen in the use of the *long bow,* for which, in one acceptation of the term, they are very justly remarkable. Received a note on arrival here from Kelat-i-Gilzie, mentioning that a most determined attack had been made on that fort, by a large body of *Ghilzies*, on the morning of the 21st. The manner in which this noble little garrison repulsed the assault, added to the laurels they had already won for themselves, by the gallant and determined manner in which they maintained their position during the whole winter, although exposed to cold and privations unequalled by any of the victorious troops in Affghanistan.

24th of May. Marched to Assielmie, ten miles; road good, but near our encamping-ground much intersected with ravines and water-courses. At this place, Colonel Wymer, in May 1841, with a wing of the 38th B.N. I., two guns, and some cavalry, engaged, and totally defeated, an immensely superior force of *Ghilzies*.

25th of May. To Asseerzy, thirteen miles, road good, encampment still on the Turnuk; we could plainly see Kelat-i-Gilzie from our camp.

26th of May. Marched to Kelat-i-Gilzie, twelve miles; a few of the intrepid defenders of the fort came out to meet and welcome our force; encamped to the westward of the fortress.

The small fort of Kelat-i-Gilzie was built on a high table-hill, rising abruptly from the plain, about one hundred and fifty feet above its level. From the centre of this table-land, rises to about the height of one hundred feet a small conical hill, which formed the citadel. It was formerly one of the largest forts or villages in this district, and, at one time, was the principal stronghold of the *Ghilzie* clan of Tukhu. When occupied, however, by our troops, on first entering the country, it was a mass of ruins, and had been long uninhabited. Barracks were constructed here for about one thousand men, and would have been tolerably comfortable quarters during the winter, but for the excessive cold, which, owing to the want of doors and windows, and the almost total absence of fuel, it was impossible to moderate. The place was surrounded by a deep dry ditch, inside which it was intended there should have been permanent wall defences; there had not, however, been time to construct them, and the fortifications round Kelat-i-Gilzie, which had been hurriedly got up by its defenders, were essentially temporary. Inside the fort were springs of excellent water.

The attack, from the testimony borne by the garrison to the gallantry of the besiegers, must have been most determined; indeed, the numbers of dead bodies of the enemy, which were still lying unburied near the principal point of attack, sufficiently attested the spirit with which the attempt to carry the place had been made and persisted in. The clearest and best account of this gallant affair is to be had from the despatch of Captain Craigie, the commander, which is annexed.

The garrison were delighted to see us. Their position was daily becoming more precarious; they had been made aware of the defeat of General England, but had not learned of his subsequently being enabled to come on to Candahar, and were not prepared to find that we could so soon march to their relief;—their supplies were nearly exhausted, indeed, the last sheep was killed the day before our arrival.

The country in the neighbourhood of Kelat-i-Gilzie is hilly, and with the exception of a very limited portion near the river Turnuk, barren and rocky.

On the 27th, the small garrison of Kelat-i-Gilzie marched out of the scene of their triumph with flying colours, and receiving three honest, hearty cheers from the relieving brigade, moved to the ground on the left of our camp, which had been marked out for them.

On the morning of the 28th, fatigue parties under the superintendence of Major Saunders, chief engineer, commenced the destruction of the fort. This duty was continued under his direction on the 29th, 30th, and 31st, when the force received orders to march the following morning. Ghuznee we had all fondly hoped was our destination; but our steps on the morning of the 1st of June were redirected to Candahar; which city, returning by the same route we had come, we reached on the 12th of June, without having met the opposition promised. Indeed, instead of seeing the vaunted thousands of *Ghilzies* who were to drive us back on Candahar—if they should condescend to leave any to drive,—I think I rather exceed the number when I state, that during our absence from Candahar in the *Ghilzie* country, we did not see more than ten natives.

At Teer-un-daz we learned that Prince Sufter Jhung, and Actar Mahommed, had been joined by Ukbar Khan, chief of Zemindawur, and that under the idea that Candahar had been left very badly off for troops, they had proceeded to the attack of that place;—that General Nott had moved out to meet them, and that these chiefs had been completely defeated.

The success attendant on the promptitude and energy that distinguished General Nott's operations, by which alone General England was enabled to reach Candahar; the repulse of the attack on Kelat-i-Gilzie; and the defeat of the united rebel army at Candahar on the 29th of June,—had completely broken the spirit of the insurgents in that part of Afghanistan.

Negotiations were entered into by Saloo Khan,—the Kojuk chief who had deserted our cause during the winter—to forward regularly the mails from Quettah: camels and stores were also brought up in considerable numbers after our return, lightly-equipped brigades being sent down for them; flocks of sheep and supplies of a better description were brought in; and the winter troops soon began to benefit from the improved living this change of circumstances produced, the wholesome meat that was now issued offering a pleasing contrast to the almost carrion, on which we had been feeding for months.

Three or four days after our return, part of the force, consisting of three regiments of infantry and the whole of the mounted troops, having in charge all our baggage-cattle, moved out under Colonel Wymer, partly for the purpose of destroying some forts which during the winter had been the strongholds of our enemies, but more for the facilities afforded in feeding our cattle. Little of interest occurred with the troops remaining in garrison and cantonments. The reports as to our destination were numerous and varied, the only certain thing being,—move somewhere out of this we must.

At fives-playing we continued really indefatigable, and had many excellent matches.

Some days after returning to Candahar, I was surprised and delighted, to be accosted by an old friend, Dr. Campbell Mackinnon, whom I had not seen for many years, and who had accidentally heard of my being at Candahar.

I was perfectly aware that he was in this country, but having understood that he was one of the Cabul prisoners, if not one of the unfortunate victims of our disasters there, I was more than astonished to find him safe at Candahar, and to learn that he was one of the participators in the ever-memorable defence of Kelat-i-Gilzie.

In July, the 40th regiment lost by his death the valuable services of Quartermaster Philips; death and burial follow each other in the East with a necessary precipitancy, which would disgust and horrify, by its apparent indecency, our friends at home; this is succeeded by a species of oblivion, yet not forgetfulness of the deceased, which, while betokening no want of feeling, proves how fortunate it is, that we are so constituted that events so distressing even as the loss of esteemed friends, do not interfere with our performance of the usual routine of duties.

Chapter 17

Advance on Cabul

Towards the latter end of July all the old guns in Candahar were destroyed, the repairs in progress in the fortifications were discontinued, and everything betokened a move, but the question was—whither?

It was well known that General Nott had all along urged upon Government the propriety, nay, the very necessity of advancing a British Army on Cabul: the means of carriage, which had lately been put at his disposal, placed him in a position to make that advance himself; and the Candahar Division gloried in the hope that he would be enabled to carry out his wish.

At length, on the 30th of July, orders were received for the troops to hold themselves in readiness to *return to India*. Part of the force, including the sick, under General England, was to retire by Quettah, and the Bolan Pass; the main body, composed of "*the best troops*" under General Nott, it was said, were to proceed to Dehra Ishmael Khan, and there cross the Indus.

The particular object to be gained by adopting this latter route it was difficult to divine, and the generally received impression among the officers, perhaps because the one most desired, was, that our General was to lead us on to Cabul, and that the mention of Dehra Ishmael Khan was merely to throw dust in the eyes of the natives; indeed, it was afterwards accounted for, whether justly or not, by this fact—that if the Louhanies, upon whom we were dependent for a large proportion of our camels, had had an idea that our intention was to have marched on Ghuznee and Cabul, they would have declined accompanying our army.

The craven portion of the press of India had long been urging the policy and propriety of withdrawing our armies from Affghanistan;

its columns teemed with letters, purporting to be from officers of our division, proclaiming the foul falsehood, that our army desired to return unavenged. For the honour of the cloth it is to be hoped that those letters never were written by officers; from whomsoever they emanated, they were but the productions of hearts in which the spirit of a soldier had never existed; and the general enthusiasm with which the prospect of our advance on Cabul was hailed, gave the lie to the dastardly assertions they contained.

Our gallant chief had "*not contemplated falling back*;" he had succeeded by his representations to Government in proving, that all that was required to enable him to advance, and strike the grand blow, for the honour of "*dear Old England*," was carriage; that he had now procured; and the sanction of Government to his forward movement had been obtained. On the small army he had, he knew that he could place the utmost reliance,—that he could confidently trust to its gallantry—its aspirations for the glory of its country—its desire to wipe off the stain from our arms—and its devotion to himself: and he knew well, too, its ardent wish to uphold him triumphantly through one of the most daring, because one of the most thoroughly independent and unsupported operations, carried through the heart of an enemy's country, which any general had ever attempted.

On the 3rd, H.M. 40th, 2nd, and 16th regiments evacuated cantonments,—and encamped close to the walls of Candahar; the same day the troops, proceeding with General England, also moved out of garrison and encamped. On the 4th, General Nott came into camp, leaving two or three regiments as a guard in the city over the stores, ammunition, &c., which had not yet been brought into camp.

An event occurred this day that might have been most serious in its results. A large quantity of damaged powder, which had been laid aside to be used by the engineers in some experiments previous to our departure, was ignited by the carelessness of an artilleryman: a vast explosion followed, the shock of which was felt for miles,—a mass of stones and dust was hurled far up into the air, there was not a window in the city that was not destroyed, several of the inhabitants were killed, and numbers, thinking it the signal for a general massacre by the British, in revenge for all we had suffered, rushed frantically to the officers on guard, and implored mercy for themselves and families. The panic was at length dispelled, and order and confidence restored in the town. It is a most fortunate circumstance that the flame from this explosion did not communicate with the main magazine, close adjoining, in which was a great part of our ammunition.

On the 6th, a few of us rode out to take a "last *fond* look" of our cantonments; part of them were occupied by the followers of some chief, ready to enter the city when we retired. Near the Baboowalla Pass we met a considerable body of horsemen, and several, on our approach, dashing out from their ranks at full speed, galloped towards us; not being very certain of our friends, we were in what the Yankees would call a *fix*, and began to think whether it would not be prudent to turn to the right about, and trust to our horses to take us into camp; the cavaliers, however, suddenly drew up, and made us a most profound *salaam*, thereby assuring us of their friendly regard.

On the 7th, the remainder of our troops were withdrawn from Candahar. Prince Timour Shah, eldest son of Shah Soojah, with his family, joined General England's camp, with which he was to proceed to Hindostan; and the command of the garrison was assumed by Prince Sufter Jhung, who, towards the end of last month, had returned to Candahar. He was not, however, in the most remote manner acknowledged by General Nott.

On the 9th, we broke ground, General England's camp moving towards Deh-i-Hadjee; that of General Nott marching on Abdoolah Kaureez, four miles on the road to Cabul.[1] The latter consisted of Leslie's troop, horse-artillery (Bombay); Anderson's troop of horse-artillery (Native, late Shah's); Bengal company, European, with four eighteen-pounders, Bombay company (Blood's); four nine-pounders and two twenty-four-pounders, howitzers,—the whole under Major Sotheby: Bengal artillery, 3rd Bombay cavalry (Delamaine); part of Skinner's horse (Haldane); irregular regiment of cavalry, late Shah's, (Christie);—the whole under Captain Delamaine: H.M. 40th regiment (Hibbert); 16th Bengal (McLaren); 38th Bengal (Burney); 3rd, late Shah's regiment (Craigie);—forming the first brigade, under Brigadier Wymer: H.M. 41st (Gore Browne); 2nd Bengal (Lane); 42nd Bengal (Clarkson); and 43rd Bengal (Nash);—forming second brigade, under Brigadier Stacey: also some sappers and miners.

On our occupation of Candahar, during the winter of 1841 and 1842, we could look back with pride and satisfaction. During the long and eventful period that, to maintain the honour of our arms we had to contend with the most trying difficulties and privations, no reverse had occurred to sully their brightness, no excess had been committed

1. We carried with us sixty days' provisions, and had a retinue of 10,000 camels, besides other beasts of burden.

by which our humanity or integrity could be impeached; nor was the general absence of crime from our troops, and the extreme devotion to our cause of the native soldiery, even when rumours of the most desponding character reached our garrison, the least gratifying part of our associations and connections with Candahar. In entering on our present undertaking, we remembered how much depended on its success. We knew the intense interest with which our movements were watched by our countrymen at home; we felt a pride in sharing the responsibility that our noble chief had dared to incur; and we were inspirited by the conviction that, under his direction, victory would attend this momentous enterprise.

Uctar Mahommed, it was said, was in the neighbourhood of Candahar, waiting for our final departure before entering the city; not liking to trust himself within the walls while we were near, for fear that we should return and secure him.

On the 10th we continued our march, and pursuing the same route that the force under Brigadier Wymer took in May last, we reached Kelat-i-Gilzie on the morning of the 17th of August. Since our last visit, the crops had been removed from the ground. The natives, of whom we saw many, had suddenly become our greatest friends and admirers, and they brought into camp supplies of grain, &c. in abundance. A few of our camp followers, how- ever, who chose to wander among the hills during our stay here, got cut up for their temerity.

The fort we found exactly in the same state as we had left it in June.

On the 19th we marched over a good, though rather a hilly road to Sir-i-Usp, nine miles. There was a very decided and pleasing change in the temperature here; the thermometer, which latterly at Candahar had been 115°, being now only about 95°. Our encampment was good, and we had abundance of water, being pitched near the Turnuck.

20th. Eight miles to Nourouk,—the road very hilly, but the country not so barren as in the neighbourhood of Kelat-i-Gilzie. The river near Nourouk is very winding in its course; encamping ground good, and water abundant. The natives continued to bring in supplies of grain, &c. A futile attempt was made by some *Ghilzies* today to carry off camels; they were detected in the act, and a few were put to the sword. A number of *sepoys*, who were spared during the massacre at Ghuznee, and who were made slaves, escaped from their masters, and joined our camp today. The report now was, that the negotiations for the release of our Cabul prisoners, between General Pollock and Akbar Khan, were at an end, in consequence of the displeasure of the latter at General Nott's advance, Akbar declaring that he would not permit any British army to approach Cabul! One of my camels came down in a *nullah* today, and in its fall a bottle of brandy was broken. Thus I lost all my stock of *inspiriting* liquid, and there was no possibility of replacing it;—the only consolation being, that the water was good.

21st. To Abée Tazee, eleven and a half miles; road good, along the banks of the Turnuck. It was from this place that Colonel MacLaren determined on his retrograde movement in November. Our encamping ground satisfactory; water plentiful. Supplies were now beginning to be scarce, the villages, as we advanced, being generally deserted.

22nd. To Shuftal, road very bad, being intersected with ravines. Still near the Turnuck. Villages on today's march quite deserted. A native brought intelligence into camp today, that the enemy were assembling in great force at Ghuznee, and preparing to give us a warm reception. *Sepoys*, formerly of the Ghuznee garrison, continued to join our camp; it was gratifying to be the means, as we moved along, of releasing these poor creatures from their bondage.

23rd. To Chusma-i-Shadie, "*the fountain of delight*;" road good, over a wide and open plain, flanked by bold hills. Encampment clear, and near the river. Several villages near, from which we obtained supplies in abundance. Not far from camp was a large cave, in which, according to the tradition of the natives, some immense treasure is concealed.

25th. To Chusma-i-Gunja, seven miles; the road very good, the valley widening as we advanced. Reports improved today,—Shumshoodeen Khan being all ready to exterminate us on our arrival at Mookur, where he had assembled a large army, said to be increasing daily. By last returns it was four thousand matchlock men, fifteen hundred *Jizailihies* (riflemen), four nine pounders, and a host of cavalry.

Encampment near the Turnuck; obtained supplies from the villages in small quantities.

26th. To Ghozan, fourteen miles; road excellent, over an extensive and level plain, bounded on either side by high hills, and studded with numerous forts and villages. Passed, on today's march, a very neat little fort, which had been built by Major Leech for the protection of

Dawks and *Cafillas*; it had been the scene of the murder of Guddoo Khan, one of our adherents, when carrying despatches from Ghuznee to Candahar, on the breaking out of the insurrection. It was now deserted, and the walls were much dilapidated. Near our camp was the scene of a victory gained over some Affghans by a Goorkha regiment which accompanied Lord Keane. Excellent grazing for our camels in the vicinity of camp.

Rumour still asserts that we are to have work tomorrow.

27th. Mookur, twelve miles. After advancing a few miles, about three hundred of the enemy's cavalry were seen in front, and we began to prepare for action. Light companies were formed in advance, parties of our cavalry were on our flanks, and two guns were added to the rearguard. A *cossid* came in and reported that the horse in front were merely a reconnoitring party, and that Shumshoodeen's army was some marches in advance. We moved on and encamped close to the source of the river Turnuck, and near the large village of Mookur, which was quite deserted.

There, however, we got quantities of grain and forage, without the trouble of paying for them,—an admirable system, in the estimation of the greater part of the officers, whose supply of the "*needful*" owing to the arrears of pay due to us, was rather limited. In the front of our camp was a high barren hill, rising abruptly from the plain, on the top of which were a few natives, one of whom, with his long loose drapery floating in graceful negligence in the breeze, occasionally discharged his matchlock in the direction of camp. He went through a series of gesticulations, seemingly denouncing us, and heaping imprecations on our heads. A body of cavalry and infantry made an attempt on the baggage, but were driven off with some loss by our rearguard, and without having secured any booty. During the night we were annoyed by the firing of the enemy into camp, but we sustained no injury.

28th. To Oostam Khan, or Killa Azeem, about fourteen miles. Having marched a short distance, a party of the enemy, amounting to about two hundred or three hundred cavalry and infantry, were observed to our left front, moving along under a range of hills running parallel to our line of march, about a mile distant. They gradually drew off to our rear, shouting, beating *tom-toms*, and the horsemen occasionally dashing out from the ranks, caracoling gracefully about, and anon discharging their matchlocks in the air, in token of defiance and contempt.

Approaching nearer, they made some demonstrations on our baggage, and, as they increased in numbers, we were obliged to move on slowly, to enable our baggage to keep close up to us. At length they became over rash, and some of our cavalry were slipped at them, and coming upon them, put to the sword about sixty of their number, principally infantry,—the remainder, taking advantage of the *nullahs* which intersected the plains, succeeded in escaping to the hills. Our loss did not exceed five or six killed, and a few wounded.

We could plainly see the marks of the wheels of Shumshoodeen's guns on our march today.

Encamped about 11 a. m., at some distance from some small forts.

After breakfast, a report was brought in that a part of Shumshoodeen Khan's army had attacked our grass-cutters a short distance in front of camp. Captain Delamaine, commanding the cavalry, immediately ordered a portion of them out, and moved to the scene of action, having, however, *adopted the precaution* to dispatch a messenger to the adjutant-general, intimating, for the information of General Nott, the step he had taken, of course in the expectation that, should it be approved, he would be supported; if not, that there was time for his recall before he could have reached the enemy. *This communication was, however, not made at the time to the general.*

Meanwhile Captain Delamaine, with the whole cavalry, moved out, and, coming up with the enemy, repulsed and drove them back with loss. Elated by success, our troops lost the advantage they had gained by pursuing their opponents too far; and being met by the whole of Shumshoodeen's army, in a difficult country full of ravines which were lined with matchlock men, were overwhelmed and overpowered.

We had all been attracted to the front of camp by the firing we heard, but for a long while could distinguish nothing of what was going on, from the masses of dust which veiled everything from our view; at length, a number of horses with empty saddles were seen to emerge from the clouds of sand, galloping wildly towards camp. Shortly after a report was brought in, that our cavalry had met with a severe check, that they had sustained the loss of several officers, and that they had been driven into the plain, where we could now see them re-forming.

The general *being now apprised* of what was going on, issued orders for a considerable portion of his force to move out: the "assembly" was sounded throughout camp, and all was hurry and activity. Then it was that marching down with three regiments and some guns towards the cavalry, we learned the extent of our losses. Among those who had fallen gallantly cheering on their men, were Captains Bury and Reeves of the 3rd Bombay Cavalry, old and intimate friends of my own and most of my brother officers,—the life and soul of all our manly sports and amusements at Deesa, and possessing that ardour and daring promptitude and resolution, so peculiarly and inseparably connected with the character of good cavalry officers. Among the wounded were Captain Ravenscroft and Lieutenant M'Kenzie, 3rd Cavalry, and Lieutenant Chamberlain of the Irregular Cavalry, who seemed to have the *good fortune* to be wounded on every occasion he was engaged.

As the general with his reinforcements advanced, Shumshoodeen with his army retired, satisfied, doubtless, with the success he had already obtained. The grass-cutters having mentioned that the villagers in some of the neighbouring forts had been most busy in assisting Shumshoodeen, that several of our followers had been slain by them, and a number of cattle stolen, the general directed a part of the force to move down and ascertain the truth of the report, while a regiment of infantry, with some guns, proceeded to recover the bodies of our fallen comrades.

On approaching the fort, some of the inhabitants came out proclaiming their innocence, and with *Korans* on their heads imploring for mercy. General Nott informed them, that he merely wished to assure himself whether they had in any way assisted our enemies, or committed the depredation on our property of which they were accused, and if he found they had not, that of course they should not be molested. Captain F. White with the light company of H. M. 40th regiment, was now ordered in to inspect the fort, the habitants of which, who consented to this step, having been warned, that should they offer any opposition to his progress, the place should be stormed, and not a man be spared.

White had scarcely entered the fort ere he was assailed by a volley from the matchlocks of the infatuated wretches. Immediately on hearing this, I was ordered in with my company to support him, and was followed by the light company of H.M. 41st, and a few companies from other corps. A heavy fire was opened on us from the houses in the different detached forts, but our loss in killed and wounded was fortunately very small. The men were exasperated by the events of the morning, but no excess disgraced their conduct; under any circumstances the destruction of human life must be painful, but there is always a satisfaction in knowing that blood has not been needlessly or wantonly spilt.

The entry of our troops into the fort had been sanctioned by the inhabitants,—that entry had scarcely been effected, ere our soldiers were treacherously fired upon, and a continual discharge of match-locks kept up on our men from the houses in the fort. Those in arms against us were v necessarily sacrificed, but we are guiltless of the blood of the women and children, notwithstanding the numerous calumnies asserted to the contrary. During the whole of the operations of this day, I saw but one woman killed, and that was purely accidental: none of the officers experienced the slightest difficulty in restraining their men; on the contrary, to my knowledge, the lives of several men were spared at the prayer of the women and children, who were mingling with our troops.

Numbers of our camels were found in the fort; and concealed among the lucerne were several of the dead bodies of our followers. The troops were at length withdrawn; supplies of forage, grain, &c. which we required for our cattle, and which had been refused to us in the morning, were taken out; the residue was fired as a punishment to the villagers, and a warning to those in advance: and the darkness of the night was illumined by the flames which issued from the burning ruins of the fort.

While we were engaged at the fort, the mutilated corpses of our fallen soldiers were brought into camp,—mangled, inanimate remains of what they had been, and exhibiting mournful proofs of the utter barbarity of those against whom we were opposed. Deprived of heads, hands, and otherwise fearfully disfigured, their limbs were sent through the country as trophies. At Ghuznee poor Reeves's head was exhibited as that of General Nott, who, it was said, had been entirely defeated near Mookur, himself killed, his army dispersed, and the whole of his artillery captured.

At dead of night, the remains of the gallant Reeves and Bury were, in sadness, silence, and sorrow, consigned to their last resting place. No monument in that far land points out where they have been laid, but they died the death of brave soldiers, and they will live long in the memory of the friends who mourned their loss. The observation that "*war cannot be made without loss*" is truly applicable here,—it is also very painful.

Our loss in the disastrous affair of this day must have been of officers and men nearly fifty killed.

On the 29th, moved camp to Oba, a distance of three miles, and encamped near ground which had evidently been occupied the night before by the enemy,—the marks of the gun-wheels being distinctly visible. Shumshoodeen, in great force, was in the ridge of hills about three miles in front of camp; during the day, his followers amused themselves by discharging their matchlocks, firing salutes, &c., in honour of the success they obtained yesterday. Tomorrow is the day fixed on by our opponents for our entire destruction.

30th. To Karabaugh, near Goaine. During this morning's march, the enemy, in great force, moved along a ridge of hills parallel to us, and encamped about four miles from our halting-place. The country is extensively cultivated, and filled with forts, generally small rectangular defences, with round towers at each angle. On coming to our ground, we sent to some of them for supplies, but were most insultingly refused. The general gave the villagers until the rearguard came up to think better of their determination. About two p. m., still persisting in refusal, the general moved out with Anderson's troop of horse-artillery (late *Shah's*), two eighteen-pounders, Blood's battery of four nine-pounders, one twenty-four-pounder howitzer, all the cavalry, H.M. 40th, and 41st regiments, and the 16th, 38th, and 3rd, late *Shah's*;—the 2nd brigade being left in charge of camp. Having moved under cover of a deep hollow, part of the infantry, and the heavy guns, took up position within breaching distance of the small port of Goaine; the remainder of the troops being so placed as to enable the lighter guns to play on the fort, and cut off the retreat of the enemy.

At this time the battlements and towers were crowded, but in an instant they were swept by the beautifully correct fire from the light guns, directed by Lieutenant Turner, of the Bengal Artillery, in the *Shah's* service.

The order was given to effect a breach with the eighteen-pounders, which, with my company, I was directed to assist in placing in position. While engaged in working one of them over a ditch, a fire was opened from the guns of Shumshoodeen Khan, who, at the head of about twelve thousand men, now appeared on the hills in front of our position. Their first shot was rather short, but the second, which was finely directed, plunged into the centre of my company and the artillerymen, whom we were assisting with the guns. I fully expected to have found that I had lost a few of my men, but, when the clouds of dust it had raised cleared off there, we were all right, not even the gun-carriage splintered. Crowded together as we were at the time it came among us, it was matter for surprise how the ball got inside the knot we formed round the gun, without grazing any one, and much more how it should have bounded on without inflicting any injury.

The eighteen-pounders made little or no impression on the mud walls, the fire was not concentrated, and the balls merely made small holes in different parts of these efficient defences.

Lieutenant Terry volunteered to blow open the gate with the twenty-four-pounder howitzer, if a company of infantry was sent to support him. Lieutenant Wakefield therefore accompanied him with the grenadiers of the 40th; they approached the gate, but Shumshoodeen Khan advancing, caused the general to abandon the fort for the present, and direct his whole force against the Ghuznee chief.

During the whole time that the guns were playing on the battlements, one man, who seemed to bear a charmed life, in the midst of the shrapnel that was bursting around him stood uninjured and undismayed, ever and anon addressing us in a fine clear-toned voice, and waving his sword in scorn and derision at our futile attempts to enter his stronghold. Occasionally he held up to view the skin of some animal stuffed with straw. The particular point of this, however, we never could discover; though, during our progress through Affghanistan, we observed similar objects in several of the deserted forts we visited.

Meanwhile Shumshoodeen's artillery was directed on the regiments of infantry which, during the attempts to breach, had been ordered to pile arms and *stand at ease*, a military manoeuvre which generally can be effected with facility, but which is difficult of continuance when under the fire of an enemy.

We were all young soldiers, and few had ever been exposed to the influence of round shot; it was most amusing therefore to see the graceful but involuntary obeisance made along the whole of our line, as each succeeding shot from the enemy's guns seemed almost to graze our heads.

Anderson's troop was now brought up on our right, our guns were opened on the hill, whence the fire of the opposing army proceeded, and for a time the artillery on both sides had all the fun to themselves.

At length Shumshoodeen advanced into the plains, his troops, as they approached our line, beating their *tom-toms*, and uttering the most discordant yells. An attempt was made by them to pass our right flank and gain our camp; this was however frustrated, and our infantry, covered by the light companies and guns, advanced in open columns of divisions towards the right, where the enemy were now in position. The practice from the guns under Lieutenant Turner's direction, was at this time most beautiful, both from its precision and the celerity with which the movements of his troop were executed. As we neared the enemy, we formed a widely-extended line, and continued to move steadily on; we were received with shouts and many volleys from the matchlock-men, but, as usual, their fire was ill-directed. Having gained the bottom of the hill, on the crest of which the opposing army had made their stand, a loud hurrah burst from our line; this was succeeded by an irresistible British charge, and the enemy, succumbing to the superiority of the bayonet over the sword and shield, broke and fled.

Here we much felt the want—from which we had so long suffered—of cavalry in sufficient numbers to reap the advantage of our victories. If the British had had a few more squadrons, not many of their enemies would have escaped this day.

One of the guns which was abandoned fell into the hands of the light company; another, through the gallantry of Captain Christie, and Lieutenant Chamberlain with the Bengal cavalry, formerly in the *Shah's* service, was captured late in the evening. The enemy attempted to take it off the field, but Lieutenant Chamberlain dashing forward, succeeded in cutting the traces of one of the horses, and the cavalry, who were close behind, cut up the artillerymen—most of whom (Mussulmen) were deserters from our service—and secured the gun. The practice of the enemy's guns was exceedingly fine, but that they did not do much execution, was on account of the great elevation they required from being fired at such a long range, and the front of our position being ploughed fields, the softness of which prevented the balls ricocheting.

The whole of the enemy's camp, all their ammunition, which was principally British and had been taken at Ghuznee from our garrison, and two of their guns, fell into our hands.

We returned home late at night, the light companies, under Captain White of the 40th, having been left to bring in the guns, &c., which had been captured. Ammunition we did not require, so the remains were destroyed after the men had filled their pouches.

In the dispatch of General Nott, owing to some oversight, no mention is made of H.M. 41st having been engaged at Goaine, nor is any allusion made to the services of Captain Christie and Lieutenant

Chamberlain. General Nott when spoken to on the subject of the 41st, by the gallant commander of that distinguished regiment, expressed his regret at the omission, and immediately volunteered writing to Government, the Commander-in-chief, &c.

With reference to Captain Christie and Lieutenant Chamberlain, it certainly was a matter of regret their not being mentioned. General Nott has been much blamed for the omission of the names of several officers in his dispatches; I do not mean to argue that the present is a case in point, but I conceive that many of the omissions complained of were more to be attributed to the commanding officers of brigades and corps, who failed to send in the names of deserving officers, than to the general, who could not possibly see everyone.

The dispatches of General Nott, notwithstanding the many faults which have been attributed to them, will be generally confessed, from their singular clearness and conciseness, to be the most soldier-like productions with which of late years we have been favoured.

The intention was to have attacked the fort of Goaine on the morning of the 31st, but during the night it was deserted. Halting on the 31st, we employed that day in restocking our commissariat from such supplies for our necessities as we found in Goaine. The guns which we had captured were burst today.

We were joined today by a party of Huzaurehs, a tribe inhabiting the Paropamisan Mountains between Cabul and Ghuznee; but they are quite a distinct race from the Affghans, being much smaller, and not such fine-looking men; their features denote their Tartar extraction, but little appears to be known of their real origin. Their women, it is said, are handsome, and the few of the chiefs we saw appeared to be quite of a different nation from their followers, being tall, handsome men, their features rather of the Grecian character.[1] They pro-

1. The women are often very handsome, and, what is surprising in a tribe so nearly savage, they have an ascendancy unexampled in the neighbouring countries. The wife manages the house, takes care of the property, does her share of the honours, and is very much consulted in all her husband's measures. Women are never beaten, and they have no concealment. It is universally agreed that they are by no means remarkable for chastity, but I have heard different accounts of their libertinism. In the north-east, which is the most civilized part of the country, the women would prostitute themselves for money while their husbands were out of the way; but the men, though not jealous, would probably put a detected adulteress to death. In other parts of the country there prevails a custom called Koorro Bistaun, by which the husband lends his wife to the embraces of his guests. At all times, if a husband of that part of the country finds a pair of slippers at his wife's door, he immediately withdraws. Both sexes spend a great deal of their time (continued next page),

fessed the greatest possible friendship for us; their regard, however, was more likely to be the result of their detestation of the Affghans, for whom they entertain all that inveterate hatred which difference in faith, and the most rancorous bigotry, never fail to produce, and which, under the hallowed but abused name of religion, is even in our civilized country so sacrilegiously, so intolerantly, and so impiously indulged.

They strongly urged upon us the propriety of exterminating all Soonees, they themselves being most enthusiastic followers of Ali, and consequently Sheeahs. They also expressed a hope that we should rase Ghuznee to the ground; and, above all, that we should destroy or carry off Jubber Jhung, the large brass gun (sixty-four pounder), in that fort, for which they appeared to entertain a most religious horror.

The numerous forts in the valley, which were deserted, they set fire to, and expressed with much warmth their astonishment at our forbearance. We remonstrated with them on the wantonness of the destruction, and pointed out the probability of the retribution which would await them on our departure. To all our representations the answer given was, "Very true, but revenge is sweet, and we shall never have such another opportunity." A strong party of this tribe followed in our train nearly to Cabul, spreading destruction through the country, (the villages in which were generally deserted,) unsanctioned, however, by us, although by our presence they were empowered to do so. They were the means of inflicting a fearful punishment on the Affghans for those disasters which we ourselves had advanced to punish, and afterwards avenged with more dignified severity.

1st September. Marched to Chuppa Khanna in the country of the Huzaurehs, who, being our *friends*, received us most kindly; from their numerous villages we received supplies of grain, forage, &c., in abundance. Our encampment was near the hills, and prettily situated. The valley presented a most curious appearance; on our left were the nu-

---

in sitting in the house round a stove. They are all great singers and players on the guitar, and many of them are poets. Lovers and their mistresses sing verses to each other of their own composing, and men often sit for hours railing at each other in extemporaneous satire.

Their amusements out of doors are hunting, shooting deer, and racing. They clear a spot for the last-mentioned amusement and ride bare-backed: the stake is often a great many sheep, oxen, or suits of clothes. They also shoot at marks for similar wagers. They are all good archers and good shots: every man has a matchlock. Their other arms are a Persian sword, a long narrow dagger in a wooden sheath, and sometimes a spear.—*Elphinstone's Account of the Kingdom of Caubul, &c.* vol. ii.

merous Huzaureh forts, enjoying a temporary quiet and prosperity; while on the right, were those of the Affghans, emitting clouds of smoke and flame. In the darkness of the night the spectacle presented by the lurid glare from those burning towers was exceedingly grand, but the misery and privation which were to follow on this destruction of property, was subject for painful contemplation.

The thanks of the general to the troops, for their conduct at Goaine, was conveyed to them today in a most laconic order.

2nd. To Nooshakee.—Country richly cultivated, and dotted with numerous forts, all of which, not belonging to the Huzaurehs, shared from them the same fate as those near our halting- ground.

3rd. To Nam a, twelve miles over a barren, uninteresting country: a reconnoitring party of about two hundred horse from Ghuznee took a look at us, *from a distance*, today. Several *sepoys* of the 27th came into camp today; they stated that numbers of their brethren had been murdered by the Affghans as soon as our advance was known, and that they owed their safety to having escaped into the Huzaureh country.

4th. Made a short march of eight miles, near the end of which we came in full view of Ghuznee; encamped about two miles from the city, close to some gardens, from which our light company had to drive a few of the enemy.

The plain was studded with small forts, and was extensively cultivated; there were also some fine orchards, particularly near Rosah, which added much to the beauty of the scenery.

On the range of hills to the north-east of Ghuznee, is the village of Behlole; here we could see numbers of the enemy, and a tolerable display of banners. There did not appear to be many people inside the fortress, which, with the exception of the citadel and walls, seemed to be in ruins.

Contrary to our expectations, we were unmolested during the day. In the afternoon numerous small parties, principally of infantry, were observed to be moving towards Ghuznee, from which we concluded that we should have some work in storming the place. We found quantities of lucerne, grain, vegetables, grapes, &c., lying about in great profusion in the gardens near us.

5th. Moved today for the purpose of pitching our camp on the Cabul road, previous to commencing seriously the capture of Ghuznee; had to cross over a very difficult country for the guns, it being much intersected with deep and broad water-courses, most of which were filled with water.

Major Saunders, chief engineer, with the 16th Bengal regiment, proceeded to reconnoitre the fort, for the purpose of selecting a point for breaching. As he approached the village of Behlole, strong parties from the enemy, who had come out of garrison and occupied the heights to the north-east of the city, advanced to meet him, and the 16th soon became engaged with much superior numbers. Captain White, 40th regiment, with the light companies, moved to their support; and at length the General advanced with some of the other corps, leaving a portion to protect the baggage and camp, which was being pitched. The affair now became general. The 16th and the light companies, drove the enemy from Behlole; and H. M. 40th and 38th regiments—whose advance I had the honour to cover—with the grenadiers, under Lieutenant Wakefield, and No. 1, (my own company,) stormed and carried the heights on the extreme left of the enemy's position; some of the corps belonging to the 2nd brigade being as actively and successfully employed against other parts of the hill.

Shumshoodeen Khan, who had been considerably reinforced by Sultan Jan, from Cabul, now retired with his infantry within the walls; the cavalry remaining outside, and making some slight attacks on the baggage and rearguard, which were, however, gallantly repulsed.

One of the batteries in the fort completely enfiladed the heights above Behlole, and a well-directed fire therefrom compelled us to *hug mother-earth* most affectionately: by scattering and lying down we escaped without receiving much injury.

About one p. m., the 40th was relieved from the heights and marched into camp, being exposed to a heavy fire from the fort in moving along the plain between the heights we had stormed and where our tents were pitched.

The enemy waited patiently until they saw all our tents up, and everything in camp made snug. Not thinking of any interruption, we had commenced breakfast, when, of a sudden, a loud report was heard, and a most unwelcome messenger in the shape of a sixty-four-pound shot from the great brass gun, Jubber Jhung, came whizzing through the air, grazing the ridge-pole of our mess-tent, and landing at length among some camels in rear, destroying several. Some would-be comforter assured us that from the difficulty of managing this gun, a space of twenty minutes at least elapsed between each shot,—this, however, we soon found to be a traveller's tale, and shot after shot succeeded with astonishing rapidity. Such an accompaniment did not at all add to the comfort of our meal. On our native servants, who are not much famed for courage, Jubber Jhung produced a startling effect;—acting like a *powerful alterative*, and transforming them at once, at least as far as complexion was concerned, into Europeans. There was an intensity of anguish in their looks, and an expression of the deepest concern and regret that they had been induced to come so far from home.

The balls were made of wrought iron, and had been formed roughly with the hammer; of course, from their many points and angles, the hissing noise that they made whirling through the air, was something extraordinary, if not terrific.

Orders were given to move camp near Rosah, and during a considerable experience in marching, I never saw any camp struck with such celerity. As soon as we got to our new camp, our followers made a rush to the orchards of Rosah, and commenced helping themselves to the grapes, &c.: this, however, was immediately put a stop to by the general.

Two of our nine-pounders were placed on the heights on the N.E. and soon succeeded in silencing the enemy's battery; the former with two corps of infantry were left for the night in possession of the heights and village of Behlole.

Major Saunders having selected an advantageous point for breaching, fatigue parties were warned to move down at dark, to commence the work of digging the trenches. The remainder of the infantry in camp were ordered to parade early the following morning, to place in position the eighteen-pounders, which it was hoped we should be able to open on the fort the following day.

During the night we were unmolested, and the work of digging the trenches went on most favourably. On the morning of the 6th the division paraded according to order, when, to our astonishment, we saw that the fort was already in our possession. The following extract from the memorandum of Major Saunders explains the circumstances better than I can hope to do—so I copy it:—

> Early on the evening of the 5th a brisk matchlock fire was kept up from the citadel on the hill, but this gradually slackened, and at ten p.m. had entirely ceased. The enemy's infantry had been observed at dark, crossing the river near the water-gate, with the intention, it was supposed, of attacking the working party during the night; but towards the morning of the 6th, there

were grounds for believing the fort was evacuated: at daylight this was ascertained to be the case by Lieutenant North of the Engineers, who took possession at that hour of the water-gate without opposition, leaving Lieutenant Newton and twenty *sepoys* of the 16th Native Infantry in charge of the gateway, and returning to the battery for further assistance. The whole of the working party was immediately moved into the town, of which, and of the citadel of Ghuznee, they were in possession before sunrise.

Thus was accomplished the capture of Ghuznee, and thus had one of our "*past disasters been retrieved and avenged*" on one of the "*scenes on which they were sustained*."

The general rode down, accompanied by some of the senior officers, to inspect the renowned fortress of Ghuznee. The Cabul Gate by which Lord Keane's army had entered, the enemy had determined should not be the place of ingress for a second victorious British army; they had built up outside it a brick-wall, and the gates were doubly secured and barricaded inside with beams of wood.

Great quantities of our own powder were found in the magazine in the citadel, a portion of which was appropriated this morning to blowing up the Cabul Gateway. In the forenoon I visited this scene of our successes.

Ghuznee is built on the slope of a hill nearly eight thousand feet above the level of the sea, and is surrounded by stone walls, and a deep wet ditch, which is filled from a tolerably rapid stream that flows along the north-east face of the fort.

The wall was very strong, and presented few places where a practicable breach could have been easily made; indeed the judgment of our engineer was evinced by selecting perhaps the only point where this could have been effected with the means at our disposal, and the short period we could command to achieve such an undertaking. The entrance by the different gates was through high, vaulted, but narrow and tortuous passages;—all the approaches to the gates were commanded, and the walls in every direction loop-holed. The citadel is on the right of the entrance to the Cabul Gate; it is built much higher than the town, and is approached by a very steep ascent, at the top of which is cut out of the hill, a large platform; here our *friend* Jubber Jhung was placed, a fine piece of brass ordnance, beautifully ornamented. Several other guns were near this, and others distributed over different parts of the defences. Most of the guns, I believe, were manufactured at Herat.

The town, as we supposed, was in ruins; there were the remains of three very mean-looking bazaars and a *charsoo.* A great proportion of the inhabitants at the time of the massacre were Hindoos, who, in this country, are generally the most wealthy men; they were all killed by the *Gazees* (Moslem fanatics) and their houses destroyed,—miserable mud huts, but transformed by an Indian journal in noticing our destruction of this city, into "the noble edifices" of Ghuznee.

The buildings in the citadel alone were in a state of preservation; many of the rooms were lofty and well-proportioned, the ceilings of some were beautifully ornamented with a sort of mosaic work,

Here had our officers been imprisoned, and on the walls were written their names, and statements of Colonel Palmer having been put to torture, and of other indignities to which they had been subjected,—offering a striking contrast to the treatment received by the Cabul prisoners at the hands of Akbar Khan.

Little is left to tell of the grandeur of this ancient city.[2] The mighty

2. Ghuznee itself, which eight centuries ago was the capital of an empire reaching from the Tigris to the Ganges, and from the Ioxartes to the Persian Gulf, is now reduced to a town containing about fifteen hundred houses, besides suburbs without the walls. The town stands on a height, at the foot of which flows a pretty large stream. It is surrounded by stone walls, and contains three bazaars of no great breadth, with high houses on each side, and a covered *chaursoo*, besides several dark and narrow streets. Some few remains of the ancient grandeur of the city are still to be seen in its neighbourhood, particularly two lofty minarets, which stand at some distance from each other, and are of different heights, the least upwards of one hundred feet high. The tomb of the Great *Sultan* is also standing, about three miles from the city. It is a spacious but not a magnificent building, covered with a *cupola.* The doors, which are very large, are of sandal-wood, and are said to have been brought by the *Sultan* as a trophy from the famous temple of Somnaut in Guzerat, which he sacked in his last expedition to India. The tombstone is of white marble, on which are sculptured Arabic verses from the Koraun, and at its head lies the plain but weighty mace which is said to have been wielded by the monarch himself. It is of wood, with a head of metal so heavy that few men can use it. There are also some thrones, or chairs, inlaid with mother-of-pearl, in the tomb, which are said to have belonged to Mahmood. The tombstone is under a canopy, and some Mollahs are still maintained, who incessantly read the Koraun aloud over the grave.
There are some other ruins of less note, among which are the tombs of Behlole Dauna (or Behlole the Wise) and that of Hukeem Sunauee, a poet still greatly esteemed in Persia; but nothing remains to show the magnificence of the palaces of the Guznavide kings (which at one time were the residence of Ferdausee, the Homer of Asia), or of the mosques, baths, and caravansaries, which once adorned the capital of the East. Of all the antiquities of Ghuznee, (continued next page),

warrior by whom it was founded, its beauty and its glory, have lived and passed away, and but for books,—those memorials of what has been—one would not recognize in the crumbling ruins and mounds of rubbish about Ghuznee, the remains of the former capital of a powerful empire.

To the north-east of the town are two lofty and very exquisitely-sculptured minarets,—"they mark the spot where stood the celebrated Mosque, impiously called 'The Celestial Bride.'"

About three miles from Ghuznee is the beautifully situated village of Rozah, surrounded by magnificent orchards. Here, in a spacious but not elegant building, under a tomb of white marble, on which are engraved some verses from the *Koran*, rest the mortal remains of the once mighty Sultan Mahmood.

7th. The destruction of the town and citadel of Ghuznee was commenced. In the course of the day I visited the tomb of Mahmood, and saw the elaborately-carved sandal-wood gates of Soomnauth, our appropriation of which afforded such an excellent opportunity for vituperative comment to that Pharisaical portion of the community, who, assuming a moral superiority over their fellowmen, with characteristic hypocrisy and uncharitableness ever distort and denounce the actions of others.

8th. During the night we experienced considerable annoyance from the firing of the enemy into camp one sentry was shot at his post and several others were wounded.—All the guns found in Ghuznee were burst today, and the commissariat was replenished from the supplies of grain, flour, &c. which were left in the town. Copies of the treaties made with our officers were found in the citadel, also a few portions of camp equipage.

During our halt at Ghuznee, upwards of three hundred of our *sepoys*, who had been sold into slavery, escaped from their masters and joined our camp.

On the 9th we broke ground and advanced two miles on the Cabul road; the defences of Ghuznee had now been completely destroyed, and the citadel reduced to a heap of smouldering ruins. In the forenoon we took the sandal-wood gates from the tomb of Sultan Mah-

---

the most useful is an embankment across a stream, which was built by Mahmood, and which, though damaged by the guns of the Ghoree kings at the capture of Ghuznee, still supplies water to the fields and gardens round the town.—*Elphinstones Account of the Kingdom of Caubul,* vol. ii.

mood of Ghuznee, amid the wailings and tears of the numerous *fakeers* attending the shrine, who regarded them as their most valuable treasure. They were carried from the tomb, escorted by a company of H.M. 40th regiment, and doubtless, "curses, not loud but deep," from the Moslem priests were sent after us, for our abstraction of these precious memorials of Mahommedan ascendancy, from the sanctuary where, eight hundred years before, they had been placed in triumph.[3]

3. For Despatches *vide* Appendix.

Chapter 18

Lady Sale and the Female Captives

On the morning of the 10th September, we left the neighbourhood of Ghuznee, carrying with us the "Gates of Somnauth,"—proud and memorable trophies of our successes. On the subject of these gates, a great deal of the most sickening cant has been expended, and, in their mean desire for finding fault, some writers and many speakers have most effectually overreached themselves, and been singularly successful in displaying their ignorance of the topic they attempted to discuss. Much was heard of the insulted feelings of our Mahommedan *sepoys*. In what had those violated feelings been shown? They were to be found expressed in that general elation of heart with which they, in common with their European and Hindoo brethren, regarded these proofs of victory,—in the joy that they had been wrested from the hand of our enemies,—and, in the intensity of their anxiety, that they should be transported in triumph and safety over the mighty Indus.

Our march today was to Shushgao, twelve miles. The ascent on this march is very great. About half-way we entered a narrow defile of about two miles in length, the road through which is very stony; and we ascended higher than we had yet been, the point of greatest altitude in today's march being considerably more than eight thousand feet above the level of the sea. At the top of the Pass is an old and very small fort which commands it both ways; it is now, however, a complete ruin, and part of the walls fell down in consequence of the vibration caused by our heavy guns passing near it. Our encampment was considerably lower than the pass, in a narrow valley in which there were a number of mud forts, all of which we found deserted, but fortunately for us full of grain, lucerne, &c.; the hills to the right and left of the valley are barren and uninteresting. We heard today that Akbar Khan had ordered the prisoners off to Bamean.

11th. To Puttonah, thirteen miles. During the night we were much annoyed by the continual firing of the enemy into camp. Our road skirted the hills, from which a number of beautifully clear springs gushed out. The undulating country improved much as we advanced; the crops were mostly off the ground when we passed, but there were proofs of its being extensively cultivated. There were numerous forts dotting the country in all directions; they were, however, generally deserted, but the inhabitants had most kindly and considerately left in them supplies of grain, &c. needful for our cattle. The weather had now become very cold, and we began to feel the advantage of our *nimchees.*[1] The news we received today was, that General Pollock had commenced his march on Cabul.

12th. To Seyedabad, eleven miles. Departed from the usual routine-marches laid down, and halted here in order to blow up a small fort in which Captain Woodburn, 24th Bengal N. I., and nearly two hundred *sepoys*, had been murdered in November, 1841, on their way to Ghuznee. He had been attacked outside by a superior force, and was received into the fort with promise of protection; but no sooner had he entered it than he was fired upon, and he and all his followers treacherously massacred. The fort, which was one of the strongest and most picturesque we had seen, was deserted; in one of the small huts inside, was found poor Woodburn's will, his forage cap, a teacup, and several of the *sepoys'* breast-plates.

Fatigue-parties were employed today in the destruction of the fort, and in the evening one of the bastions was blown up, and the houses inside fired. The road today was exceedingly heavy, passing through a tortuous and narrow valley covered with large loose stones. The scenery, however, was truly beautiful, and there were evidences of very extensive cultivation. Our encampment was badly selected, being intersected and surrounded by deep ravines; and as the night advanced we found the disadvantages of our position, for the enemy, exasperated by the destruction of one of their best forts, seemed determined to avenge their loss. Soon after dark they assembled on all sides in great numbers, uttering the most fiendish yells as they advanced; and during the night, they attacked our piquets several times, pouring into them an incessant fire from their matchlocks, to be answered unremittingly by a roll of musketry from our men.

1. A *nimchee* is a small fur cloak. During rain the hairy side is worn outside; on other occasions it is worn inside. Every officer and soldier in the division wore one during the campaign.

Ever since leaving Mookur, we had been accustomed to have our camp fired into at night, and had become so used to it, that it seldom interfered with the rest of those who did not happen to be on duty. But at Seyedabad, there was a something in the jackal howling which accompanied the enemies' expenditure of ammunition, which most effectually prevented any one from indulging in balmy sleep. The nature of the ground, too, was favourable to any attempt to enter camp, it being perfectly impossible to guard the innumerable ravines, under cover of which it would have been easy to effect an entrance. Volley succeeded volley, and the most dreadful shrieks rent the air; every instant we expected a portion of our assailants would be among our tents, and there were few if any who were not prepared for *active service at a moment's warning.*

Under cover of the darkness of the night and the excessive badness of the ground, the enemy were enabled, unseen in some instances, to get close up to our sentries, two of whom were shot on their posts, notwithstanding great care and judgment had been evinced in placing them by Lieutenant Todd of the 40th, who was on piquet. Towards morning the firing discontinued, and ere "the General" had beat it had ceased altogether.

During the day, two men of H. M. 41st, who wandered a short distance from camp, were slain near the place where Colonel Herring, of the Bengal service had been barbarously murdered in 1839 or 1840.

13th. Continued our march through the valley of Logur nearly eight miles; crossed the river near Shirkabad, and moving for about two miles, encamped on clear ground. The part of the vale through which we passed today was very narrow, with high steep hills on either side; these were occupied in great numbers by the enemy, who greeted the columns with a continued discharge from their matchlocks, *gingals*, and *jessails*,—but we did not sustain much injury. The road generally was heavy and contracted, and where it wound along the banks of the Logur river, precipitous and crumbling. Our rearguard met with considerable annoyance today, the narrowness of the valley, and the badness of the road, making it tedious and difficult for the passage of our interminable baggage.

Turner, Bengal Artillery, who was in charge of the guns, with the rearguard, got some opportunity of displaying his prowess in the art of gunnery, and did considerable damage in the ranks of our opponents. The villages as usual deserted, but we had no difficulty in procuring supplies for our cattle. Our sheep did not improve by marching, and the joints on our mess-tables shewed more of the bone and less of the meat than accorded well with our excellent appetites.

The attack on camp last night was, we ascertained today, planned by a deserter from our cause, formerly a native officer[2] in the 27th regiment, which he had left at Ghuznee.

In the evening the hills in rear of camp were occupied in some force by the enemy. Captain Malet, 3rd Bombay Cavalry, was sent with a squadron to clear the heights, and afterwards, as the hilly and broken nature of the ground was not considered well adapted for cavalry operations, I was directed with four companies of the 40th to move after him. As we advanced the enemy retired, and we took possession of the heights, after exchanging a few long shots. We maintained our position until dark, when we retired quietly, with the loss of one trooper killed and a few men wounded. During the night we were unmolested, and had not even the usual entertainment of being fired into. Received a deputation from the Kuzilbaches tonight, intimating that they had withdrawn their allegiance from Akbar Khan, and were anxious to aid us in every way in their power; a proof of the decay of his cause, and that our new allies were not of

The frien's we can trust
When the win's o' adversitie blaw.

14th. To Beni-badam, thirteen miles; our road close to a range of high hills on the left. As we advanced, we saw detached bodies of horse and foot with their many banners moving along the hills; but as we received authentic intelligence of the defeat of Akbar Khan at Tezeen, by General Pollock, and of the intention of the latter to enter Cabul on the 14th or 15th, we did not anticipate that we should meet with any further opposition in our progress to the capital.

As we approached our encamping ground we observed the enemy in great force on a high rugged hill, upwards of a mile in front of where we were to pitch. Close to a small fort at the foot of this hill was Shumshoodeen Khan and Sultan Jan with their cavalry,—the latter, however, drew off as we advanced. General Nott having determined on clearing the heights, Captain F. White, 40th regiment, who commanded all the light companies of the force, was directed to perform this duty, which he did in the most gallant style, with some

---

2. He afterwards gave himself up, and was shot pursuant to the sentence of a general court-martial, by which he was tried.

slight loss. General Nott moved off to camp, shortly after which Brigadier Wymer ordered Lieutenant Wakefield with the Grenadiers of H.M. 40th, to clear a detached hill on which there was a considerable number of the enemy, who were firing on our baggage as it passed; this service was effected in an equally spirited manner,—Lieutenant Eager, one of the officers of the grenadiers' company, being severely wounded. In the dispatches[3] announcing this success, no mention is made of the services of the grenadier company; this, however, may perhaps be accounted for, by General Nott having left the field before it was employed, under the impression that all the heights had been secured; or possibly by his not having been made acquainted with the circumstances previous to transmitting his dispatch.

Very shortly after the Affghans had been driven from their position, the light companies and the grenadiers were withdrawn under cover of the Artillery, who kept up a brisk fire on the heights: all the troops then moved into camp, and the enemy of course reoccupied the hills.[4]

Our encampment was situated in the centre of a large plain, surrounded by high and barren hills: towards the afternoon they seemed to swarm with the enemy, who kept up from them a continual but harmless fire the rest of the day. As evening approached, their numbers increased; and their monotonous and wolf-like shrieks wafted on the breeze broke most unpleasantly on the ear.

Anticipating that it was their intention to attempt an attack on camp during the night, guns were placed in different positions after sunset, so as to command those points which appeared most favourable to the enemy's approach. At night, the hills by which we were surrounded had a peculiar and beautiful appearance, from the thousand campfires of the enemy gleaming like meteors in the darkness on the mountain sides.

As night advanced, there was a lull in the firing and discordant yells, and shortly after the twinkling of the enemy's matchlocks was distinctly seen in a ravine some distance to the rear of camp: on this one of our eighteen-pounders was brought to bear; a shrapnel was discharged, which, bursting in the very gorge, was succeeded by a shriek of horror from the mass among whom it had so unexpect-

---

3. See Appendix F.

4. It seemed extraordinary that the general should have taken the trouble to occupy the heights, they being at such a distance from our ground. It was said that he had done so, not having correctly understood the position camp was to occupy.

edly exploded. Silence followed, and the rest of the night was passed unmolested.

In the dispatch of the events of this day, I was delighted to see honourable mention made of my old and valued friend Ferdinand White; and in after months I was equally rejoiced to find his name among those who were rewarded for distinguished services during the campaign.

It was a subject of great regret to us all, that General Pollock had deemed it *expedient* to move on to Cabul before our arrival there, we having expected from the arrangement entered into, if not made by him, with General Nott, that both armies were to enter that city on the same day.

15th. To Maidan, six miles; moved close to the range of hills on our right, which were occupied by small parties of the enemy. A few of them came down into the plain, and commenced firing on us, which was reciprocated with interest by our skirmishers. Having advanced about five miles, there is a narrow gorge in the mountain through which we passed from the valley wherein we had been encamped yesterday *en route* to Maidan. The River Cabul flows through this pass. Here are the remains of a stone bridge, now perfectly impassable; on the left bank on a high hill is a small fort commanding the river here, at the only point where it is fordable; this in the morning was occupied by the enemy, but they evacuated on our approach .

Having crossed the river, which was up to our men's pouches, we continued our march through *paddy-fields*. Had the enemy been so inclined, they had a much better country in today's route to annoy us, than in yesterday's,—the latter part of our march being unavoidably up to our knees in mud, through fields which were over-hung with steep and rugged hills. A very slight opposition was, however, offered; and the numerous forts in the rich and beautiful valley of Maidan were quickly secured by our troops.

Our quartermasters were driven in today, and their gallant leader, Captain Adamson, H. M. 40th, now 21st Fusiliers, who was acting quartermaster for the 40th, had a narrow escape, a matchlock ball having passed through the peak of his forage cap. The rearguard were also more closely pressed than usual: the axle-tree of one of the nine-pounders under Lieutenant Terry broke, and the enemy gaining confidence from this mishap, rushed into the plain in immense numbers, hoping to secure the prize; they were allowed to come on, and when sufficiently near, were received with a withering fire of musketry and grape from a second gun, which compelled them to fall back. After this unexpected repulse we received less annoyance.

The chief of Maidan, who had been most actively employed yesterday, and even today, against us, when he saw that further opposition was hopeless, came out to meet us and request protection for his forts. *The days of conciliation and concession* were, however, at an end, and the general informed him that he could have no intercourse with him; he then retired. The crops in the valley were cut down and appropriated to our cattle, and at night the picturesquely situated forts of Maidan, which had been but half seen through the clusters of poplars and willows, were enveloped in smoke and flame.

Received the cheering intelligence today that some of the prisoners had been recovered, and were now in General Pollock's camp, who had taken possession of the Balla Hissar, at Cabul.

16th. To Urghundee, eleven miles; road much intersected with ravines. On our march today passed the ground where Dhost Mahommed abandoned his guns, on the approach of Lord Keane's army, in 1839. Our encampment was good, situated on a plain near a number of small forts, all of which were occupied, and the inhabitants of which most *friendly*. Had to pay today for grain, forage, &c., for our camels—a thing that to us, from want of practice in monetary payments of late, appeared rather strange.

Today it was reported that Sir Richmond Skakespeare had passed near our camp during the night, with five hundred or six hundred *kuzilbashes*, to effect the release of the remaining prisoners, who were confined in a fort near Bamean.

17th. Marched this morning, and encamped within three or four miles of Cabul. Our encampment was in a lovely plain, extensively cultivated, full of luxuriant gardens, and surrounded by hills beautifully diversified by ravines and hollows.

Here we procured the most refreshing and luscious fruits:—

The grapes of gold, like those that shine
On Casbin's hills; pomegranates full
Of melting sweetness; and the pears
And sunniest apples that Cabul
In all its thousand gardens bears.
—Moore

Shortly before reaching camp, General Nott received a note from General Pollock, congratulating him on his arrival at Cabul, and mentioning the circumstance of Sir Richmond Shakespeare having proceeded to Bamean, in the hope of obtaining the release of the prisoners.

Owing to the severe indisposition of General Nott, General Pollock waived ceremony as senior officer, and on the morning after our arrival, came over to the "Candahar" camp, where he was received with a guard of honour and the usual salute. The interview between the two illustrious chiefs lasted for about two hours. It afterwards transpired, that in alluding to Sir Richmond Shakespeare having moved to the release of the prisoners, General Pollock suggested that General Nott should dispatch a brigade, with some cavalry and guns, towards Bamean, to act in concert with Sir Richmond Shakespeare, in the event of that gallant officer succeeding in securing the prisoners. To this our general objected, on the principle that to the folly of despising our enemy, and sending out small parties of troops, many of our disasters in Affghanistan were to be attributed; and *he offered to move with the whole of the Candahar division next morning*, should General Pollock wish.

At the same time General Nott represented that his troops had made a long and arduous march from Candahar of upwards of three hundred miles,—it might almost be said, without a halt, those days on which they did not march being employed in some fatigue duty; and he suggested that a portion of General Pollock's force, which had not traversed more than one-third of the distance, and had already rested three days at Cabul, should be dispatched on this duty. General Nott also expressed surprise, that when an intention existed of sending a part of his force on the duty in question, such intention had not been communicated while he was at Urghundee, which was on the way to Bamean, instead of bringing it first to Cabul.

The conduct of General Nott has been much canvassed; and a degree of censure has been implied for his not having immediately, on hearing General Pollock's views, put a brigade in motion, to secure the return of the prisoners. Nor were there wanting the malevolently-disposed, who, judging of others by their own mean spirit, inferred that his objection to march arose either from indifference to the fate of the prisoners, or a morbid feeling of jealousy that Cabul had been occupied by General Pollock's army before the arrival of the Candahar division. Such insinuations are as false as they are unworthy, and the shafts of malice which were thus hurled at the reputation of this distinguished *captain* fell harmless and contemned.

To the fact of General Pollock having declined to permit the whole "Candahar division" moving, and finally decided on dispatching a brigade from his own force, we owe our deprivement of the honour of proceeding to the assistance of the prisoners—a matter of the deepest regret to the gallant Nott and his devoted army.

On the 19th a brigade, with some cavalry and guns—the command of which had been most appropriately given to General Sale, owing probably to the circumstance of Lady Sale and her daughter being among the prisoners,—passed our camp *en route* to Bamean. (*Lady Sale's Afghanistan* by Florentia Sale, also published by Leonaur).

On the 20th, we heard the joyful news, that all the prisoners were safe in General Sale's camp at Urghundee. In the evening, some of them came into our camp, among others, Major Eldred Pottinger, to whose decision of character and great exertions the captives were chiefly indebted for their restoration to their countrymen. The number of European prisoners now set at liberty was about one hundred and twenty. They were all dressed in the costume of the country, and we could not help remarking, how much more elegant and graceful is the loose flowing drapery of the Easterns, than the tight ungainly garments to which long use has accustomed us.

21st. Moved camp nearer Cabul and pitched in a beautiful valley, on a soft green turf,—the ground rather damp, however, from the number of little rivulets that flowed through the vale. Our camp was intersected by luxuriant hedgerows of poplar and willow. Near us were several small forts, generally deserted, but filled with lucerne, grain, &c.

This afternoon the prisoners passed our camp on their way to join General Pollock's camp; the men of our division turned out and gave them a right hearty English cheer, a compliment that was also paid to "The Hero of Jellalabad," as he moved past with his force.

All the grand objects of our advance had now been achieved; the armies of Pollock and Nott had met in triumph at Cabul—the prisoners, with but one exception, had been recovered, and thus had "all past disasters been retrieved and avenged on "every scene on which they were sustained, and "repeated victories in the field, and the capture of" the cities and citadels of Ghuznee and Cabul, "had advanced the glory and established the "accustomed superiority of the British arms."[5]

The names of Pollock, Nott, and Sale, are encircled with glory, but the brightest ray falls upon the *illustrious Nott*, who, undismayed by accounts of the dread calamities occurring around him, or unshaken by the instructions to retire, conceived, urged, and at length executed that extraordinary march, the glorious results of which were developed in the release of our prisoners, and the restoration of our national honour.

Assailed by difficulties, surrounded by perils, he saved, by his energy, wisdom, and prudence, from the most imminent destruction his own force,—that army which was for so long a time neglected, but which, nevertheless, nobly upheld our national honour, and during a period of four years, acted with the greatest forbearance and humanity to the people of Afghanistan;" and eventually, by the ever-memorable and splendid execution of his glorious advance on Cabul, he mainly contributed in removing the tarnish that sullied the brightness of our arms. "No envy can detract from this: it will shine in history, and, like swans, grow whiter the longer it endures."[6]

Mr. Nicholson, 27th Bengal Native Infantry, one of the Ghuznee prisoners, joined camp today. The treatment which the captives taken at that city received from Shumshoodeen Khan must have been harsh indeed, and afforded a singular and, as respects that chief, most unfavourable contrast with the conduct the other prisoners experienced from Akbar Khan, who appears to be a strange mixture of ferocity and kindness.

Cabul is a large city,—encompassed on three sides by an amphitheatre of high hills, along the crest of which runs a wall which is now much dilapidated:—near our camp was a narrow gorge between two high hills, through which we had to pass to enter the town. The houses here are all built of wood, the best material for constructing buildings in a country so subject to earthquakes as this is. The bazaars, four in number, are the only buildings in the town possessing any beauty, and even they do not merit that excellence as works of art, which has been attributed to them; the houses therein are all two stories high, the streets formed by them being wide, and arched over, producing a continuation of splendid arcades, separated by open spaces, in the centre of each of which is an elegant marble fountain. The fronts of the houses are very showily painted, and adorned in the usual Eastern

---

5. Lord Ellenborough's dispatches.

6. Dryden.

taste, the ceilings of the arcades being ornamented with mosaic-work, similar to the rooms I have before noticed in the citadel at Ghuznee.

The shops are, I believe, handsome, but during our stay here, the town was almost deserted, so but few of them were to be seen; in those, however, which were open, there was a goodly supply of furs, silks, horse trappings, &c. The marks of musket-balls and other indications of strife were visible on the walls. In one of these bazaars the body of Sir William M'Naughten was exposed after his murder. To the northward of the town is the Balla Hissar, surrounded by a high wall of mud, loopholed in every direction. In this are the Palace and other buildings appertaining thereto. One of Shah Soojah's sons, Futteh Jhung, who had proclaimed himself king, was enjoying the royal title for the few days we were here, so no one was admitted within the precincts of His Majesty's abode.

Near the Balla Hissar, in an open *esplanade*, were all the guns that now fell into our hands, thirty-six in number, many of which, alas! had been taken from us. There were some native guns, and among the rest two curious wall-guns, rifled, and carrying ball of about one-pound weight. Near the Palace was a sort of hall used for *durbars*; a fine oblong building, about two hundred feet long by sixty broad. The tower is used for guard-rooms, &c.; the upper room, where His Majesty held his levees, was surrounded by four open verandahs, the walls and ceilings of each of which were most elaborately and chastely painted. In rear of this building were the beautiful gardens of the palace; but these had been laid waste during the insurrection. Commanding the Balla Hissar on the top of a high hill, was an "upper citadel, used as a state prison for the princes of the blood," but which is now a heap of ruins. From the highest point on this waved "the meteor flag of England."

The view from this upper citadel was most commanding; the immense town, surrounded by hills and orchards, lay below, and in the distance stood what had been the cantonments, detached and now ruined buildings scattered over the country,—memorials of mal-arrangement and folly.

To the left of the gate by which we passed from the citadel, is an old mosque, in a narrow compartment of which is entombed Shah Soojah ool Moolk: a small mound covered with the quilt on which His Majesty reclined in his *palanquin* when he was shot, marks where he is laid, but no tablet records that here rest the mortal remains of the descendant of a long line of Kings.

In the city of Cabul, is a small colony of Armenians, an interesting account of whom is given by Mr. Allen (our chaplain) in his narrative.

23rd. Was one of a party to visit the tomb of the Emperor Baber. Our road at first was narrow, finely shaded by poplars and willows, which appear the prevalent trees in this part of the world. The hedgerows were beautiful, and on either side spread green meadows of exuberant grass and clover, through which a hundred little brooks and rills gurgled in pleasing music. Pursuing our ride we crossed the river Cabul by an ancient and picturesque stone bridge, and a little further on appeared the ruins of an old *caravanserai*, in which were several gates; passing through these, we entered the terraced and finely wooded grounds leading to the tomb of the wise and mighty Emperor Baber. The tomb is situated on a slight eminence, and is over-shadowed by a cluster of noble trees, comprising several lovely sycamores; overhanging it towers a lofty hill, and gushing out from the rock on which the Musjid is built, races a beautifully clear and limpid stream, which empties itself into a small tank, at the foot of an immense hollow sycamore,—and then, pursuing its course, rolling like pellucid crystal over the numerous terraces, murmurs softly on, and, escaping from the gardens, loses itself in the river Cabul in the vale beneath.

The Musjid is of white marble,—an elegant, chaste, and beautifully-sculptured monument; the roof is supported by three handsome arches; opposite the centre one as you enter, is the niche for prayer, and above it, carved' in Eastern characters, are a few short sentences, recounting the virtues of him whose dust now mingles with the kindred dust around. In front of this Musjid is a small square, enclosed by a simple, light, and elegant screen of open flower-work, most delicately and elaborately carved in white marble. Inside are two unpretending tombs, the one of the mighty *Sultan*, the other of his daughter.

The view of the Cabul valley from this Musjid is magnificent: the fine river winding through the picturesque plain below, ornamented and studded with its thousand gardens and orchards,—the blooming hedgerows and the park-like scenery in the grounds around the mosque, all reminded us of our fatherland. When least expected, such a scene touches a chord that recalls a world of happy associations; and, lost in the contemplation of the beauties by which we were on this bright spot surrounded, we felt as if we could linger about it for ever.

But these feelings were evanescent: in the plain below was the tented field of an avenging army, reminding us acutely that within view of this seeming earthly paradise, we had sunk under a load of adversity, involving the treacherous massacre of thousands of our gallant countrymen, whose blanched and withering bones, scattered yet unburied in the mountain passes of Afghanistan, appealed in mournful testimony to the extent of our disasters.

On the 24th, accompanied by Mr. Thomas, 40th, I went to visit our young friend Talbot, of H. M. 13th (Prince Albert's Light Infantry), who had accompanied the 40th from Kurachee to Quettah. The road passed the spot near Shere Sungh, where Shah Soojah was murdered: it is marked by a small heap of stones. This day too I had the honour of calling on Lady Sale. On leaving her tent I was met by most of the other female captives, and the poor children who were to assemble in her Ladyship's tent to be present at the baptism of some of the infants that had been born during the captivity; it was an interesting but painful sight, calling forth sympathy for their sufferings, and admiration for the truly feminine fortitude which they had exhibited.

Here were the widowed mother and orphan-child, those "for whom the prayers of thousands had gone up;"—where now is the recollection of their sufferings, their perils, and their privations? Where now the sympathy for their sorrows and irreparable losses? Are they forgotten in the hour of triumph,—or is it sufficient that the remembrance of them and the resignation with which they were endured should be concentrated and reflected in the exclusive homage which has been paid to the renowned lady of the illustrious hero of Jellalabad?—

Tiffed (lunched) with the 13th today, and enjoyed some excellent wine of the country, a cask of which had been presented to their mess by an Affghan chief. It was light, and really of very *curious* quality, not unlike Rhenish wines, but of an inferior description. Learned while in the headquarter camp that a force under General MacCaskill was to march the next day on Istaliff, and that the Candahar division was to furnish a brigade. Not being certain which brigade had been chosen, we galloped home. On our way we saw clouds of smoke issuing from a division of the city which by order of Futteh Jhung had been set fire to.

On arrival in camp, found that the 2nd brigade was to proceed to Istaliff; the 1st, to which we belonged, being ordered to move from their present ground, and encamp near Shere Sungh, about two miles from the headquarter camp.

During the night of the 26th, we had a good deal of rain, and the snow beginning to appear on the distant hills, made us seriously think of leaving the country.

27th. Moved our camp, and pitched on a marshy plain to the eastward of Cabul; had to send upwards of a mile for water, that procurable near camp being exceedingly brackish. Our 2nd brigade marched today. Captain By grave, the last of the prisoners, was sent into camp by Akbar Khan today: our joy on this matter was, consequently, completed.

30th. News arrived of General MacCaskill having gained a victory at Istaliff. Poor Evans of the 41st was among the killed.

7th October. General MacCaskill's force returned, and our 2nd brigade marched into our camp.

The halt which the combined armies of Pollock and Nott had made at Cabul, was not only much longer than we had anticipated on our arrival at the capital, but was entirely against the wish and advice of General Nott. This long delay was, however, rendered necessary by the march of General MacCaskill's division to Istaliff; an expedition, the judiciousness and expediency of which the gallant Commander of the Candahar division did not admit.

Winter was now coming on apace; the snow already appeared on the summits of the distant mountains; and when it was considered that latterly it was perhaps more owing to the inclemency of the weather than to the formidable opposition of the Affghans in the field that the number of our unfortunate troops had been reduced, there was a prevalent feeling of anxiety that the day for our departure should be named.

Before leaving, however, it was requisite that "a lasting proof of the British power should be left in Cabul,—consistent with British humanity;" and on the 9th October, commenced the demolition, by order of General Pollock, of *one of the Bazaars at Cabul.* To this work of destruction General Nott was decidedly averse, and he most strenuously urged the propriety of razing the Balla Hissar.

The springing of the first mine, was the signal for all the camp followers to rush into the town, and commence a work of the most disgraceful plunder; a result which might have been expected, and which, indeed, was predicted. Guards, it is true, were placed at the different gates, to prevent anyone entering while the work of destruction was going on; but there were many points of ingress besides the gates, and all attempts to keep out the followers were futile. It is not to be denied that *several of the soldiers* contributed to the irregularities, but the misconduct of a few men does not criminate the actions of an army.

Exasperated as our troops were, it is matter of surprise that they practised forbearance to the extent they did, and it must ever be a subject of astonishment, that when an opening for revenge was given, the city of Cabul should have been spared.

During our stay here, some soldiers of H. M. 31st, in walking about near camp, saw the marks of gun-wheels, the track of which suddenly disappeared; this induced them to make search near the spot where the impression discontinued, and after digging a little below the surface, they came upon one or two nine-pounders, with carriage, &c., complete.

While the destruction of the Bazaar was progressing, all the guns found in Cabul, *with the exception of four*, were burst; those four bearing the mark of the Honourable Company, had been presented to the late Shah Soojah by the Indian Government; they were now consigned to the King, whose authority we had in a manner acknowledged.

On the 12th October, we marched from Cabul. The defences of the Balla Hissar remained uninjured, as a proof of our clemency,—a ruined bazaar and rifled shops, constituted a worthy memorial of inconsistency; and, as a fitting climax to the long list of infatuations which had marked our career in Affghanistan, four British guns were left, as if the more surely and palpably to perpetuate the remembrance of our disgrace!

Chapter 19

March from Cabul

General Sale having moved on in advance with his division to occupy the heights of the Khourd Cabul, the remainder of the army marched from Cabul on the 12th of October, and encamped at Bootkak, the entrance to the Pass.

Consequent on its having been decided that the Headquarters Division of General Pollock's army and the Candahar Division should march the same day, the latter did not leave its camp until about twelve o'clock, in order that the former might have moved off previous to our passing through the ground it had occupied while here, and which was on our road to Bootkak. On coming up to it, however, we found that not only was their rearguard still there, but that several tents were yet unstruck: we were consequently halted for some hours; the baggage of our division got mixed with that of the division in front, and our line of march being intersected at one place by a broad marsh,—to pass across which it was necessary to move along a narrow causeway, leading to a still narrower bridge over a small stream in the centre,—the greatest confusion prevailed.

In the crush numbers of camels fell, and many were pressed into the swamp; several stuck in the mud and were never extricated; their loads being in many instances necessarily abandoned, and otherwise much injury sustained. *The gates* were in charge of a native regiment; concerning them there was a prediction by a *moolah*, that they would never get beyond Bootkak; this was very nearly being verified, as they all but fell over the bridge into the stream below, which was exceedingly deep and rapid. The baggage was all very late coming up, and among the last was our mess kit, so that we were obliged to trust to the contents of our haversacks for dinner.

On either side of the road on today's march, numerous skeletons were strewed.

13th. Halted at Bootkak to admit of General Pollock's division, which marched this morning, clearing the pass before ours; Lord Ellenborough having ordered that General Nott with the Candahar Division should have the post of honour in the rear, on withdrawing from the enemy's country.

In the neighbourhood of our encampment were numbers of skeletons, additional indications of this having been the halting-place of our doomed and unfortunate army. Ragged portions of clothing, old gloves, &c., were lying about, and even the tattered portions of *rowtees*[1] our troops had been permitted to carry with them. The weather was now exceedingly cold.

14th. Entered the Khourd Cabul Pass; the road very narrow, but better for marching than the Bolan, being less stony; as in the latter, however, there is a stream, which in its serpentine course, crosses and recrosses the road, and which we had to ford upwards of twenty times. On either side of the road, steep, nay, almost perpendicular hills tower to an immense height; in many places the path is overhung by rocks and cliffs, which it would be perfectly impossible to crown from the interior of the pass; and if well defended, it would require an army not only strong in courage, but in numbers also to carry it. Even now the cold was intense, the water forming in icicles on the wheels of the guns as they passed through the stream; judge then, what must have been the sufferings of our famished, disheartened, and devoted troops, who traversed it in the month of January, when the ground was covered with snow, and they were exposed to the heavy and too unerring fire of the Affghans.

The pass was literally strewed with the horrid remains of men,—skeletons they could not be called, for in many the features were so hideously perfect, that little difficulty was experienced in recognising in this sad and changed state, those who had been known in life. Mingling with the corpses of our comrades, were those of camels, horses, &c. In some places, the slain lay in heaps, probably marking the place where they had made a gallant, but ineffectual stand; in others, they were to be seen crowded in the caves and crevices whither they had fled from one sure death to meet another, even more dreadful and lingering. Nor were the evidences of death confined to those whose loss we were here to avenge. Several corpses of the straggling followers of

1. A small tent.

the divisions in front, who had been cut up and plundered, were lying about. All around was horror, the very birds of prey seemed scared by such a sickening, such a revolting spectacle.—

For, oh! to see the unburied heaps
On which the lovely moonlight sleeps—
The very vultures turn away,
And sicken at so foul a prey!

The painful feelings connected with our march through this appalling scene of death were augmented by its being impossible to avoid driving the guns over the remains of our slaughtered comrades: the wheels crushed the bones of those unburied masses, and the harsh, agonizing sound struck mournfully and direfully on the heart. There was no sun to impart a ray of cheerfulness to the bold and beautiful mountain scenery around—nothing to dispel the gloom and horror of our associations, and lead the mind to happier subjects for contemplation than the sad, affecting, and humiliating scene through which, in this "*Valley of the Shadow of Death,*" we had passed, and from which at length, in sorrow and in heaviness, we emerged.

On arrival at Khourd Cabul, General Pollock's rearguard was just moving off; we encamped near the ground he had occupied, in the midst of a wide plain surrounded by hills.

15th. To Tezein, fourteen miles. The first few miles of our march were very easy, through the dry bed of a river. At the end of this, we came to a high rock, at the foot of which a river flowed. The road here turned sharply to the left, and wound down an abrupt declivity, so steep, that we were detained some time in getting the guns to the bottom. We now entered what is called the Huft Kotul (or Eight Hills),—for some miles a series of formidable undulations through a country of great strength, from its innumerable ravines. At the termination of these we entered a narrow gorge (the Tezeen Pass), about two miles in length, and not more than twenty yards broad in any part, and in several not exceeding ten, with high perpendicular rocks on either side.

The road presented the same horrors as yesterday—skeletons uncountable were lying scattered about, the bones crumbling and being crunched as we were obliged to walk over them; numbers, also, of the followers of General Pollock's division, and some of his *sepoys* (one *naique* and five),—added to which, camels and horses, dying and dead, lay in putrefying masses about. From the bodies of the *sepoys* being left behind, we concluded that the rearguard of the force in front must have been exceedingly hard pressed.

Our main column met with no annoyance; but the distant booming of guns, and the sharp rattle of musketry in front and rear, told us that our own rearguard and that of the division preceding were engaged.

Our encampment was in tolerably open ground for this part of the world, and a clear rapid stream ran near it. Owing to the difficulties of the country, and the opposition experienced by our rearguard, the baggage came in but slowly. At about six p.m. an officer from the rearguard rode in to report, that towards dark the enemy had increased in numbers—that the rearguard was hard-pressed,—their ammunition nearly expended, and fresh supplies of that and reinforcements instantly required.

A wing of the 40th and two companies of H.M. 41st, under Major Hibbert, were immediately sent off. On entering the Pass, we found it choked with camels, whose drivers becoming alarmed by a report that the enemy were in their front, would not proceed: gaining confidence, however, by our appearance, they moved on towards camp. On approaching within a short distance of where we had first entered the gorge in the morning, we found drawn up the rearguard—consisting of part of the 42nd Bengal N. I., some companies from other native regiments, and two guns, the whole under Captain Leeson,—the guns occasionally firing on a high hill in the centre of and commanding the Pass, of which hill the enemy had taken possession. The grenadier company of the 40th, under Wakefield, was ordered to seize this position, and rushing at it with a cheer, soon drove the enemy from it. Lieutenant Todd, with No. 2 company, relieved a company of *sepoys* from the heights on the left; while I, with my own company, occupied those on the right, which had been held by a company of the 42nd Bengal N.I., who then withdrew. Major Hibbert, with No. 3 company of H. M. 40th, and two companies of H. M. 41st, then advanced to the head of the gorge, driving a party of the enemy before them, and returned bringing with them the bodies of some of our artillerymen and *sepoys*, who had fallen, and which from being so hotly engaged the rearguard had been obliged to abandon.

The piquet, rearguard, and other duties were most severe, two of our regiments, the 2nd and 16th, having been *borrowed* by General Pollock until arrival at Jellalabad. The *sepoys* in rear today had been out and engaged in desultory and fatiguing skirmishing since four in the morning: it was nearly ten p. m. before we relieved them, and in the meanwhile they had been totally without food and almost without water. It is not surprising, therefore, that we found them completely exhausted in body— though not in spirit, for when I intimated to the officer I relieved on the heights that he was to proceed to camp with the remainder of the rearguard of the morning, the duties of which were to be continued by the reinforcements of which my company formed a part, the *sepoys* expressed a wish that they should be permitted to remain to share in these duties, and the fatigues and perils by which they might be attended.

All the baggage and the old rearguard having cleared the Pass, our companies were withdrawn, and we also retraced our steps. I was ordered to move in advance with two companies; following me were the two guns, and bringing up the rear were the remaining companies of the 40th and the two of the 41st. During our passage through the narrow defile, a continued fire from matchlocks was kept up on us; occasionally the bullets whistled unpleasantly near, but, thanks to the intense darkness of the night, the Affghans could not take good aim. They were completely out of our sight, and it would have been useless attempting to fire at them.

One *young* soldier, notwithstanding the caution to reserve his fire, thinking he saw something moving along the top of one of the ridges, could not withstand the temptation to try and dislodge it: the flash from his musket giving the enemy a correct idea of where we were, brought down upon us a volley, but, strange to relate, only one man was hit. After running the gauntlet between the high rocks for about a mile and a half, we cleared the Pass *with only one man wounded*, although several hundred rounds had been discharged at us: so much for the Affghans as marksmen!

In our rearguard duty at Tezeen we were accompanied by our chief engineer, Major Saunders, ever among the foremost when anything was to be done. He fell on the hard-fought field of Maharajpoor, in December, 1843; and in the dispatch announcing that victory, the following short, but eloquent tribute to his noble qualities as a soldier was paid by Sir Hugh Gough:—

> In the returned of killed I have greatly to deplore the loss of Lieutenant-Colonel E. Saunders, C. B., of the Engineers—than whom this army, with its numerous list of devoted soldiers, could not boast a more enthusiastic officer.

Our loss in camp-followers today must have been immense,—judging from the numbers of these poor creatures we saw lying about, even in the short distance we traversed while proceeding to reinforce the rearguard.

16th. Seh-Baba, seven miles: the country here open, the road through the bed of a mountain-torrent. The enemy mustered in numbers on the hills: a party came down and made an attempt on the baggage,—it was unattended with success. During the day there was a great deal of firing; and towards evening our piquets on the right and rear were attacked, but the enemy were driven back with loss.

17th. Kuttey Sungh: a short march of six miles through an undulating country, similar to the Huft Kotul. Our camels were thoroughly knocked up; at the last ground there was a poisonous herb, of which many partook and died. Their feet sored from the shingle, our gun-bullocks were hardly able to move, much less to draw the eighteen-pounders. The rearguard had to assist them—indeed, it had to perform the whole work of dragging the guns along nearly the entire line occupied in marching; and we all hoped that our general would follow the example of General Pollock, who, while at Tezeen, had burst two of our eighteen-pounders that he had *borrowed*, the bullocks having become quite exhausted. These animals, it was said, he handed over to the commissariat, and they were afterwards killed and issued to the troops. If true, this was *unkind*: considering that *we* had brought them from Candahar, we ought certainly to have derived the benefit from them. However, "*it is not lost what a friend gets.*"

Had a little very pretty skirmishing today. Our encampment was irregular, and in a rugged broken country, intersected with ravines, rivulets, &c., which made it no easy matter to fix on a proper position for piquets and *videttes*.

Received the welcome and gratifying intelligence today, that a medal and six months' *batta* had been awarded to the troops for their exploits.

A medal with the mural crown points out the defenders of Jellalabad;—a similar badge "The Unconquered" of Kelat-i-Gilzie. "Victoria Vindex" tells of the glories of the avenging armies of Pollock and Nott; but there is nought to mark the long line of successes of the Candahar force during the winters of '41 and '42. Those regiments which arrived at that city, under General England, in May, and were fortunate enough to bear a part in the engagement in its vicinity on the 29th of that month, have received the same medal, and carry the same achievements on their colours, as those which maintained their position there throughout the winter.

No one grudges these laurels to our gallant companions. "*They won them well, and may they wear them long!*" yet, in the distribution of honours, though it was not for us to set a value on our own actions, nor dictate what reward should be meted out for our services, we did fondly hope that some specific distinction would have been granted, to mark the successes that attended the operations of the Candahar force previous to the arrival there of the regiments under General England.

18th. Jugdulluk, five or six miles; there are two roads—one through a short pass, by which the guns and cavalry and some of the infantry went, the other hilly and undulating like that on the last two or three days' marches; by this latter the main body of the infantry, and all the heavy baggage passed. The hills were occupied by a few of the Affghans, but we received little or no annoyance; though in the distance among the hills we could distinctly see the rearguard of the centre division engaged with strong bodies of the enemy.

Our encampment was near a ruined fort; the memorable spot where the last stand was made by the Europeans on their retreat. This was marked by a heap of their dead bodies, close to which was the skeleton of a horse, and that of his rider by his side,—probably an officer. It was here that General Elphinstone was made prisoner.

Although we left our last camp very early, and had such a short distance to march, it was late in the evening before the heavy guns came up; the bullocks were quite unable to drag them, and they were brought into camp entirely by manual labour. The camp was surrounded by steep hills, which were occupied by the enemy; on our arrival on the ground, they retired before our piquets, and for once we were allowed to pass the night in tolerable quiet.

19th. Soorkaub, sixteen miles. The commencement of our inarch was through a narrow defile, the heights on either side, though not very high, being much intersected with hollows and ravines, and covered with low brush-wood. General MacCaskill's rearguard had met with considerable opposition here yesterday. Our main column was allowed to pass through unmolested, but the baggage was afterwards attacked, and the rearguard much harassed; there were several officers wounded, among whom was Lieutenant Macgowan, 40th, and a number of men killed and wounded. Previous to leaving Jugdulluk, the rearguard burst the remaining eighteen-pounders, the bullocks being now so completely exhausted from fatigue and lameness as to be unable to work. In the defile through which we passed in the early part of this march were the remains of a breastwork, which had been thrown up the more effectually to impede the progress of the Cabul army.

20th. To Gundamuck, seven miles: the 40th, commanded by Major Stopford, formed the rearguard today. The country now became more open; the enemy came down in numbers on our baggage, but having now got more room for action we were enabled to make rather a severe example of some of them.

Crossed rather a picturesque stone bridge on leaving our old encampment; under some rocks near this, part of our rearguard were concealed,—the enemy suspecting nothing, followed and were close upon us before they found out their mistake. An opportunity was afforded us, of which we did not fail to take advantage, to pour in two or three well-directed volleys before they had time to recover from their surprise and retire. General MacCaskill we found halted here.

21st. Rejoiced both on our own account, and that of our cattle, to get a halt today. We had rather more firing into camp at night than we had of late been accustomed to.

22nd. Neemlah, five miles; encamped near a celebrated and very beautiful garden. The rearguard had a little work today, but the country had become too open for the Affghans to venture very near, especially after the lesson they got the day before yesterday. Forded one of the small branches of the Cabul River today,—there were the remains of a stone bridge over it, now perfectly useless.

23rd. Futtey-a-bad. An exceedingly bad road, and very stony, until close to the encamping ground, which was in a pleasing little valley, abundantly fertile, the hills surrounding it being nicely wooded. The distant hills of the Soliman range and Hindoo Koosh with their snow-capped summits looked picturesquely grand from this encampment. Our rearguard was very slightly annoyed today.

24th. Sultanpoor, nine miles, road good over a sandy plain; the enemy still continuing to follow us, several of them were cut up today, without doing much injury to us. Poor Ravenscroft, 3rd Cavalry, died this morning of the wounds he had received in the cavalry affair on the 28th of August last. At night all his old friends attended to pay the last tribute of respect to his memory. To guard against the remains of our comrades being disinterred, it was necessary to bury them with the greatest secrecy, the ground being afterwards carefully levelled, and generally a fire lighted on it, to mark, as it were, the spot where some of the soldiers had been cooking. Ravenscroft's grave was dug inside the mess-tent of his regiment. Here we all assembled; a few wax candles glimmered faintly round the grave, and at ten p.m. the solemn service of our church was read over his body, which was lowered by some of his troopers; the grave was then filled up and made even with the rest of the ground. In the morning the tent was struck, and a fire was kindled on another of those graves of the brave o'er which "*not a soldier discharged his farewell shot.*"

25th. Jellalabad, ten miles. The scene of the triumphs of the "Illustrious Garrison,"—a strong fort, but of course most of the defences new. Encamped on the Peshawur road. Some distance, in front of camp, runs the Cabul River, which is a broad and considerable stream here. It is not unusual to descend to Peshawur on rafts down this river, and some of our Sikh allies left by this route while we were here; its navigation, however, on account of the numerous rapids and whirlpools is exceedingly dangerous. The whole army was assembled here previous to making our last start for *home.* During our stay we had several slight shocks of earthquake.

The scenery about Jellallabad is fine, particularly on the opposite side of the river, and there I should say the country was very rich and well cultivated. We had several camels carried off here from the camelmen persisting, in defiance of orders, in crossing the river.

26th. Halted. The rain came down in torrents and prevented our marching; on the 27th and 28th we were detained from the same cause. While we were encamped here, the defences of Jellalabad were entirely destroyed. It is difficult to understand upon what ground this fort should have been demolished, while the defences of the Balla Hissar of Cabul were left uninjured.

29th. The sun at length broke out, and our tents being sufficiently dry we marched, about one p.m., five miles to Ali Baghan, over a sandy and level road: one of the regiments (2nd), and Blood's guns, (nine-pounders), which had been detached with General MacCaskill's division since we left Cabul, now rejoined us. In front of our encampment were numerous ravines, and a lofty hill beyond them was occupied by the enemy; the afternoon's amusement was to dislodge our opponents, which we succeeded in doing. The ambuscade system was practised with success today. A party of our cavalry concealed themselves in a ruined fort; the enemy came down into the plain, when the troopers under Lieutenant Graves of the 3rd Bombay Cavalry, and Lieutenant Chamberlain, Irregular Cavalry, rushed out from their ambush, and falling on the Affghans, cut up many of them.

30th. Battee Kote, eleven miles; road good, high hills on our left. Experienced very little annoyance.

31st. To Bussole, twelve miles—an excellent road. Encamped near the river; on the other bank immediately opposite our camp, rose an extensive, lofty and almost perpendicular rock, full of innumerable caves, all of which are inhabited: the dwellers in them are for the most part robbers, and must be bad indeed, as they are viewed in that light by their neighbours, whose own morality with respect to the principle of "*meum et tuum*" is sufficiently lax and questionable. A few camels were carried off today.

1st November. To Dukka, nine miles. The road at first similar to what we had had since leaving Jellalabad; after marching four or five miles it became so very narrow,—bounded on one side by high hills, and on the other by an extensive marsh, that only one camel could pass along at a time. At about ten miles from Bussole we entered a narrow gorge, upwards of a mile in length, called the Chota Khyber, or Small Khyber; this was almost choked up with large detached portions of rock, and the dead camels of the division preceding us,—the stench from which was quite overpowering. Near the entrance of the gorge and in its centre was a high-pointed hill, on the top of which, perched like an eyrie, was a small watch-tower commanding a view of the whole pass. Leaving the gorge we entered a beautifully fertile valley, enclosed on three sides by the magnificent hills of the Sufaed-Coh, and washed in front by the broad stream of the Cabul River, on the opposite banks of which were numerous mud forts picturesquely situated.

About two miles higher up the valley was General MacCaskill's division, enjoying a halt today, consequent on General Pollock having determined on dividing his force, and marching through the Khyber in advance with General Sale, who led the withdrawal of our troops from Afghanistan. On our right frowned upon us the steep and rugged hills, whose many windings and ravines form the celebrated Khyber Pass. Our rearguard did not get into camp until seven p.m., although we marched at four in the morning.

2nd November. Halted to admit of General MacCaskill's division preceding us. The 16th Bengal regiment rejoined our camp today.

3rd. To Lundie Khanna, nine miles. Entered the Khyber Pass,[2] the road through the dry bed of a mountain torrent, and very narrow the hills on either side high and exceedingly picturesque; they were occupied by *Jezailchees* (riflemen of the country in our pay) who by their presence saved our men much fatigue. Our encampment was in a narrow defile; on reaching it we found General MacCaskill's rearguard still on the ground, and likely to remain there, from the delay in getting the baggage through the different narrow dells and camel-roads. Our rearguard did not reach camp until seven in the evening.

4th. Ali Musjid. The 40th was on rearguard today; the main column moved at four in the morning. The commencement of the march was up a road cut in the side of the hill, to the top of which it wound in a

---

2. The Khyberees consist of three independent tribes, exclusive of the Upper Momunds. These are the Afreedees, Shainwaurees, and Oorookeyes. Altogether they are about 120,000 souls. The Shainwaurees are the least numerous, but they are the best people of the three, and most subject to the King's authority. The others are secured from subjugation by the strength of their country; but the importance of the Khyber Pass (the great communication between Peshawur and Caubul) renders it necessary for the King to have some control over their proceedings. They accordingly receive great pensions on condition of answering for the quiet of the road; but such are their habits of rapine, that they can never be entirely restrained from plundering passengers; and when there is any confusion in the State, it is impossible to pass through their country. The Khyber Pass is about twenty-five miles long, over steep ridges and through very narrow defiles. The road is often along the beds of torrents, and is extremely dangerous in the event of sudden falls of rain in the hills. In quiet times the Khyberees have stations in different parts of the Pass to collect an authorized toll on passengers, but in times of trouble, they are all on the alert; if a single traveller endeavours to make his way through, the noise of his horse's feet sounds up the long narrow valleys, and soon brings the Khyberees in troops from the hills and ravines; but, if they expect a caravan, they assemble in hundreds on the side of a hill, and sit patiently, with their matchlocks in their hands, watching its approach.

They are excellent marksmen, and are reckoned good hill-soldiers, though of no great account in the plain. They are often employed in this sort of warfare, as far from their country as Kote Kaungra, in the eastern extremity of the Punjaub. They are, however, more disposed to plunder than to war, and will fall on the baggage of the army they belong to if they find it unguarded. It was thus they behaved to Shah Shujah in the heat of the battle of Eshpaun, and by these means lost him the day.—*Elphinstones Afghanistan*, vol. ii.

gradual ascent for upwards of a mile; on the left were lofty rocks overhanging it,—and on the right, abrupt and frequently perpendicular descents. The guns and "gates" were soon got up, then followed the cavalry and infantry; the tedious operation of getting the baggage on now commenced:—only one camel could get up at a time; and when any of these poor animals fell, which was often the case, the whole line in rear was detained, (it being impossible to pass on either side of such an obstacle,) until the animal had been raised, or, what was frequently the alternative, rolled over the precipice to the rocks below. The ascent of our baggage commenced at a quarter past four a.m.; the last camel did not reach the top of the ascent until eight p.m. About six p.m. I was ordered to relieve Captain Thomas, commanding the *Jezailchees* on the heights, close to the top of the ascent, in order that lie might move on with his men to a ravine near Ali Musjid.

About half an hour after this, there being much firing a-head, Lieutenant Todd, 40th, was sent on with his company, and came to a deep ravine, where the enemy, having made a dash on our baggage, had succeeded in carrying off to their fastnesses several of our camels. A little after eight o'clock the piquets of the rearguard were withdrawn, and it commenced its ascent. A host of Khyberees came rushing down the hill, and annoyed our rear excessively. At the top of the ascent, lying in a ravine, was the Khazee, a large brass gun similar to that we had destroyed at Ghuznee; it had been taken from Jellalabad, but abandoned by General MacCaskill's Brigade, from want of means to carry it on.

It was, I believe, expected that we should bring this ordnance with us; but, having no means of transport, that was impossible. However, we made arrangements for bursting it, and, when completed, the main body of the rearguard moved on, and our grenadier company under Wakefield remained to protect the artilleryman who was to fire the match; which being done, the grenadiers and their charge ran in. The gun burst with a tremendous explosion, that echoed sharply through the mountains, just as the enemy must have gained the height near where it was; this had at least the effect of astonishing and frightening them so much as to keep them from annoying us until we got through a difficult, undulating, and confined part of the Pass, into which we entered after leaving the gun.

It was now quite dark, and impossible for us to see the beauties of this bold and rocky scenery. Our route lay through a succession of narrow dells: on either side were high, craggy rocks; and, when we occasionally emerged from them for a short time, our line of march was flanked by innumerable ravines, extending and conducting into the distant mountains which towered above and around us. The signal-shouts and shrill *holloas* from different bodies of our enemies echoed among the hills; and the wildness of the whole scene was increased by the peculiar appearance of the *Jezailchees*, who were posted in small parties at different turns of the road, their lighted matches glimmering like glow-worms in the darkness, and ever and anon their wild, melancholy wail, in assurance of their watchfulness, rising on the air.

Still onwards we moved; every turn spoke of a desperate struggle, or of the success of our vigilant enemies in carrying off baggage, either from our own division or the ranks that had preceded us; here and there rifled boxes were to be seen—dead and dying camels—and numbers of our murdered followers, strewing the paths. As we approached Ali Musjid, we found some of our regiments posted at different parts of the road; and at length, after being out on rearguard duty for about thirty hours, we got into Ali Musjid. Here we learned of the reverse General MacCaskill had met with the day before; two of his guns having been captured, and two officers and several men left dead on the field. The painful duty of consigning these poor fellows to the silence of the grave was reserved for us, and the melancholy task was performed by our chaplain on the evening of the 4th of November.

The first person I met on my arrival in camp was my servant, who had been wounded during the night; and he forthwith communicated the pleasing intelligence that the kit I had on my back was about the whole extent of my wardrobe, as I was numbered among the unfortunates whose camels were carried off near one of the many ravines. There was nothing, one would think, very mirth-provoking in such a communication; yet notwithstanding I had to regret the loss of my journal, which I had kept ever since the regiment left Kurachee, and a few remembrances of Afghanistan, in the shape of matchlocks, *jassails*, ancient Greek coins procured at Cabul, and other little trifles that I valued, I could not resist laughing at the ridiculous plight to which I was reduced. Unfortunately, I was not the only sufferer, several of my brother officers being losers to as great an extent as myself.

A *subscription* was set on foot for the benefit of the *unfortunates*, and in a short time a liberal supply of shirts, trowsers, &c. was collected, and distributed amongst us;—but, not being all alike in size or form, I cannot say much for the appearance of those who had thus been reduced to a dependence on the generosity of their comrades.

Halted the rest of the day at Ali Musjid; the encampment was in a valley, which we entered after passing through a very narrow gorge, between perpendicular rocks rising to a height of two or three hundred feet. The fort of Ali Musjid was built on a conical hill in the centre of the pass, but considerably lower than the hills on each side of it. On another rock was a small watch-tower; and close to the river, which ran through our camp, was an insignificant white temple built, of Chunam. During the night our piquets were attacked, but the enemy got the worst of it.

6th. To Futtehgur. The Khyberees assembled in great force this morning, and gave every indication of their intention to make a farewell dash at our baggage: they had collected in a vast multitude on one hill, and, some of the artillery having been directed to open on them, I loitered behind to see the practice from the twenty-four-pound howitzers; but observing some of the piquets driven in, and companies ascending the heights to support, I had to gallop off to join my own company, in case it should be also employed. The Khyberees were in turn driven back; our guns belched forth canister, grape, and shrapnel,—every shot telling in the ranks of the enemy. The main column wound slowly up the mountain path that led out of the valley of Ali Musjid, and, as its rear crowned the crest, a concussion was felt as if from an earthquake; a tremendous explosion succeeded, and high in the air, amid clouds of dust and flame, which rose, in one vast lurid column, were hurled the defences of the fort of Ali Musjid,—a parting salute, as the hill on which it stood was lost to our view *forever*.

About two miles from the plains of Peshawur there is a bridge over a deep ravine, which for the better security of the baggage it was necessary to guard; and two hundred infantry and some cavalry were placed under my command for this duty: on the hills in the distance were numerous small bodies of Khyberees moving about, but none ventured near my party. Very unlike an old soldier, I had started without replenishing my haversack, and did not much relish the idea of being out until night without administering to the comforts of the inner man; however, we were fated to fare better than those even who got into camp early, for one of my subs (Meason), seeing his servant crossing the bridge, secured him, and much to our delight, as all had been equally improvident, found on one of the camels a basket with some mutton chops, a few biscuits, a gridiron, a tea-kettle and some tea. A fire was soon lighted, and in a very short time an excellent breakfast was prepared and partaken of; after which we could look with more complacency from the heights, where we were posted, upon our camp, which we could see pitched some miles distant in the peaceful plains of Peshawur.

About four p. m., Major Gore Browne, 41st, came up with the rearguard, which he commanded; my party protected his flanks until he cleared the pass, when we formed in rear of his guns with the piquets, furnished by the 40th under Lieutenant Wakefield, and had the honour of being among the last of the rearguard of the rear division of "The Avenging Army of Afghanistan," to leave that country. We were accompanied out of the pass by a division of the Sikh Army, about five thousand strong; fine-looking men, particularly well equipped with French muskets, and very steady in their movements. Like most Easterns, they were excessively fond of hearing the report of their firearms, a taste they indulged to an immoderate extent on this occasion.

Terry, of the Bombay Artillery, a most superior officer, was mortally wounded; and Chamberlaine, of the Irregular Cavalry, severely. Poor Terry! he had risked much in joining at Candahar,—riding through a great extent of territory when the country was in a state of insurrection. He had been out with the Candahar force on every occasion on which it was engaged; and the last day of the campaign, and almost by the last shot that was fired, he received his death wound.

The whole British army had now withdrawn from Afghanistan; our eventful connection with that country had totally ceased. That connection will assuredly constitute a curious and important page in history—less certain is it that that page will be a creditable one to the British name. But no one will question the glorious achievements of our army: the forcing of the Khyber Pass, the defence of Jellalabad and Kelat-i-Gilzie, the successes at Candahar, are events enshrined in glory; and the extraordinary advance of General Nott, unsupported, through the heart of an enemy's country, has excited universal wonder and admiration. Nor are the merits of this army to be estimated solely by the opposition it met with, or the comparatively small number of casualties that occurred in its ranks. There are other and worse sources of suffering in a campaign than those incidental to the battlefield; and, in seeking to judge of the services of our army, these circumstances must command a degree of consideration, and, when approbation is meted for what it did achieve, justice demands a tribute of praise for *what it dared*!

Scarcely had we cleared the passes when we were assailed, by accounts in the columns of part of the Indian press, of the horrible excesses we had committed. Enormities unheard or until ought of were most unblushingly laid to our door. Men unprincipled enough had been found to detail the perpetration of crimes which they well knew had never disgraced our army;—individuals there were fiendish enough to seem "loosed out of hell to speak of horrors," which had their existence only in their own black and malignant hearts.

Such was the return for our services from a contemptible section of our countrymen!—such the gratitude of a tribe of hirelings, who, perched aloft on their tripod stools, dared to vilify the members and impugn the actions of an army, the meanest spirit in which soared immeasurably superior to their traducers! Well might General Nott with difficulty curb his indignation when he was required to answer queries called forth by the propagation of falsehoods so base and dastardly. "*I am desired to state*," writes this illustrious man, "*whether unresisting individuals were destroyed in cold blood for mere vengeance? and whether women were either violated, or murdered for their ornaments?*"—"*I will endeavour to suppress my scorn and indignation while I shortly reply to this charge, or suspicion, or whatever it may be called by the persons from whom it emanated.*"

Our armies had marched to Cabul through scenes well calculated to excite the most revengeful and bitter passions. On the one hand, the walls of the citadel of Ghuznee were written over with accounts of the indignities and ill-treatment our captive countrymen there experienced; on the other side, General Pollock advanced through passes where almost every step spoke of treachery—where the blood of our yet tombless dead was still crying aloud for vengeance. Yet forbearance and humanity undeviatingly marked our progress. The honour due for the practice of that difficult forbearance—the brightest jewel in the crown of glory which our soldiers had achieved—their malicious calumniators would fain have wrested from them;—but it was in vain. A nobler and better spirit actuated the people of England! to them the integrity of our actions needed no vindication—proudly and dearly will *they* cherish the remembrance of our services in Affghanistan. To us the recollection of those services is hallowed by the approbation of our Sovereign, and endeared by the admiration of a grateful country!

Chapter 20

Army Marches en Route to India

After leaving the Khyber Pass we encamped near the small Sikh fort of Jumrood. On the 7th we moved ground near the city of Peshawur, and encamped to the westward of it. That lamented officer of the Bombay Artillery, Terry, who had lingered, died here today, and was buried in front of camp in the evening.

On the 12th we marched nine miles, and encamped to the east of Peshawur. During our stay here we experienced the greatest hospitality from General Avitabile, an officer in the Sikh service, and Governor of Peshawur. At his table eighty or one hundred officers sat down daily while the armies halted in the vicinity. The general is, I believe, an Italian by birth, and served in early life in Napoleon's Italian legions. He is a tall, handsome man, of striking military appearance, though now rather advanced in years.

The town of Peshawur rises from an extensive plain; its circumference about five or six miles. The houses, built of mud bricks, are usually high; there was little of beauty about the city, and nothing striking, if we except the number of gibbets in the environs to which criminals were hanging. The citadel we were not permitted to enter.

On the 15th of November, the order of march having been previously arranged, our first brigade and headquarters left Peshawur *en route* for India; the 2nd brigade under Colonel Stacey being directed to keep a day's march in rear of us, arid form the last brigade of the army of Affghanistan on its march through the Punjaub.

Our first march was to Pubbee, a small village distant about nine miles and a quarter. Our road lay across an extensive plain, the country evidently rich, but neither much nor highly cultivated. Supplies of wood, &c. for the army had been laid in here. Forage for horses procurable in abundance, but very little grazing for the baggage-cattle. The commissariat found it necessary to purchase fields of *kirby* for the public camels.

The reduced strength of the rearguards was one of the many symptoms that we were now in a friendly country.—Encamping ground good and extensive.

16th November. To Nowshera, a small village, distant about eleven miles. Road for the first six or seven miles over an open, uncultivated country; after which it was flanked by extensive fields of *kirby* and other grain. Encamping ground, confined and indifferent, was close to the River Cabul, here a broad and rapid stream. The communication with the village, on the opposite bank of the river, was by means of a small ferry-boat. Found supplies of wood, barley, *bhoosa*, &c., laid in.

17th November. To Akora, distant ten miles. Road over a wide and uncultivated plain, covered with low brushwood. Encamping ground clear and extensive, near the River Cabul. Got supplies of grain, and lucerne in abundance from the small village of Akora.

18th. To Attock, eleven and a half miles. Road at commencement of march light, and country open; on approaching Attock, it became more confined, and was in many places intersected with *nullahs.* About four miles from the river Attock entered the Geedah Gullee Pass, a narrow defile of about two miles in length. In the centre of this pass the ascent is very abrupt, and we were detained some time in working up the guns. The hills on either side were prettily wooded; and the gleaming of the arms of the troops as they wound along, and the dense mass of baggage-cattle crowding on the rear of the column, added a pomp and interest to the beauty of the scenery around. On the head of the column entering the bridge of boats across the river, a royal salute was fired from the fort of Attock. Our encamping ground, which was about a mile from the river, was clear and sufficiently ample.

The fort of Attock is large and strong; the walls lofty, and built of polished stone. It commands the river, but is itself completely overlooked and commanded by a neighbouring hill.

The Cabul River empties itself into the Indus a little above Attock. The former river is fordable during the summer; but the latter rarely, if ever so. Owing to the bridge of boats admitting of only one camel passing at a time, great delay was experienced in getting the baggage up; and much extra fatigue was incurred by the cattle, many of which were laden for upwards of eighteen hours. The usual plan of march is to the right bank of the river, and to postpone crossing it till the following day; but the general was anxious to push on to India as quickly as possible.

19th. To Shumshabad, eight miles and a half; road excellent, over a fine open plain, extensively cultivated. Encamped about two miles from the village of Shumshabad, in an open country, but in heavy ploughed fields. Supplies of flour, grain, &c., laid in here, for the use of the army. Several small tanks and wet *nullahs* in the neighbourhood, in which were immense numbers of wild duck, which afforded amusement for the Nimrods. The country, however, below the passes, as far as we have yet been able to judge, is almost destitute of game.

20th. Futteelah, twelve miles. Road at first excellent: after marching about six miles it became much intersected with ravines, and was crossed by a small clear stream; after crossing which, the country became more open. Encamping ground dry and open.

On the line of march today an incident occurred which showed, that, although we were now in a friendly country, it was still necessary to guard against the hostility of our old enemies. My friend Seymour went some distance from the column with his greyhounds, in the hope of having some sport. Passing through some ravines, he came suddenly on a party of plunderers, who, not yet relinquishing all hopes of securing a few of our camels with their loads, were concealed, ready to take advantage of any favourable opportunity of carrying off a stray prize to their neighbouring hills.

Immediately Seymour came upon them, their swords flew from their scabbards. The country behind him was too broken to admit of his getting off easily; so, although unarmed (having given his sword to his horse-keeper to carry), he determined on dashing through his foes, in the hope of gaining the open country before him. Fortunately, he was riding a pony that had long been looked upon in the regiment as public property, and which had, in the course of its *multifarious duties*, been highly educated in tricks: among others, the art of kicking and plunging to a furious extent on being pinched on the back. Seymour, recollecting this accomplishment of his steed, dashed at the bandits, and as he neared them placed his hand behind the saddle; the animal, lunging out behind and before, cleared a passage, when his rider, plunging his heels into his steed's flanks, galloped off in safety, the only injury sustained being a slight sabre *scratch* on the quarter of his pony.

21st November. Wah, ten miles; road generally bad and confined, and much intersected with *nullahs*, which, from their precipitous banks impeding the progress of the guns, delayed us much. About five miles from Wah crossed a broad river—not deep, and with good bottom and shelving banks; after which the road is over a plain, covered with a forest of bauble jungle. At the little village of Punjab is a small and elegant temple; near this, shaded by some noble trees, an elaborately-ornamented, but not extensive, tank, containing numbers of small fish, which are held sacred. Encamping ground close to the river, and, owing to its many windings, very inconvenient.

22nd. Jaunee Ka Sung, thirteen miles: a long and tedious march; the country, which was covered with bauble jungle, being much intersected with ravines that caused considerable delay in the passage of the guns. About half-distance, came to a narrow causeway, over which it was necessary to pass, and where only two camels could go abreast. Within two or three miles of Jaunee Ka Sung the country became more open, and free from jungle; but, owing to the numerous *nullahs*, the encamping ground was confined and bad. Water very brackish.

23rd. Rawul Pindee, fourteen miles. Road at first through high tree jungle, after which it became very light and open; crossed two deep ravines, and close to the village the River Lea, with high precipitous banks. Encamping ground, to the right of the village, clear and extensive. Rawul Pindee is a large town, prettily situate, and the houses have a singularly clean and neat appearance. Numbers of beautifully-worked shawls, slippers, &c., the produce of Cashmere, were brought into camp, and offered for sale by the natives.

24th. Halted. Brigadier Stacey's division closed up today. Small-pox had now broken out throughout the whole Affghan army; but, although many were attacked, and several of our men died from this dangerous disease, we did not suffer so severely as the different brigades preceding us, which sustained great loss both in officers and men.

25th. To Hoormuck, eight miles; road at commencement very bad, being crossed by three or four deep ravines. The country in the neighbourhood of Rawul Pindee is more undulating and wild than we had of late traversed. Six miles from Rawul Pindee moved through a narrow gorge, where there was room for only one camel to pass at a time. At the bottom of the gorge is the river, which at this season is generally narrow and shallow; after crossing the river the road improved. Encamping ground satisfactory. Left Brigadier Stacey's division at Rawul Pindee.

26th. Maunicyaula, ten miles; country covered with large loose shingle, and much intersected with ravines. At about five miles from Hoormuck, near a small village, the road becomes better. Encamping ground good and open: more cultivation in this neighbourhood than we had yet seen. About two miles from our encampment, passed the celebrated Tope of Maunicyaula, (see note below), a large and singular-looking dome, built of hard stone supposed to be a Grecian structure, coeval with the time of Alexander the Great. Near camp were the extensive ruins of an ancient city.

Note:—The height from the top of the mound to the top of the building was about seventy feet, and the circumference was found to be one hundred and fifty paces. It was built of large pieces of a hard stone common in the neighbourhood (which appeared to be composed of petrified vegetable matter), mixed with smaller pieces of a sandy stone. The greater part of the outside was cased with the first-mentioned stone, cut quite smooth; and the whole seemed intended to have been thus faced, though it had either been left incomplete, or the casing had fallen down. The plan of the whole could however be easily discovered. Some broad steps (now mostly ruined) led to the base of the pile: round the base is a moulding, on which are pilasters about four feet high and six feet asunder; these have plain capitals, and support a cornice marked with parallel lines and headings.

The whole of this may be seven or eight feet high from the uppermost step to the top of the cornice. The building then retires, leaving a ledge of a foot or two broad, from which rises a perpendicular wall about six feet high: about a foot above the ledge is a fillet formed by stones projecting a very little from the wall; and at the top of the wall is a more projecting cornice, from which the sphere springs. The stones of the facing are about three feet and a half long, and one and a half broad, and are so put in that the ends only are exposed. The top is flat, and on it the foundations of walls are discoverable enclosing a space of eleven paces long by five broad: a third of this area is cut off by the foundation of a cross wall.

There was nothing at all Hindoo in the appearance of this building: most of the party thought it decidedly Grecian. It was indeed as like Grecian architecture as any building which

Europeans in remote parts of the country could now construct by the hands of unpractised native builders.

(Mr. Erskine, in a paper read to the Literary Society of Bombay in 1821, pronounced this building to belong to the worship of Boodh, an opinion which has since been fully substantiated. It was opened in 1830 by the Chevalier Ventura, a general officer in the service of Runjeet Sing, who found it contained, besides religious relics, many ancient coins of great interest; and the zeal and liberality with which he promulgated his discoveries, quickly led to similar investigations in other quarters. By the active and persevering researches of Mr. Masson and Dr. Martin Honisberger, a great number of *topes* resembling this one have been discovered in the tract extending between the river of Caubul and Hindoo Coosh, from the Hydaspes to Caubul. The oldest coin found in those buildings of which the date is known is one of the second Triumvirate in the first century before Christ, and the last is of Khoosroo Purbeez, in the sixth century after Christ. The construction of the *topes*, therefore, was probably within those epochs).

The natives called it the Tope of Maunicyaula, and said it was built by the gods.

("*Tope* is an expression used for a mound or barrow as far west as Peshawer, and Maunicyaula is the name of an adjoining village)."—*Elphinstone's Afghanistan, Introduction.*

27th November. Serai Pucka, thirteen miles; road principally through the beds of *nullahs*, and tedious for guns and baggage. Encamping ground indifferent, close to the River Ragie, a small stream.

28th. Shumuk, fifteen miles.—Road for the first two miles terribly bad, similar to that through which we passed yesterday. After this it became more open until we crossed the river, when it again became broken. Today's was the most trying march for the cattle we have had since leaving the passes.

29th. Bukrala, nine miles. Road easy, with the exception of a very steep descent at the commencement; where, owing to its being necessary to lock the gun-wheels, and only one camel being able to move down at a time, considerable delay was experienced. At the bottom of the descent we entered the bed of a river, dry at this season, along which the road lay. The cattle were much fatigued by this day's march. Encamping ground clear.

On the 30th we reached Ooderana, nine miles. Road still along the bed of the river, but good and wide. Encamping ground open and extensive.

1st December. Rhotas, nine miles. Road for about six miles through the bed of the river, when we emerged into a fine open plain. Excellent encamping ground on the right bank of a small branch of the Jheelum River, called Kussee.

Rhotas has formerly been a place of great strength, but its defences are now nearly in ruins. The gateways, which, with the other parts of the walls, are constructed of solid masonry, are still very beautiful, as specimens of the architecture of the age in which they were built. The country in the neighbourhood of Rhotas is exceedingly fertile.

2nd December. Jheelum, twelve miles. Road crosses the River Kussee several times, and at length continues along its bank until it joins the river Jheelum;—country studded with villages and topes of trees, and very extensively cultivated. Employed this day and the next in crossing the river Jheelum (Hydaspes) in boats. There was a ford about a mile below our encampment, but, owing to the bed being composed of adhesive mud, it was exceedingly precarious; and, although many camels got over it, numbers stuck and were eventually sacrificed. The stream at this season was very sluggish.

On the 4th we marched to Khowar, twelve miles; road generally light, crossed by a few ravines, but none of any importance. We passed a small fort, after which the country became jungly. Our encamping ground was confined and indifferently good, with a small branch of the Jheelum in rear.

On the 5th we reached Dhinga, fourteen miles and a quarter; road heavy and over a continuation of sand-hills, covered with low jungle. Our encamping ground today was clear, and the country in the neighbourhood much cultivated.

On the 6th we marched twelve miles to Paree Walla. Road through a rich and well-cultivated country, occasionally varied by tracts of jungle.

7th December. Ramnuggur, twelve miles. Excellent road all the way to the river Chenab (Acesines), where we found numbers of boats awaiting us, in which we crossed. This river is not so broad as the Jheelum, but is much more rapid. The right bank is very precipitous and high, but *ghats* were cut in it to facilitate the operation of loading, &c. The cattle and horses crossed by a ford about a mile down the stream.

Road from the left bank to the encamping ground was about three miles in length, and, being through deep sand, was very heavy. Here the cattle became very much exhausted.

On the 8th we halted; Brigadier Stacey's division crossed the river.

On the 9th we continued our route to Nyemala, thirteen miles. We passed numerous villages, and the road was very easy, through a fine and well-cultivated country.

On the 10th we inarched to Thabool, eleven miles and a quarter; and on the 11th to Mutta, eleven miles; the road and encamping ground continuing extremely favourable, and the country clear and well cultivated. Supplies of grain, forage, &c. were brought in great abundance.

12th. Burra Mullear, thirteen miles. Road light; country open and highly productive. Encamping ground clear, and excellent grazing for the cattle in the jungle in neighbourhood of camp.

13th. Halted. Several officers went out for the purpose of hog-hunting or shooting. There appeared to be but very little game in the country; and, owing to the density of the jungle, it was impossible to get the wild-hog to break cover. Brigadier Stacey's division closed up.

On the 14th we resumed our march to Dheenga, fourteen miles,—a tedious journey; the country, although richly cultivated, not being diversified by many villages, or possessing any striking scenery. Brigadier Stacey's division halted at Burra Mullear.

We reached Surrukpoor on the 15th, thirteen miles; the road principally over a fine level country. Near camp was a very extensive grass jungle, in which numbers of hog were found; but it was impossible, with the limited number of beaters at our disposal, to drive them out of cover. Today our encampment was fourteen miles from Lahore, but no one from our force was allowed to visit that capital.

On the 16th we marched to Rungulpoor, ten miles; road excellent through a highly cultivated country, but encamping ground, on the left bank of the river Ravee (Hydraotes), very confined, and intersected with numerous ravines. Crossed the river by an excellent bridge of boats, constructed of sufficient breadth to admit, if necessary, the passage of two camels abreast; little delay was consequently experienced in getting the guns and baggage over.

On the 17th we proceeded nine miles to Jungateh,—the road easy through a level brushwood-covered plain; and on the 18th we arrived at Lalleaune, the march tedious through an uncultivated country covered with high jungle.—Our encamping ground was extensive and clear. There was a heavy fall of rain in the afternoon.

On the 19th we reached Kussoor, after a tolerably light march of ten miles and a half; and on the 20th we halted to enable Stacey's division to close up. The whole Candahar division halted on the following day and night, throughout which it continued to rain heavily and with little intermission.

It was on the 22nd of December that we reached Gunda Sing Walla. Owing to the heavy rain which fell during the night, the country was very slippery, and we were unable to march until one p.m. Passed the ruins of Kussoor, which cover a great extent of ground. From our encamping ground, which was close to the Suttlege (Hypasis), among strong reed grass, we could see the bridge of boats over which we were to pass in the morning, and which was ornamented with innumerable flags. On the left bank of the river, close to the bridge, was a large canopy, composed of cloth of the colour of the "Riband of India," and a vast field of white canvass pointed out the position of the "Army of Reserve."

From the high reputation of the late ruler of the Punjaub, I was prepared to find in the country over which he reigned some nobler result of his military genius—some more lasting and more honourable memorial of the benefits of his rule—than the mere establishment of military posts and construction of fortresses. No roads secured a communication between the different parts of the country through which we had marched; and the lamentably small proportion of cultivated territory bore evidence that, even under him, there was an absence of that feeling of security ever symptomatic of a wise and good government. It is but just, however, to consider from what discordant materials he had succeeded by his energy and ability in uniting and raising to consequence a number of divided and formerly powerless chiefships,—and, by the force of his genius, assumed for the Punjaub among the nations of the East a position of the most formidable importance.

But with him the glory of his rule has departed. Since the passage of "the Army of Afghanistan" through that territory, its history has been one continued tale of misrule and blood: ruler after ruler has been removed by the hand of the assassin; every day some fresh proof is adduced that the "master hand" is no longer there; and uninterrupted anarchy and confusion evidence the utter and hopelessness of any party in that formerly flourishing state establishing a secure government.

The history of British connection with India has been one of continued, gradual, but compulsory augmentation;—the very existence of our power has forced upon us the *expediency* of extending our territory. The hearty co-operation of the natives in our efforts to emancipate them from the thraldom of tyrannical oppression and misrule vindicates the justice of this aggrandisement.

The security of our power in the East—*secure* only by our ever being impressed with and acting on the conviction of its *insecurity*—must, sooner or later, impose upon us the necessity of an interference in the affairs of the Punjaub: the placing it under British control and influence, if not indeed the complete annexation of it to our existing mighty territory, is inevitable.

Early on the morning of the 23rd, during parade, a fog rose from the river, which for its dense intensity could not have been surpassed even in London. At length the burning sun of the East dispersed the mist, and the Candahar division marched in triumph on to the British territory; the Governor-General, attended by his staff, the commander-in-chief, &c., received our illustrious chief, and a salute from a distant battery told that the last of the gallant Affghan army had now returned.

Chapter 21

Conclusion

The first great act in Lord Ellenborough's administration was now at an end. By his prudence in placing a discretionary power in the hands of his generals, the honour and renown of the British arms had been retrieved in Affghanistan. "I defy any man, if Nott had failed in his advance, to attribute any blame to Lord Ellenborough; and, if no blame could attach to him in failure, surely no merit should accrue to him from success." Such is the specious argument formed for this event. But would such reasoning have been adopted or admitted had failure, instead of success, attended the operations of General Nott?

Lord Ellenborough's government in the East has now terminated, but the benefits arising from the wisdom which distinguished it will long be felt. On his arrival in India, disasters, defeats, and revolts met him on all sides; added to which, the public treasury was nearly exhausted. What an altered—what an improved appearance have affairs since then assumed! Our Eastern Empire, after two years of continued triumphs, has risen to, and now enjoys, a state of prosperity which it had not known for years. Such is the best proof of the sagacity of his Lordship's administration; and, if further evidences are wanting, they are to be found in the importance which has been attached to trifles—the elaborate criticisms which have been levelled at his proclamations (in which if there do exist objections, they are merely in style, and *in one* it is but just to consider to whom it was addressed),—and in the undignified and puerile attacks that have been made upon him for the preference and regard which he showed for that profession by which India has been won, and by which India must be preserved.

How paltry is that jealousy of the army, in the expression of which an ungenerous and unchivalrous *sneer* is implied on the profession of arms by a writer in an Indian Review, who sums up an article on Lord

Ellenborough's administration in these words:—

> To leave behind him no monument of his greatness *but a few captured cannon*, a volume of proclamations, *and an infinite quantity of parti-coloured ribbon*, is but a poor achievement after all; and, when years hence we inquire what great works are associated with the name of Ellenborough, we may point to a *fantastical gun-carriage*, a new road to Government House, *and an immense number of half-crown pieces pendant from manly breasts in every ballroom in the country!*

We live in an age of faction; the time has not yet arrived when the acts of Lord Ellenborough's administration can be viewed calmly and dispassionately: but when the veil is withdrawn, which is now thrown over them by the prejudice or bitter acrimony of party, they will elicit that universal admiration which their wisdom and beneficial results so justly merit; and Lord Ellenborough, *the regenerator of India*, will be classed among those distinguished men whose names are inseparably associated with the glory of our Eastern Empire.

During our stay at Ferozepore, I was unable, from indisposition, to participate in the gaieties of the place; but I had the pleasure of witnessing the review of all the troops assembled here, amounting to nearly forty thousand men of all arms,—one of those glorious *spectacles* which man has but seldom an opportunity of beholding.

The camps of the Affghan divisions were pitched apart from that of the army of reserve, and our old stained and tattered tents bore a striking contrast to the new white dwellings of our brethren. The service camps appeared, however, to be the subject of much interest, if not amusement, to the fair sex, who of an evening generally honoured us by riding through our lines, and passing their comments on the extreme shabby-gentility of our turn-out; our poverty of outward appearance not being confined merely to tents and camp-equipage, but extending itself to our personal attire, from which the gloss of newness had long since departed, and which in many cases had an appearance singularly responsive to the description of Joseph's coat of many colours.

At length the order was issued for breaking up the immense army which had now assembled at Ferozepore, and the different regiments comprising it moved gradually off to the stations to which they had been ordered to proceed.

Our more immediate comrades of the Candahar division were

separated from us, and of that army the 40th Regiment alone remained at Ferozepore.

Our chief had been rewarded for his services by a high appointment at the Court of the King of Oude; and on the 2nd of January, 1843, previous to proceeding to assume its duties, he issued the following order to his companions in arms:—

> Major-General Nott, having received permission to join the appointment assigned him at the Court of the King of Oude, cannot leave the Candahar force without returning his best thanks to the officers and men composing it, for the assistance he has constantly received from them, which has enabled him upon all occasions to uphold the honour of our country and the reputation of British arms.
>
> It is with feelings of deep regret and admiration that the Major-General now bids farewell to his brave and gallant comrades of the Candahar army.

My health was now in such an enfeebled state that I was recommended to return to England. At the same time orders were given to H. M. 41st to proceed down the Indus to Kurachee. In consequence of this the greatest difficulty was experienced in obtaining boats, so many being taken up for the public service. My friend, Mr. Allen, having also been ordered down on duty to Scinde, kindly offered me a passage, and I prepared to accompany him.

On the 9th, our Chaplain, Colonel Hibbert, Lieutenants Seymour and Carey, 40th, Mr. Andrew, 78th, and myself, left Ferozepore; the Colonel, Seymour, Carey, and self, being *en route* to England. Delightful as was the anticipation of revisiting our native land, it was not without unfeigned sorrow that I parted with those with whom ten of my best and happiest years had been passed. The remembrance of the generous and universal expression of regret at our departure, and the cheers from our men as they accompanied us far out of camp, will never be forgotten. It was indeed one of those events which "fate allows but seldom here," and which leave a lasting and indelible impression.

On the morning of the 10th we sailed, and, after floating down the stream, reached Sukkur on the 30th without incident, save being stuck, not unfrequently, for hours together, on a mud-bank, and perhaps occasionally breaking a rudder or oar. The country on either side of the Indus is flat and uninteresting, covered with extensive forests of mangrove. At Sukkur we were most hospitably entertained by our old friends of the 20th and 21st Bombay regiments stationed there.

The general impression then seemed to be that not a shot would be fired in Scinde. We did not, therefore, hesitate pursuing our journey down the river, and sailed for Tatta on the morning of the 2nd; our party now consisting of Seymour and Carey, 40th, Knox, 42nd Bengal, and myself. On the 6th we reached Tatta the natives along the river treating us very civilly. During our passage down we observed numbers of Beloochees, armed to the teeth, crossing at different places; with the exception of one party who hooted us as we passed, they were remarkably courteous. Poor Ennis of the Bombay 21st, who left Sukkur some days after us, *en route* to Bombay, in bad health, was not, however, so fortunate; he was attacked by a party of these Beloochees, and murdered. On approaching Tatta we looked in vain for the town; at length, seeing some Europeans walking on the banks, we asked them where Tatta Bunda was, and they answered that we were now there. We pulled up, and getting on shore found that we should have to walk two miles at least to the conductor's house, whom we wished to consult as to the probability of our being able to get boats for Bombay at Gorah Barree.

This house, when Seymour went up the river with our right wing at the end of 1840, was overhanging the banks of the Indus, which had since then so completely changed its course.

The conductor having assured us that we should obtain boats at Gorah Barree, we sailed from Tatta Bunda on the 7th, and reached our destination on the 8th; there we found only one boat of fifty *candees*—about ten or twelve tons—and open. We determined on tempting the waves in this cockleshell, and our own party of four, increased by Captain Werge, 39th, and Mr. Webbe, one of the Affghan hostages, with all our servants, got in and sailed for Bombay on the 11th. We reached that port on the morning of the 17th, the day on which Sir C. Napier gained his first glorious victory in Scinde. We left Gorah Barree only just in time, for a day or two after an European conductor and small guard of *sepoys* stationed there were attacked by a strong party of Beloochees, overwhelmed and sacrificed.

Of the six officers composing the party from Gorah Barree to Bombay, only four now remain: poor Werge died of smallpox at Trieste on his way to England, and Seymour, one of my earliest and most valued friends, fell a victim to the liver complaint he had contracted in India—a few months after his return home, and shortly after he had obtained his promotion in a corps, which, alas! he was destined never to join. He and I were old brother subs in the Grenadier Company, and during a long and arduous service in the East, the greatest intimacy and friendship had subsisted between us. Tall and handsome in form, amiable in disposition, warm in his friendships, and gallant and zealous in the discharge of his duties, his death was sincerely and deeply felt by his old comrades of the 40th. It may be some consolation to his relations, however melancholy, to know of the still ardent sympathy for the loss they have sustained, of those who so long knew and esteemed Henry Seymour.

If the perusal of the foregoing pages should afford pleasure to any one of my countrymen, I shall be more than repaid for the time I have expended in writing them. This is my first attempt at authorship—in all probability it will be my last; I ask the indulgence generally extended to the *premier essai*, and in the hope, gentle reader, that you have censured lightly the many imperfections my narrative contains, I now say—farewell.

Appendix

(A.)

Declaration

Of the Right Honourable the Governor-General of India, on the Assembly of the Army of the Indus.

Scinde, Oct. 1, 1838.

The Right Honourable the Governor-General of India having, with the concurrence of the Supreme Council, directed the assemblage of a British force for service across the Indus, his Lordship deems it proper to publish the following exposition of the reasons which have led to this important measure.

It is a matter of notoriety, that the treaties entered into by the British Government, in the year 1832, with the Ameers of Scinde, the Nawab of Bahawulpore, and Maha Raja Runjeet Singh, had for their object, by opening the navigation of the Indus, to facilitate the extension of commerce, and to gain for the British nation, in Central Asia, that legitimate influence which an interchange of benefits would naturally produce. With a view to invite the aid of the *de facto* rulers of Afghanistan to the measures necessary for giving full effect to those treaties, Captain Burnes was deputed, towards the close of the year 1836, on a mission to Dhost Mahomed Khan, the chief of Cabool. The original objects of that officer's mission were purely of a commercial nature.

Whilst Captain Burnes, however, was on his journey to Cabool, information was received by the Governor-General that the troops of Dhost Mahomed Khan had made a sudden and unprovoked attack on those of our ancient ally, Maha Raja Runjeet Singh. It was naturally to be apprehended that his Highness the *Maha Raja* would not be slow to avenge this aggression; and it was to be feared that the flames of war being once kindled in the very regions into which we were endeavouring to extend our commerce, the peaceful and beneficial purposes of the British Government would be altogether frustrated. In order to avert a result so calamitous, the Governor-General resolved on authorizing Captain Burnes to intimate to Dhost Mahomed Khan that, if he should evince a disposition to come to just and reasonable terms with the *Maha Raja,* his Lordship would exert his good offices with his Highness for the restoration of an amicable understanding between the two powers. The *Maha Raja,* with the characteristic confidence which he has uniformly placed in the faith and friendship of the British nation, at once assented to the proposition of the Governor-General, to the effect that, in the mean time, hostilities on his part should be suspended.

It subsequently came to the knowledge of the Governor-General, that a Persian army was besieging Herat; that intrigues were actively prosecuted throughout Afghanistan, for the purpose of extending Persian influence and authority to the banks of, and even beyond, the Indus; and that the Court of Persia had not only commenced a course of injury and insult to the officers of Her Majesty's mission in the Persian territory, but had afforded evidence of being engaged in designs wholly at variance with the principles and objects of its alliance with Great Britain.

After much time spent by Captain Burnes in fruitless negotiation at Cabool, it appeared that Dhost Mahomed Khan, chiefly in consequence of his reliance upon Persian encouragement and assistance, persisted, as respected his misunderstanding with the *Sikhs,* in urging the most unreasonable pretensions, such as the Governor-General could not, consistently with justice and his regard for the friendship of Maha Raja Runjeet Singh, be the channel of submitting to the consideration of His Highness; that he avowed schemes of aggrandisement and ambition, injurious to the security and peace of the frontiers of India; and that he openly threatened, in furtherance of those schemes, to call in every foreign aid which he could command. Ultimately, he gave his undisguised support to the Persian designs in Afghanistan, of the unfriendly and injurious character of which, as concerned the British power in India, he was well apprized, and by his utter disregard of the views and interests of the British Government, compelled Captain Burnes to leave Cabool without having effected any of the objects of his mission.

It was now evident that no further interference could be exercised by the British Government to bring about a good understanding between the Sikh ruler and Dhost Mahomed Khan, and the hostile policy of the latter chief showed too plainly that, so long as Cabool remained under his Government, we could never hope that the tranquillity of our neighbourhood would be secured, or that the interests of our Indian empire would be preserved inviolate.

The Governor-General deems it in this place necessary to revert to the siege of Herat, and the conduct of the Persian nation. The siege of that city has now been carried on by the Persian army for many months. The attack upon it was a most unjustifiable and cruel aggression, perpetrated and continued, notwithstanding the solemn and repeated remonstrances of the British envoy at the Court of Persia, and after every just and becoming offer of accommodation had been made and rejected. The besieged have behaved with gallantry and fortitude worthy of the justice of their cause, and the Governor-General would yet indulge the hope that their heroism may enable them to maintain a successful defence until succours shall reach them from British India. In the mean time, the ulterior designs of Persia, affecting the interests of the British Government, have been, by a succession of events, more and more openly manifested.

The Governor-General has recently ascertained by an official dispatch from Mr. McNeill, Her Majesty's envoy, that his Excellency has been compelled, by the refusal of his just demands, and by a systematic course of disrespect adopted towards him by the Persian Government, to quit the Court of the Shah, and to make a public declaration of the cessation of all intercourse between the two Governments. The necessity under which Great Britain is placed, of regarding the present advance of the Persian arms into Afghanistan as an act of hostility towards herself, has also been officially communicated to the *Shah*, under the express order of her Majesty's Government. The chiefs of Candahar (brothers of Dhost Mahomed Khan, of Cabool) have avowed their adherence to the Persian policy, with the same full knowledge of its opposition to the rights and interests of the British nation in India, and have been openly assisting in the operations against Herat

In the crisis of affairs consequent upon the retirement of our envoy from Cabool, the Governor-General felt the importance of taking immediate measures for arresting the rapid progress of foreign intrigue and aggression towards our own territories. His attention was naturally drawn, at this conjuncture, to the position and claims of Shah Shooja-ool-Moolk, a monarch who, when in power, had cordially acceded to the measures of united resistance to external enmity, which were at that time judged necessary by the British Government, and who, on his empire being usurped by its present rulers, had found an honourable asylum in the British dominions.

It had clearly been ascertained, from the information furnished by the various officers who have visited Afghanistan, that the Barukzye chiefs, from their disunion and unpopularity, were ill fitted, under any circumstances, to be useful allies to the British Government, and to aid us in our just and necessary measures of national defence; yet, so long as they refrained from proceedings injurious to our interest and security, the British Government acknowledged and respected their authority. But a different policy appeared to be now more than justified by the conduct of those chiefs, and to be indispensable to our own safety. The welfare of our possessions in the East requires that we should have on our western frontier an ally who is interested in resisting aggression, and establishing tranquillity, in the place of chiefs ranging themselves in subservience to a hostile power, and seeking to promote schemes of conquest and aggrandizement.

After a serious and mature deliberation, the Governor-General was satisfied that pressing necessity, as well as every consideration of policy and justice, warranted us in espousing the cause of Shah Shooja-ool-Moolk, whose popularity throughout Afghanistan had been proved to his Lordship by the strong and unanimous testimony of the best authorities. Having arrived at this determination, the Governor-General was further of opinion, that it was just and proper, no less from the position of Maha Raja Runjeet Singh, than from his undeviating friendship towards the British Government, that His Highness should have the offer of becoming a party to the contemplated operations. Mr. Macnaghten was accordingly deputed, in June last, to the Court of His Highness, and the result of his mission has been the conclusion of a tripartite treaty by the British Government, the *Maha Raja,* and Shah Sooja-ool-Moolk, whereby his Highness is guaranteed in his present possessions, and has bound himself to co-operate for the restoration of the *Shah* to the throne of his ancestors.

The friends and enemies of any one of the contracting parties have been declared to be the friends and enemies of all. Various points have been adjusted, which had been the subject of discussion between the British Government and His Highness the *Maha Raja,* the identity of whose interests with those of the Honourable Company has now been made apparent to all the surrounding states. A guaranteed independence will, upon favourable conditions, be tendered to the Ameers of Scinde; and the integrity of Herat, in the possession of its present ruler, will be fully respected; while by the measures completed, or in progress, it may reasonably be hoped that the general freedom and security of commerce will be promoted; that the name and just influence of the British Government will gain their proper footing among the nations of Central Asia; that tranquillity will be established upon the most important frontier of India; and that a lasting barrier will be raised against hostile intrigue and encroachment.

His Majesty Shah Soojah-ool-Moolk will enter Affghanistan, surrounded by his own troops, and will be supported against foreign interference and factious opposition by a British army. The Governor-general confidently hopes that the Shah will be speedily replaced on his throne by his own subjects and adherents, and when once he shall be secured in power, and the independence and integrity of Afghanistan established, the British army will be withdrawn. The Governor-General has been led to these measures by the duty which is imposed upon him of providing for the security of the British Crown: but he rejoices that, in the discharge of this duty, he will be enabled to assist in restoring the union and prosperity of the Affghan people.

Throughout the approaching operations, British influence will be sedulously employed to further every measure of general benefit; to reconcile differences; to secure oblivion of injuries; and to put an end to the distractions by which, for so many years, the welfare and happiness of the Affghans have been impaired. Even to the chiefs, whose hostile proceedings have given just cause of offence to the British Government, it will seek to secure liberal and honourable treatment, on their tendering early submission, and ceasing from opposition to that course of measures which may be judged the most suitable for the general advantage of their country.

By order of the Right Honourable the Governor-General of India.

W. H. Macnaghten,
Secretary to the Government of India,
with the Governor-General.

(B.)

Dispatch

Relative to Fight at Candahar.

Headquarters, Candahar. May 29, 1842.

Sir, Akbar Khan, chief of Zamindawur, having assembled three thousand men, crossed the Helmund, and joined the rebel force under Prince Suftur Jung and Atta Mahomed, on the right bank of the Urghundab, taking advantage of the absence of Brigadier Wymer, who had been detached into the Ghilzie province with a large portion of my force, and nearly the whole of my cavalry. The enemy, under an impression that we had not a sufficient number of men to hold the city, and at the same time to attack them in the field, took possession of some steep rocky hills within a mile of the city walls. I instantly moved out with the troops noted in the accompanying field return, leaving Major-General England, K.H., in command of the city. The Ghazees had about 8000 in position, and 2000 men guarding the Babawullee Pass and roads leading to their camp. Our troops carried all their positions in gallant style, and drove them in confusion, and with great loss, across the Urghundab River.

I was ably assisted by Brigadier Stacey and every officer present. Major Rawlison, political agent, with his accustomed zeal, was in the field, and gallantly led a small body of Persians and Affghan horse to the charge. I am, &c.,

(Signed) W. Nott, Major-General,
Commanding Lower Affghanistan and Scinde.

(C.)

Dispatch of Captain Craigie, &c.

Notification, Secret Department, Allahabad.

July 2, 1842.

The Governor-General has great satisfaction in making public the following dispatch from Major-General Nott, and the report from Captain Craigie, Commanding the garrison of Khelat-i-Ghilzie, of the gallant and successful defence made by that garrison against a large force of Affghans by which it was assaulted. On this occasion the late Shah Soojah's 3rd Regiment of Infantry, and the Detachment of the Bengal 43rd Regiment Native Infantry, displayed that decided superiority over their enemies, which has been uniformly manifested by the several corps composing Major-General Nott's Army.

By order of the Right Hon. the Governor-General,

T. H. Maddock,

Secretary to the Government of India,

with the Governor-General.

From Major-General W. Nott, commanding Lower Affghanistan and Scinde, to T. H. Maddock, Esq., Secretary to the Government of India, with the Governor-General, Headquarters.

Sir,—I have the honour to acquaint you, for the information of the Right Honourable the Governor-General of India, that an attack was made on the Fort of Kelat-i-Ghilzie on the morning of the 21st instant, by a body of four thousand *Ghilzies*: the accompanying letter from Captain Craigie details the result. I am, &c.

(Signed) W. Nott, Major-General,

Commanding Lower Affghanistan and Scinde.

Candahar, May 27, 1842.

From Captain J. H. Craigie, commanding Kelat-i-Gilzie, to Captain Thomas Polwhele, Deputy Assistant Adjutant-General.

Sir,—I have the honour to report, for the information of Major-General Nott, commanding in Lower Afghanistan and Scinde, that Kelat-i-Ghilzie was attacked at a quarter before four o'clock this morning, in two places, *viz.*, at the long neck to the north-east, and at an outwork constructed last winter by the *sepoys*, to give a raking fire in rear of the barracks.

The enemy advanced to the assault in the most determined manner, each column consisting of upwards of two thousand men, provided with thirty scaling ladders; but, after an hour's fighting, were repulsed and driven down the hill, losing five standards, (one of which was planted three times in one of the embrasures,) and the whole of which are now in our possession.

Of the enemy's loss I am unable to give any correct account, as their killed and wounded, during the greater part of the attack, were immediately taken to the rear; but one hundred and four (104) dead bodies were left on the slope of the hill, and from six a.m. till three p.m., the enemy were employed in carrying off such of their dead and wounded as had been taken to the rear.

The greatest gallantry and coolness were displayed by every commissioned, non-commissioned officer and private (both European and Native) engaged in meeting the attack of the enemy, several of whom were bayoneted on the top of the sandbags forming our parapets.

On our side, I am happy to say, only six (6) *sepoys* were wounded, *viz.*, two of the detachment 43rd N.I., and four of the 3rd Infantry.

A body of about three hundred of the enemy, when driven back, took shelter under the rocks below the outwork, but were immediately dislodged by a company of the 3rd Infantry, which I detached for that purpose.

I have, &c.,

(Signed) J. Halket Craigie, Captain,
Commanding Kelat-i-Ghilzie.

Kelat-i-Ghilzie, May 21, 1842.

(True Copy.)
(Signed) Thos. Polhwele, Captain,
Officiating Deputy Assistant Adjutant-General.

(True Copies.)
T. H. Maddock,
Secretary to the Government of India, with the
Governor-General.

(D.)

Dispatches

Relative to Goaine, Etc.

From Major-general W. Nott, commanding Field Force, Afghanistan, to T. H. Maddock, Esq., Secretary to the Government of India, with the Governor-General.

Headquarters, dated Camp Kareez Oosman Khan,
August 29, 1842.

Sir,—I have the honour to acquaint you, that on the morning of the 28th instant a body of the enemy attacked our rear guard. I directed the officer in command of the cavalry to detach a party to assist in dispersing it.

The accompanying letter from Captain Christie details the result.

I have, &c.

(Signed) W. Nott, Major-General,
Commanding Field Force, Affghanistan.

From Captain J. Christie, commanding the Detachment, to Captain Delamaine, Senior Officer of Cavalry.

Dated Camp Kareez Oosman Khan, August 23, 1842,

Sir,—Agreeably to the instructions conveyed to me through Lieutenant Forbes, Adjutant 3rd Light Cavalry, I proceeded to the rear with two *ressallahs* of the 1st Bengal Irregular Cavalry and three *ressallahs* of my own regiment, and now do myself the honour to report the result as follows, for the information of Major-General Nott.

I proceeded at a trot for about a mile and a half, when we were closing well with the enemy; all of a sudden we came on a ravine with steep sides, which for a time completely brought us up; however, we managed to file down and form again on the opposite side. This delay allowed the enemy to move a long way ahead; but getting the detachment into a smart gallop, we succeeded in coming up with them just as the foremost of them had reached the bottom of the hills.

We cut up about 50 of them; Lieutenant Chamberlain's party from the other flank destroyed 12 more. The enemy, I should think, amounted to about 300 horse and foot. Every man did his duty, so it is impossible to offer any remark on individuals, and I shall only add that I was quite satisfied with the conduct of all. I beg to return lists of the killed and wounded.

I have, &c.

(Signed) J. Christie, Captain.

(True copy.)

(Signed) Thomas Polwhele, Captain,
Deputy-Assistant Adjutant-General.

FROM MAJOR-GENERAL NOTT, COMMANDING FIELD FORCE, AFGHANISTAN, TO T. H. MADDOCK, ESQ., SECRETARY TO THE GOVERNMENT OF INDIA, WITH THE GOVERNOR-GENERAL.

Headquarters, dated Camp, Goaine, 31 miles S.W. of Ghuznee,
August 31, 1842.

Sir,—I have the honour to acquaint you, for the information of the Right Honourable the Governor-General of India, that Shumshoodeen, the Affghan Governor of the fortress of Ghuznee, brought nearly the whole of his army, about twelve thousand men, into the vicinity of my camp yesterday, at 3 o'clock p. m.

I moved out with one half of my force; the enemy advanced in the most bold and gallant manner, each cheering as they came into position, their left being upon a hill of some elevation, their centre and right along a low ridge until their flank rested on a fort filled with men. They opened a fire of small arms, supported by two six-pounder horse-artillery guns, which were admirably served.

Our columns advanced upon the different points with great regularity and steadiness, and after a short and spirited contest completely defeated the enemy, capturing their guns, tents, ammunition, &c. &c., and dispersing them in every direction. One hour's more daylight would have enabled me to destroy the whole of their infantry.

Shumshooden fled in the direction of Ghuznee, accompanied by about thirty horsemen.

I enclose a list of killed and wounded on the 28th and 30th instant, also a return of ordnance, ammunition, &c. &c., taken from the enemy.

The behaviour of the troops, both European and Native, was such as I anticipated, and afforded me complete satisfaction.

I beg leave to bring to the favourable notice of the Right Honourable the Governor-General of India the under-mentioned officers. Many of them have served under my command for the last three years, and have been conspicuous for their zeal and gallantry in the various affairs which have occurred with the enemy during that period, and especially in the action of the 12th of January last, and have invariably upheld the reputation of our arms and the honour of our country.

Brigadier Wymer, commanding the 1st Infantry Brigade; Lieutenant-Colonel MacLaren, commanding 16th Regiment Native Infantry; Major Hibbert, commanding Her Majesty's 40th Regiment; Captain Burney, commanding 38th Regiment Native Infantry; Captains Christie and Haldane, commanding corps of Bengal Irregular Cavalry; Major Sotheby, commanding the Artillery; Captain Blood, commanding Bombay Foot Artillery; Major Sanders, Bengal Engineers; Lieutenants North and Studdert, Bombay Engineers. Majors Leech and Rawlinson, of the Political Department, attended me in the field, and rendered me great assistance in conveying my orders.

My best thanks are due to my staff, Captain Polwhele, deputy-assistant adjutant-general, Captain Waterfield, *aide-de-camp*, Lieutenant Tytler, Deputy Quartermaster-General.

Annexed is a letter from Brigadier Wymer, speaking in the highest terms of his Brigade-Major, Captain T. H. Scott, of the 38th Regiment Native Infantry. I fully appreciate this excellent officer's merits; he has been with me in four actions. I trust I shall not be thought presumptuous in expressing a hope that he will receive some mark of the favour of Government, by brevet or otherwise.

I cannot close this despatch without expressing my admiration of the dashing and gallant conduct, rapid movement, and correct practice of Captain Anderson's troop of Bengal Horse Artillery; nothing could exceed it, and I beg leave to bring this officer and Lieutenant Turner, attached to the same troop, to the particular notice of his Lordship, as officers who have on many occasions rendered me most essential service.

I have, &c.

(Signed) W. Nott, Major-General,
Commanding Field Force, Affghanistan.

FROM BRIGADIER G. P. WYMER, COMMANDING 1ST INFANTRY BRIGADE, TO MAJOR-GENERAL NOTT, COMMANDING FIELD FORCE.

Dated Camp Chuppotkhana, September 1, 1842.

Sir,—Adverting to the division orders of yesterday, expressive of your praise and thanks to the troops employed under your command in action with the enemy on the afternoon of the 30th instant, I hope you will not consider it ill-judged on my part bringing to your favourable notice the valuable assistance I derived from the active services of Captain Scott, Major of Brigade to the 1st Infantry Brigade under my command, whose exertions during the fight on that day demand and merit my best praise and acknowledgments. This being the second time of the display of Captain Scott's abilities when in action with the enemy as my personal staff, will, I hope, plead my apology for recommending him to your notice, and the favourable consideration of Government, in any way you may have it in your power to mention him as a meritorious and deserving officer.

I have, &c.

(Signed) G. P. Wymer, Brigadier,
Commanding 1st Infantry Brigade.

RETURN OF KILLED, WOUNDED, AND MISSING OF THE FIELD FORCE, UNDER THE COMMAND OF MAJOR-GENERAL WILLIAM NOTT, IN THE ENGAGEMENTS WITH THE ENEMY ON THE 28TH AND 30TH OF AUGUST, 1843.

2nd Troop Bengal Irregular Horse Artillery.—1 groom and 1 horse wounded.

3rd Company 1st Batt. Bombay Artillery.—1 bearer killed, 1 gunner, 1 bugler, 1 private, 1 driver, and 2 horses wounded.

3rd Regt. Bombay Light Cavalry.—1 captain, 1 lieutenant, 1 native officer (*jemadar*), 4 *havildars*, 1 farrier, 10 troopers, and 6 horses killed; 2 lieutenants, 1 *jemadar*, 1 trumpeter, 5 troopers, and 4 horses wounded.

1st Regt. Bengal Irregular Cavalry.—1 *duffadar* (*havildar*), and 11 troopers killed; 1 *jemadar*, 2 *duffadars*, 12 troopers, and 16 horses wounded; 9 horses missing.

Christie's Horse.—2 *duffadars*, 5 troopers, and 19 horses killed; 1 lieutenant, 1 *jemadar*, 13 troopers, and 17 horses wounded; 4 horses missing.

H. M.'s 40th Regt. of Foot.—1 lieutenant, 2 corporals, and 10 privates wounded.

H. M.'s 41st Regt. of Foot.—1 corporal, 3 privates, 1 tent lascar, and 1 *bheestie* wounded.

16th Regt. Bengal N. I.—2 privates wounded.

42nd Regt. Bengal N.I.—1 private wounded.

Total Killed.—1 captain, 1 lieutenant, 1 *jemadar*, 7 *havildars*, 1 farrier, 26 troopers, 1 bearer, and 25 horses.

Total Wounded.—4 lieutenants, 3 *jemadars*, 2 *havildars*, 3 corporals, 1 gunner, 2 trumpeters, 47 privates, 1 tent lascar, 1 *bheestie*, 1 groom, 1 driver, and 40 horses.

Missing.—13 horses.

Grand Total of Killed and Wounded.—104 officers and men, and 65 horses; and 13 horses missing.

Officers Killed.—Captain H. Bury, 3rd Regt. Bombay Light Cavalry; Brevet Captain G. O. Reeves, 3rd Regt. Bombay Light Cavalry.

Officers Wounded.—Brevet Captain G. S. Ravenscroft, 3rd Regt. Bombay Light Cavalry; Lieutenant T. A. Mackenzie, 3rd Regt. Bombay Light Cavalry; Lieutenant Meason, H. M.'s 40th Regt. of Foot; Lieutenant N. B. Chamberlain, Christie's Horse.

(Signed) Thomas Polwhele,
Captain Deputy-Assistant Adjutant-General

(Signed) W. Nott,
Major-General, commanding Field Force.

RETURN OF ORDNANCE, AMMUNITION, &C. CAPTURED IN ACTION WITH THE ENEMY BY THE FIELD FORCE UNDER THE COMMAND OF MAJOR-GENERAL NOTT, ON THE 30TH AUGUST, 1842.

Camp Gonine, August 31, 1842.

Carriages, field, with limbers, 2. One carriage, broken by our shot, left on the field.

Cartridges, balled, musquet (as originally packed in the H. C/s magazines), 4000. Destroyed on the enemy's encamping ground.

Cartridges, filled, 6 prs., 132. Destroyed on the enemy's encamping ground.

Harness, sets, 4. Unserviceable.

Horses, 4.

Ordnance, 6 pr. brass, 2.

Shot, common case, 6 pr., 9. Unserviceable.

Shot, round (hammered), 6 prs., 24. Unserviceable.

Exd. (Signed) F. S. Sotheby, Major,
Commanding Artillery.

(Signed) T. Brougham,
Lieutenant-Adjutant, Artillery Division.

(True copy.)
(Signed) T. Polwhele, Captain,
Deputy-assistant Adjutant-General.

COPY OF A LETTER FROM MAJOR-GENERAL NOTT, TO MAJOR-GENERAL POLLOCK, C.B., COMMANDING IN AFGHANISTAN.

Camp Nanee, September 3, 1842.

My Dear General,— have been favoured with your letter of the 23rd *ult.* We were engaged with the enemy on the 27th, near Mukoor. On the 30th, Shumshoodeen, Governor of Ghuznee, came into the vicinity of our camp with his whole army. I moved out with about one-third of my force; the enemy came on boldly enough, but we soon entirely defeated them, taking the two field guns they brought with them from Ghuznee, and the whole of their ammunition, tents, &c. &c.

Our *sepoys* behaved with much steadiness and gallantry.

Yours sincerely,
(Signed) W. Nott.

Killed.—Captain Bury, 3rd Bombay Cavalry; Captain G. Reeves, 3rd Bombay Cavalry.

Wounded.—Captain Ravenscroft, 3rd Bombay Cavalry, severely; Lieutenant Mackenzie, 3rd Bombay Cavalry, severely; Ensign Chamberlain, 1st Bengal Irregular Cavalry, slightly; Lieutenant Meason, Her Majesty's 40th, severely.

(True copy.)
(Signed) H. Rawlinson.

(True copy.)
(Signed) R. C. Shakespear,
Military Secretary.

(True copies.)
(Signed) T. H. Maddock,
Secretary to the Government of India, with
the Governor-General.

(E.)

Dispatch

Relative to Capture of Ghuznee.

From Major-General W. Nott, commanding Field Force, Affghanistan, to T. H. Maddock, Esq., Secretary to the Government of India, with the Governor-General.

Headquarters, dated Camp Ghuznee,
September 8, 1842.

Sir,—My dispatch of the 31st *ultimo* will have informed you of my having defeated the Affghan army commanded by Shumshoodeen.

On the morning of the 5th instant I moved on Ghuznee. I found the city full of men, and a range of mountains running north-east of the fortress covered by heavy bodies of cavalry and infantry; the gardens and ravines near the town were also occupied. The enemy had received a considerable reinforcement from Cabool, under Sultan Jan.

I directed Major Sanders, of the Bengal Engineers, to reconnoitre the works, under escort of the 16th Regiment of Native Infantry, and a party of irregular cavalry. This brought on some smart skirmishing, in which our *sepoys* behaved to admiration. Captain White, of H. M.'s 40th Regiment, commanding the light companies of the army, was pushed forward, accompanied by Anderson's troop of Horse Artillery, to support the reconnoitring party, and I at once determined on carrying the enemy's mountain positions before encamping my force. The troops ascended the heights in gallant style, driving the enemy before them until every point was gained.

The village of Bullal is situated about six hundred yards from the walls of Ghuznee, upon the spur of the mountain to the north-east, and observing it to be a desirable spot for preparing a heavy battery to be placed three hundred paces in advance, I ordered it to be occupied by two regiments of infantry and some light guns, and retired the columns into camp.

The engineer officers, sappers and miners, and infantry working parties, were employed under the direction of Major Sanders, during the night of the 5th, in erecting a battery for four eighteen-pounders; these guns were moved from camp before daylight on the morning of the 6th, but before they had reached the position assigned them, it was ascertained that the enemy had evacuated the fortress.

I directed the city of Ghuznee, with its citadel and the whole of its works, to be destroyed. I forward the engineer's report.

In these operations our loss has been much less than might have been expected from the number and positions of the enemy, and the fact of the troops having been necessitated to move under range of the guns of the fortress.

I enclose a list of killed and wounded.

The exertions of Major Sanders, of the Engineers, were as usual most zealous, and my thanks are due to him and the department under his charge.

I beg to notice the following officers: Brigadier Wymer; Major Hibbert, commanding Her Majesty's 40th Regiment; Captain Evans, in temporary charge of the 16th Regiment Native Infantry; Captain White, Her Majesty's 40th Regiment, commanding the light companies of the force; Major Sotheby, and officers of the artillery.

I have every reason to be satisfied with my Staff, Captain Polwhele, Deputy-Assistant Adjutant-General; Captain Waterfield, *aide-de-camp*; Captain Ripley, and Lieutenant Kay, Deputy-Judge Advocate-General.

I continue to receive the greatest assistance from Major Leech.

I have, &c.,

(Signed) W. Nott, Major-General,
Commanding Field Force, Affghanistan.

P. S.—I have recovered about three hundred and twenty- seven of the *sepoys* of the 27th Regiment Bengal Native Infantry, who had been sold into slavery and dispersed in villages thirty and forty miles round Ghuznee.

(Signed) W. Nott.

Camp Rozeh, near Ghuznee, September 9, 1842.

MEMORANDUM.

On the morning of the 5th September 1842, General Nott moved his camp to take up a position before Ghuznee. An advanced party was ordered to protect a reconnoissance of the works undertaken by the engineer department. On the approach of this party to the hills north of the city, it was opposed in force, but was immediately supported by the General, and thus reinforced, cleared the hills of the enemy, and took possession of the village of Bullal, within four hundred yards of the city.

The General immediately directed this important point, with the heights near the village, to be maintained, and they were occupied by two regiments of native infantry and two nine-pounder guns.

Whilst these operations were going on, the camp was established at Rozeh, two and a half miles from the city. The guards required for the protection and general duties of the camp absorbed so many men, that but few were available for the duties of a siege. The General, therefore, determined not to invest the place in form, and directed the Engineer to concentrate the resources at his disposal in one spot, where protection might be most conveniently afforded to the siege operations.

With advertence to these instructions, the Engineer proposed to establish a battery on the ridge of the hill north of the town, in advance of the village of Bullal, and distant about three hundred and fifty yards from the nearest point of the walls. From this battery it was expected that the four eighteen pounders would lay open the thin flank wall connecting the citadel on the west with the town wall in a few hours. The defences of the citadel could be swept from the same point by the light artillery, and the lines of loop-holed wall which would bear on the advance of the storming party were all viewed in enfilade from the site selected for the battery. The advance of the party to the assault would have been greatly facilitated by the existence of a thick dam of earth across the ditch, immediately opposite the point marked out for the breach.

It was further proposed that the principal assault should be supported by two other attacks; one, an attempt to blow in the water gate, (both the others having been strongly built up, and the causeways in front of them cut through,) another, to escalade a weak point near the Cabool gate, which would have been greatly aided by the fire of the artillery from the hill.

This project met the General's approval, and at dusk on the evening of the 5th September, a working party composed of the sappers, and of 160 men from the regiments occupying the hill, commenced work on the battery. By four a.m., on the

6th September, cover for the party had been secured across the ridge of the hill, and so much progress made in the execution of the work as to lead to reasonable expectations that the four eighteen-pounder guns, and two twenty-four-pounder howitzers would be established in position, and ready to open their fire during the day.

Early on the evening of the 5th, a brisk matchlock fire was kept up from the citadel on the hill, but this gradually slackened, and at ten p.m. had entirely ceased. The enemy's infantry had been observed at dusk crossing the river near the water gate, with the intention, it was supposed, of attacking the working party during the night; but towards the morning of the 6th, there were grounds for believing the fort was evacuated. At daylight this was ascertained to be the case by Lieutenant North, of the Engineers, who took possession at that hour of the water gate without opposition, leaving Ensign Newton and twenty-five *sepoys* of the 16th Native Infantry in charge of the gateway, and returning to the battery for further assistance. The whole of the working party was immediately moved into the town, of which, and of the citatel of Ghuznee, they were in possession before sunrise.

(Signed) Edward Sanders, Major, Engineers.

FROM MAJOR E. SANDERS, ENGINEERS, TO MAJOR-GENERAL W. NOTT, COMMANDING FIELD FORCE, GHUZNEE.

Dated Camp Rozeh, near Ghuznee,
September 9, 1842.

Sir,—On the occupation of the fortress of Ghuznee by the troops under your command, I received orders from you to take measures for the destruction of the citadel, to as great an extent as the means at command, and the time afforded by a halt of two days, would permit.

2. I have now the honour to report, that the engineer department attached to your force has been employed during the 7th and 8th instant on the work of demolition, and to state the progress effected.

3. Fourteen mines have been sprung in the walls of the citadel, all with good effect. The Upper Fort has been completely destroyed; the second line of .works extensively breached in two places; and the outer and lower walls have their revetments blown down and greatly injured in three places.

4. In several spots remote from the mines, the walls, though they have not fallen, are so seriously shaken by the explosions, that unless immediate and energetic measures are adopted, on the departure of your force, for their repair and security, they must crumble down during the ensuing winter.

5. The gateways of the town and citadel, and the roofs of the principal buildings, have been fired and are still burning.

I have, &c.

(Signed) E. Sanders, Major, Engineers.

RETURN OF THE KILLED, WOUNDED, AND MISSING OF THE FIELD FORCE UNDER THE COMMAND OF MAJOR-GENERAL WILLIAM NOTT, IN THE ENGAGEMENT WITH THE ENEMY BEFORE GHUZNEE, ON THE 5TH SEPTEMBER,

2nd Troop Bengal Irregular Horse Artillery.—1 horse killed; 1 private, 1 *sycee*, 5 horses, wounded.

1st Troop Bombay Horse Artillery.—1 *sycee* wounded.

3rd Regt. Bombay Light Cavalry.—1 horse killed; 1 horse wounded.

1st Regt. Bengal Irregular Cavalry.—1 private, 1 horse, 1 *jemadar*, killed; 5 privates, 7 horses, wounded.

H. M. 40th Regt. of Foot.—1 private killed; 3 privates wounded.

H. M. 41st Regt. of Foot.—3 privates wounded.

2nd Regt. Bengal N.I.—4 privates wounded.

16th Regt. Bengal N.I.—1 private, killed; 1 ensign, 1 *havildar*, 4 *naiques*, 11 privates, wounded.

27th Regt. Bengal N.I., doing duty with the 16th N.I.—1 private wounded.

42nd Regt. Bengal N.I.—2 privates wounded.

43rd Regt. Bengal N.I.—4 privates wounded.

Total of Each.—3 privates, 3 horses, 1 *jemadar*, killed; 1 ensign, 1 *havilidar*, 4 *naiques*, 34 privates, 2 *syces*, 13 horses, wounded.

Grand Total of Killed and Wounded.—46 officers and men, and 16 horses.

Ensign Stannus, 16th Regt. Bengal N.I., wounded.

(Signed) W. Nott, Major-General,
Commanding Field Force,

(Exd.) T. Polwhele, Capt. Deputy-Assistant Adjutant-General.

Return of Ordnance Ammunition captured in the Fortress of Ghuznee by the Force under command of Major-General Nott, on the 6th of September, 1842.

Camp Ghuznee, September 6, 1842.

Bags, cartridge, dungaree, 40; blue-lights, 300; boxes, ammunition, musquet, (filled) 15; boxes, ammunition, gun, (filled,) 25; boxes, ammunition, gun, empty, 15; boxes, treasure, empty, with straps, 20; cartridges, balled, musquet, 25,000, 15,000 of these are unserviceable; cartridges, balled, gun and *jingal*, about 2000; carriages, field-pieces, 6; carriages, garrison, 1; charcoal, *maunds*, 6; hides, buff, 5; *jingals* or wall-pieces, 7; lanterns, tin, 9, unserviceable; lead, pigs, 8; musquetry, musquets, without locks, 30; ordnance, brass, light field-pieces, mounted, 3, 3, 6, and 8-pounder; ordnance, brass, heavy, mounted, 1 68-pounder; ordnance, iron, light field-pieces, mounted, 3, *ditto*, dismounted, 1, 2, 6, and 8-pounders; powder, ordnance, country, (jars,) 10, about 150lbs. each; rope, cotton, (pieces,) 1; saltpetre, (bags,) 1; shot, round, English, (6 pr.) 60; *ditto*, of sorts, 550; ditto, *jinjal*, and 1 2-pr. 300; sponges, gun, of sorts, 12; *jezails*, 5.

(Exd.) T. Brougham, Lt.
Adjutant, Artillery Division.

(Signed) F. S. Sotheby,
Major commanding Artillery.

(True Copy.)
(Signed) Thomas Polwhele, Captain,
Deputy-Assistant Adjutant-General.

(F.)

Dispatch

Relative to Beni Badam.

From Major-General W. Nott, commanding Field Force, to Major-General Pollock, C.B., commanding West of the Indus.

Camp Urgundee, September 16, 1842.

Sir,—I have the honour to acquaint you that Shumshoodeen, Sultan Jan, and other Affghan chiefs, having assembled about 12,000 men, occupied a succession of strong mountains intercepting my march upon Benee Badam and Mydan, on the 14th and 15th instant. Our troops dislodged them in gallant style, and their conduct afforded me the greatest satisfaction.

The artillery distinguished themselves, and I beg to mention the names of Captains Leslie, Bombay Horse Artillery, Captain Blood, Bombay Foot Artillery, and Anderson and Turner, of the Bengal Horse Artillery, and the 38th and 43rd Bengal Native Infantry. I beg to bring under the favourable notice of Government, Captain White, of Her Majesty's 40th Regiment, in command of the light companies of her Majesty's 40th and 41st Regiments, and of the 2nd, 16th, 38th, 42nd, and 43rd Bengal Native Regiments, for the able manner in which he carried my orders into effect, and for the gallantry displayed by him and the companies under his command, in ascending the mountains and driving the enemy from their positions. I have every reason to be pleased with the conduct of all the troops, European and Native. I forward a list of killed and wounded—I am, &c.

(Signed) W. Nott,
Major-General, commanding Field Force.

RETURN OF KILLED, WOUNDED, AND MISSING OF THE FIELD FORCE, UNDER THE COMMAND OF MAJOR-GENERAL WILLIAM NOTT, IN THE ENGAGEMENTS WITH THE ENEMY ON THE 14TH AND 15TH SEPTEMBER, 1842.

Killed.—1 private 3rd Regiment Bombay Light Cavalry,
2 privates H. M 40th Regiment, 1 private H. M. 41st Regiment.

Wounded.—1 lieutenant and 3 privates, H. M. 40th Regiment; 2 lascars, 2nd battalion Bengal Foot Artillery; 3 privates, 1st battalion Bombay Foot Artillery; 1 corporal and 4 privates, 1st Regiment Bengal Irregular Horse; 1 private, Christie's Horse; 1 corporal and 1 private, H. M. 41st Foot; 1 lieutenant and 1 private, 2nd B.N.I.; 1 Serjeant and 1 private, 16th B. N. I.; 1 Serjeant and 11 privates, 38th B. N. I.; 1 serjeant and 2 privates, 42nd B. N. I.; 1 lieutenant, 1 subadar, 1 serjeant, and 15 privates, 43rd B. N. I.; 5 privates, 3rd Irregular Infantry; and 24 horses.

Officers wounded.—Lieutenant E. Eager, H. M. 40th regiment, severely; Lieutenant Mainwaring, 2nd Regiment, slightly; Lieutenant G. Holroyd, 43rd, *ditto, ditto.*

(G.)

Proclamation by Lord Ellenborough.

Secret Department.

Simla, October 1, 1842.

The Government of India directed its army to pass the Indus in order to expel from Affghanistan a chief believed to be hostile to British interests, and to replace upon his throne a Sovereign represented to be friendly to those interests, and popular with his former subjects.

The Chief believed to be hostile became a prisoner, and the Sovereign represented to be popular was replaced upon his throne; but after events which brought into question his fidelity to the Government by which he was restored, he lost by the hands of an assassin the throne he had only held amidst insurrections, and his death was preceded and followed by still existing anarchy.

Disasters unparalleled in their extent, unless by the errors in which they originated, and by the treachery by which they were completed, have, in one short campaign, been avenged upon every scene of past misfortune; and repeated victories in the field, and the capture of the cities and citadels of Ghuznee and Cabool, have again attached the opinion of invincibility to the British arms.

The British army in possession of Afghanistan will now be withdrawn to the Sutlej.

The Governor-General will leave it to the Affghans themselves to create a Government amidst the anarchy which is the consequence of their crimes.

To force a Sovereign upon a reluctant people would be as inconsistent with the policy as it is with the principles of the British Government, tending to place the arms and resources of that people at the disposal of the first invader, and to impose the burthen of supporting a Sovereign without the prospect of benefit from his alliance.

The Governor-General will willingly recognise any Government approved by the Affghans themselves, which shall appear desirous and capable of maintaining friendly relations with neighbouring states.

Content with the limits nature appears to have assigned to its empire, the Government of India will devote all its efforts to the establishment and maintenance of general peace, to the protection of the Sovereigns and chiefs its allies, and to the prosperity and happiness of its own faithful subjects.

The rivers of the Punjaub and Indus, and the mountainous passes and the barbarous tribes of Afghanistan, will be placed between the British army and an enemy approaching from the West, if indeed such enemy there can be, and no longer between the army and its supplies.

The enormous expenditure required for the support of a large force in a false military position, at a distance from its own frontier and its resources, will no longer arrest every measure for the improvement of the country and of the people.

The combined army of England and of India, superior in equipment, in discipline, in valour, and in the officers by whom it is commanded, to any force which can be opposed to it in Asia, will stand in unassailable strength upon its own soil, and forever, under the blessing of Providence, preserve the glorious empire it has won in security and in honour.

The Governor-General cannot fear the misconstruction of his motives in thus frankly announcing to surrounding states the pacific and conservative policy of his Government.

Afghanistan and China have seen at once the forces at his disposal, and the effect with which they can be applied.

Sincerely attached to peace for the sake of the benefits it confers upon the people, the Governor-General is resolved that peace shall be observed, and will put forth the whole power of the British Government to coerce the state by which it shall be infringed.

By order of the Right Honourable the Governor-General of India.

(Signed) T. H. Maddock,
Secretary to the Government of India,
with the Governor-General.

(H.)

General Order

Relative to Rewards, Medals, Etc., Granted to Troops in Affghanistan.

General Orders by the Right Honourable the Governor-General of India.

Simla, October 4, 1842.

The Governor-General, earnestly desirous of evincing the gratitude of the Government of India towards the general officers, officers, and non-commissioned officers and privates, engaged in the operations of the present campaign in Affghanistan, is pleased, after communicating with his Excellency the Commander-in-Chief, to declare the following resolutions:—

1. All the general officers, officers, non-commissioned officers and privates, serving under the command of Major-General Pollock, of Major-General Nott, and of Major-General England, between Attock and Ali Musjid. and in and above the Khyber Pass, and in and above the Bolan Pass, on the 8th of September, shall receive a donation of six months' *batta,* payable on the 1st of January, 1843.'

2. In perpetual commemoration of their distinguished services, the 2nd and 16th regiments of Bengal Native Infantry shall be hereafter regiments of Grenadiers, and the 38th, 42nd and 43rd regiments of Bengal Native Infantry shall be hereafter regiments of Light Infantry.

3. The regiment of Bengal Irregular Infantry, lately known as the 3rd Regiment of Infantry, in the service of Shah Shoojah, shall, in consideration of the valour, discipline, and fortitude manifested by that regiment on many occasions, and especially in the defence of Kelat-i-Ghilzie, continue embodied under its present commandant, Captain J. H. Craigie, and be brought on the strength of the Bengal army as an extra regiment, and be denominated the "Regiment of Kelat-i-Ghilzie." The future establishment of the Regiment of Kelat-i-Ghilzie, and other details consequent upon this resolution, will be made known in a separate Order.

4. Major-General Nott will communicate to the Governor-General the designations of every corps engaged in the several actions with the enemy in the vicinity of Candahar, between the 1st of January and the 10th of August, 1842, specifying the particular actions in which such corps were engaged; and the Major-General will state which of such corps are, in his judgment, entitled to bear hereafter the word "Candahar" upon their standards or colours and appointments, in commemoration of their services.

To such corps of the Indian army as the Major-General may name, the honour of so bearing the word "Candahar" will be immediately accorded by the Governor-General.

5. The several corps of the Indian army which on the 6th of September occupied Ghuznee, and the several corps which on the 16th of September and the following days occupied Cabool, will hereafter bear upon their standards or colours and appointments the word "Ghuznee" and "Cabool" respectively, with the figures "1842" underwritten.

The several corps under Major-General Nott which reached Cabool subsequently to the 16th of September, will be equally entitled with the troops previously occupying that city to the honour of bearing the word "Cabool" with the figures "1842" underwritten, upon their standards or colours and appointments.

6. Major-General Pollock will communicate to the Governor-General the designations of the corps under his command, which were engaged in the operations preceding the occupation of Cabool, but did not advance to that city, and will name such of these corps as he may deem entitled to bear the word "Cabool," with the figures "1842" under written, upon their standards or colours and appointments, as having contributed to the capture of that city by their previous service in this campaign; and to such corps, being on the Indian Army, as the Major-General may so name, the honour of so bearing the word "Cabool" will be immediately accorded by the Governor-General.

7. To every general officer, officer, non-commissioned officer and private, present on the occasions abovementioned in action with the enemy in the vicinity of Candahar, will be presented a silver medal inscribed "Candahar, 1842:" and to every general officer, officer, non-commissioned officer and private, present with the army under Major-General Nott in the operations leading to the capture of Ghuznee and the occupation of Cabool, will be presented a similar silver medal inscribed "Ghuznee, Cabool, 1842." Where the same person shall be entitled to both distinctions, one medal only will be presented, and such medal will be inscribed, "Candahar, Ghuznee, 1842." Major-General Nott will transmit to the Governor-general nominal lists of the several general officers, officers, non-commissioned officers and privates, so entitled, respectively.

8. Major-General Pollock will transmit to the Governor-General a nominal list of the general officers, officers, non-commissioned officers and privates, present in action with the enemy, in the several operations of his army leading to the occupation of Cabool, and to every person named in such list, a silver medal will be presented, inscribed "Cabool, 1842." On the reverse of these several medals will be inscribed the words "Victoria Vindex."

9. To every officer, non-commissioned officer and private, present within Kelat-i-Ghilzie, and forming part of the garrison thereof, during the late investment and blockade of that fort, will be presented a silver medal bearing a mural crown, with the superscription of "Kelat-i-Ghilzie," and on the reverse the word "Invicta, 1842." Captain J. H. Craigie, late Commandant of the fort of Kelat-i-Ghilzie, will transmit to Major-General Nott a nominal list of the officers, non-commissioned officers and privates, so present in Kelat-i-Ghilzie, and so entitled to the medal above granted, and to every person named in such list, when sanctioned by Major-General Nott, the medal will be given.

10. All the medals abovementioned are to be worn suspended to a ribbon similar to that which will be given with the Jellalabad medal, which will be henceforth the military ribbon of India.

11. The regimental colours of the regiment of Khelat-i-Ghilzie will be composed of three colours of the military ribbon of India, and in the centre thereof will be inscribed the word "Khelat-i-Ghilzie."

12. The Governor-General will, after communication with, and in conjunction with his Excellency the Commander-in-Chief, represent to the authorities in England the high services rendered by the officers of Her Majesty's and of the Indian army in the operations of the present campaign in Afghanistan, in order that they may be duly submitted to the gracious consideration of Her Majesty.

13. Medals similar to those presented to the general officers, officers, non-commissioned officers and privates of the Indian army, will be prepared for the general officers, officers, non-commissioned officers and privates of Her Majesty's army having respectively similar claims to the honour of wearing such medals; but the authority to wear such medals depends upon Her Majesty's most gracious pleasure.

The regiment of Kelat-i-Ghilzie will be completed to 800 privates by drafts from the other corps of the late Shah Shoojah's service, as detailed below; the European commissioned officers and staff sergeants, now serving with it, will continue to hold their present appointments, and the native-commissioned and non-commissioned officers their present rank.

The detail of the late 6th regiment below, which formed part of the Jellalabad garrison, will be incorporated with the extra regiment, and the 1st and 2nd and 5th regiments of the late *Shah's* infantry will each furnish the necessary number of *sepoys* for Captain Craigie's corps.

1 *Subedar.*
1 *Jemedar.*
4 *Havildars.*
6 *Naicks.*
38 *Sepoys.*

In consequence of this measure it will be necessary to modify the scale of distribution of the infantry portion of the late *Shah's* force, as notified in the Governor-General's Order of the 16th of June last: and to admit of this being effected, the officers now in command of the 1st, 2nd, and 5th regiments of the late *Shah's* force will immediately on the receipt of the order, forward to the adjutant-general of the army, a present state of their respective corps; and his Excellency, the commander-in-chief, is requested to give the necessary orders for drafting the remaining native commissioned, non-commissioned officers, drummers, and *sepoys*, into native infantry corps of the line, according to the principle laid down in the Governor-General's Order above quoted. The following is to be considered the establishment of the extra regiment of native infantry.

A Commandant, a Second in Command, an Adjutant, a Quartermaster, a Serjeant-Major, a Quartermaster Serjeant, 8 *Subadars*, 8 *Jemadars*, 40 *Havildars*, 40 *Naicks*, 16 Drummers, 800 *Sepoys*.

(Signed) J. Stuart, Lieut. Colonel,
Secretary to the Government of India, Military
Department, with the Governor-General.

(I.)

Dispatch

Relative to Huft Kotul and Tezeen Passes.

From Major-General W. Nott, commanding Division of the Army, to Captain G. Ponsonby, Assistant Adjutant-General.

Camp, Giant's Tomb, October 15.

Sir,—I beg to report for the information of Major-General Pollock, C. B., that the rearguard of the force under my command was yesterday attacked by large bodies of the enemy in the Huft Kotul Pass. I sent 200 *sepoys* and a wing of Her Majesty's 40th Regiment, and two companies of Her Majesty's 41st, under command of Major Hibbert, to the assistance of Captain Leeson of the 42nd Regiment Native Infantry, who had charge of the rear. Our *sepoys* defeated and dispersed the enemy. Captain Leeson speaks in high terms of the gallantry of the officers and *sepoys* under his command.

Major Hibbert and the wing of Her Majesty's 40th Regiment, and the two companies of Her Majesty's 41st, under Captain Blackbourne, behaved with their accustomed gallantry. My thanks are due to all the troops engaged. I enclose a list of killed and wounded.

I have, &c.

Return of Killed and Wounded during the Attacks of the Rearguard of Major-General Nott's Force, on the Evening of the 15th and Morning of the 16th of October.

Total of each Killed.—12 men and 3 horses.

Wounded.—2 lieutenants, 1 assistant-surgeon, 4 *havildars*, 5 *naicks*, 36 gunners, troopers, &c.; 1 horse-keeper, 10 horses.

Grand total of Killed and Wounded.—61 officers and men, and

13 horses.

Officers Wounded.—Lieutenant and Brevet-Captain W. Jervis, 42nd Regiment of Bengal Native Infantry; Lieutenant N. W. Chamberlain, Christie's Horse; and Assistant-Surgeon J. H. Serrell, 42nd Regiment of Bengal Native Infantry.

N. B.—One *havildar*, one *naick*, and one *sepoy* of the 27th Native Infantry, doing duty with the 42nd Native Infantry, are included in the above.

(K.)

RETURN OF CANDAHAR DIVISION TO INDIA.

Camp Ferozepore, December 23, 1842.

This day Major-General Nott passed the Sutleje at the head of his whole force.

The Major-General was received at the foot of the bridge by the Governor-General and his Excellency the Commander-in-chief, attended by their respective staffs and escorts.

The Governor-General was accompanied by Jye Singh Rao Ghatkee, by the Rajah of Jheend, and other chiefs of Sirhind.

The troops and followers of the Rajah of Jheend, and of the other chiefs, were formed in two lines beyond the escorts of the Governor-General and the Commander-in-chief.

The gates of the Temple of Somnauth passed the bridge under the escort directed to be formed by the Governor-General's order, the escort of infantry being composed of volunteers from the 2nd Regiment of Grenadiers. The following are the officers selected by Major-General Nott to accompany the escort:—

Major Leech, political agent; Captain R. N. MacLean and Lieutenant J. Travers, 2nd Native Infantry; Assistant-Surgeon M. A. B. Gerard; and the same are appointed accordingly.

The Governor-General delivered to the senior *Jemadar* of the escort of the infantry a flag of the three colours of the military riband of India, having inscribed thereon "Ghuznee," in English, Persian, and Hindee; and informed Captain MacLean, commandant of the escort, that on their return to their regiment the flag was to be retained by the 2nd Grenadiers as a third colour, in commemoration of their distinguished services.

Major-General Nott, appointed Resident at the court of Lucknow, will bear the title of Envoy to the King of Oude, and that of "Excellency" in all communications with His Majesty.

(L.)

Alleged Excesses of the British Army in Affghanistan.

Copy of a Letter from General Nott to Major-General J. B. Lumley, Adjutant-General of the Army.

Lucknow, April 4.

Sir,

I have the honour to acknowledge the receipt of your letter, No. 817, of the 29th *ult.*, calling upon me, by directions of the Right Hon. the Governor-General of India, to report on certain excesses said to have been committed by the British troops on retiring from Afghanistan. I will confine my remarks to that veteran, gallant, and highly disciplined army which I had the honour to command for so long a period; and I will leave it to my gallant comrade, Sir G. Pollock, G.C.B., to defend the honour of the troops he commanded.

1st. I am called upon to state upon what private property, and upon what private buildings, injury was inflicted by my orders, or under my toleration, at Ghuznee. I answer, upon none.

2nd. I am desired to state "whether unresisting individuals were destroyed in cold blood, for mere vengeance; and whether women were either violated or murdered for their ornaments?" I will endeavour to suppress my scorn and indignation while I shortly reply to this charge on suspicion, or whatever it may be called, by the persons from whom it emanated. And this is the return made by the people of England, or rather, I would believe, by a few individuals, to the gallant Candahar army,—that army which was for so long a time neglected, but which, nevertheless, nobly upheld our national honour, and, during a period of four years, acted with the greatest forbearance and humanity to the people of Afghanistan!

Colonel Palmer, at the head of a brave garrison, surrendered Ghuznee to various tribes of Affghans. The city was occupied by these people for months; it was vacated by the enemy on the arrival of the army under my command. On its being entered by the British troops, it was found that not a single person was in the city. Neither man, nor woman, nor child. There was no property, and I do not believe there was a house left completely standing in the town; the whole had been unroofed and destroyed by the contending Affghans, for the sake of the timber,

&c.

I have said there were no inhabitants in Ghuznee, and therefore "unresisting individuals could not have been destroyed in cold blood; women could not have been murdered and violated for their ornaments." These, I boldly say, are gross and villainous falsehoods, whomsoever they emanate from.

I ordered the fortifications and citadel of Ghuznee to be destroyed. It had been the scene of treachery, mutilation, torture, starvation, and cruel murder, to our unresisting and imprisoned countrymen. Look at the contrast,—see the conduct of the noble British soldier; and are calumny and gross falsehood to rob him of the honour? They shall not, while I have life to defend his fame.

The extensive town or village of Rosa is situated about two miles from Ghuznee, and is lovely to behold. When this city was taken by the force under my command, Rosa was full of inhabitants, men, women, and children; my troops were encamped close to its walls; its gardens and its houses were full of property; its barns and farmyards were well stored; its orchards were loaded with fruit; its vineyards bent beneath a rich and ripe vintage; the property taken from our murdered soldiers at the Ghuznee garrison was seen piled in its dwellings. Were not these tempting objects to the soldier who had undergone four years of fatigue and privation?

Some of these soldiers had seen, and all had heard of the treacherous murder of their relations and comrades by these very people; but why should I enlarge? Four days the victorious Candahar army remained in camp close to this village, with all these temptations before it and at its mercy; but not a particle of anything was taken from the Affghan, the fruit brought for sale was paid for at a rate far above its value; no man, no living thing was injured. Much more I could say, but so much for the noble British soldier, for Ghuznee, and for the beautiful, rich, and tempting town of Rosa.

I did not command at Cabul. I did not interfere in its concerns. I never was in its bazaars. My division was encamped at a distance, with the exception of one regiment, against which corps I never received a complaint. My division was not in Cabul after Sir George Pollock's troops left, General Pollock's army and my troops marched the same day. No man under my command was ever detected plundering without being immediately punished.

Nor am I to have patience to reply to "Whether Affghans were permitted to be wantonly treated or murdered?" Is this a proper question to put to a British general officer who has ever had the honour of his country uppermost in his mind, and deeply impressed on his heart? "Permitted," indeed! is it supposed that I am void of religion; that I am ignorant of what is due to that God whom I have worshipped from my childhood? Am I thus to have my feelings outraged because a few people in India and in England have set forth villainous falsehoods to the world? I have confined my reply for the present as much as possible to the questions in your letter. I would only further say, that never did an army inarch through a country with less marauding and less violence than that which I commanded in Afghanistan.

In Lower Afghanistan, or the Candahar districts, I put down rebellion,—quelled all resistance to the British power in spite of the fears and weakness of my superiors. By mild persuasive measures, I induced the whole population to return to the cultivation of their land and to live in peace; I left them as friends and on friendly terms. On my leaving Candahar, no man was injured or molested,—no man was deprived of his property,—and my soldiers and the citizens were seen embracing.

It is on record that I informed the Indian Government that I could hold the country for any time; it is on record that I informed Lord Auckland, as far back as December 1841, that I would with permission reoccupy Cabul with the force under my command;—there was nothing to prevent it but the unaccountable panic which prevailed at the seat of Government; and now I am rewarded by a certain set of people in England, taxing me with that which would be disgraceful to me as a religious man, as an honourable gentleman, and a British officer.

I am, Sir,

Your obedient Servant,

(Signed) W. Nott, Major-General.

To Major-General J. B. Lumley,
Adjutant-General of the Army.

An Adventure in Afghanistan

By M. Laing Meason
(Late 40th Regiment).
From *The English Illustrated Magazine,* November, 1885.

The 40th Regiment, in which I was then a subaltern, arrived at Candahar in October, 1841. We had been encamped at Quetta since the month of February, and our first experiences of Afghanistan were by no means pleasant. During the six months we were at Quetta, the battalion, which on its arrival at that place numbered one thousand effective rank and file, lost no less than a hundred men and three officers, nearly all of whom died from a very virulent form of dysentery, said to be brought on by the water of the locality, which was chiefly composed of melted snow from the mountains. When we arrived at Quetta in February, there were not more than two *per cent*, of the whole corps on the sick list, but when we started to march for Candahar in the following September, at least a fourth of the regiment had to be carried on *doolies*, or camels, and quite as many more were allowed to get along on foot as best they could, without arms or accoutrements, being all what in England would be called outdoor patients of the regimental hospital.

In the ranks, and fit for duty, we had not more than five hundred men out of the thousand we had mustered a few months previously. The march to Candahar lasted about thirty days. Our commanding officer, acting on the advice of the medical men, ordered that the regiment should halt every fourth day, and the result of this judicious arrangement, together with the climate, which improved more and more as we got further to the north, was that nearly all the men who had started from Quetta more or less sick were fit for duty, and able to take their places in the ranks before our arrival at Candahar. When our corps arrived at the latter place we found, to our great delight, that cantonments, such as they were, had been provided for us. We had all been upwards of a year under canvas, and a wing of the regiment that had preceded the other half of the corps, had been for more than two years dwellers in tents. It is only those who have gone through a prolonged trial of the kind that can appreciate the blessing of having a roof over their heads, and being surrounded with stone, instead of canvas walls.

Our cantonments at Candahar were very much the reverse of what can be termed luxurious; they had been built for Shah Sooja's native troops, and could boast of not even the most common conveniences of Indian life. But the very fact of every officer having a room to himself, and of the men having space to hang up their arms and stow away their other belongings, made them appear veritable palaces to us. At Candahar we found none save Bengal troops. General Nott was in command of the garrison and the division. The latter consisted of the 2nd, 16th, 42nd, and 43rd Bengal Native Infantry, together with some few local corps, raised for the service of Shah Sooja, the king, whom we had placed on the throne of Afghanistan, and who eventually cost us so much in money, men, and prestige, by trying to maintain him as ruler of that country. The 40th had, since its arrival in India, some ten or more years previous to the period I am writing of, served in the Bombay Presidency, and was looked upon as a regular Bombay regiment. But nothing could exceed the kindness and good fellowship of the Bengal officers, amongst whom we were now thrown.

General Nott, in particular, was most kind and considerate in the manner he received us, and the invitations to different messes, as well as the offers to make us honorary members of the same, were so numerous, that it look the president of our mess committee no little time to reply to them. I make mention of all these details, trifling as some of them may appear, in order to let my readers understand the exact state of the case, as regards Candahar and its garrison, when we arrived there, and, as will be seen presently, to show the why and the wherefore of certain events which took place shortly after we formed part of the force that held the place. Since the days of which I write, the world is some forty-four or forty-five years older. Men who were then young smooth- faced lads, fresh from school, with their lives all before them, are now long past middle-age, and are looking forward to the probably not far-off end of their sojourn in this world. Hence it is that what was then a mere matter of passing history, must be now pretty well forgotten, and the prologue of the drama has to be told before the present generation can be expected to take any interest in what happened so long ago.

In less than a month after our arrival at Candahar, we heard the news from Cabul that our army there, under General Elphinstone, was daily getting into worse and worse trouble, and that their total defeat was merely a matter of time. Coming—as these reports did—through natives, and our communication with British India being cut off, we hardly knew what to believe. But in time, and before long, too, the very worst news we had heard proved only too true. The story of the English force trying to retreat to the Khyber Pass being cut up almost to a man, and many of the principal officers being taken prisoners, reached us in due time, and very shortly our own troubles commenced, although certainly on a smaller scale than those of the Cabul force. By the first day of December, Candahar was surrounded by thousands of Afghans. It is true that they kept a comparatively respectful distance from us. But they were not more than a very few miles from the city, and at times were quite close to our quarters.

Our force was divided into two brigades; one of these, consisting of the 40th Regiment, the 2nd, 16th, and 38th Native Infantry, occupied the cantonments; the other, composed of the 42nd and 43rd Bengal Native Infantry, together with two of Shah Souja's regiments, which were officered by Englishmen, was in the town, which was surrounded by high walls, and was not more than five hundred yards from the cantonments. Two or three times General Nott led a large portion of the force under his command against the enemy, but so little good was effected by the movements, and there was so much danger of our stores and supplies falling into the enemy's hands, that this plan of operation was abandoned, and we remained throughout the winter on the defensive.

As a matter of course, it was strictly forbidden for anyone to go beyond a certain distance from the town or the cantonments. But what will not Englishmen venture in case of sport? About three miles from our lines there was a broad—but very shallow—river, on the banks of which snipe, it was reported, were very numerous, and of a size rarely, if ever, seen in other parts of the world. Now and again, when the enemy was reported to be a considerable distance off, a few venturous spirits amongst us would risk our lives—to say nothing of the certainty of being tried by court-martial if we were found to have disobeyed orders—for the purpose of bagging a few of these birds. One of these adventures I have a very vivid recollection of, as it very nearly proved, not only the last day's shooting I should ever do, but, for some time, made me and my companion believe that our respective careers in this world had come to an end.

A camp-follower, who had a couple of dozen or so of snipe for sale, came to the cantonments one afternoon, and—as he could speak a little Hindustanee—gave us to understand that he had shot these birds in the course of about four hours. The birds were certainly very fine indeed of their kind. No snipe of such a size or in such admirable condition had ever been seen by even the most experienced shots amongst us, either in India or England. The gun with which he had killed his game was a wretched, old, single-barrelled affair, with a very bad flintlock, and the only shot he had was much larger than ordinary peas. The temptation proved too strong, at any rate, for two of us, of which I was one. It seemed that if this half-caste camp-follower, with his almost useless gun, could make a good bag of snipe, we, with our percussion, well made fowling-pieces, would be able to do a very great deal belter.

As a matter of course, the intended trip had to be kept a secret, for it was a direct violation of orders. But as none of the enemy had been seen for some days past, we thought that a venture to try what could be done was practicable, and determined to try our luck. My companion, and the leader and director of the affair, was also a 40th man—"Horace" Seymour[1]—a brother, if I am not mistaken, of General Sir Frank Seymour, who holds a high position as Master of Ceremonies to Her Majesty. Seymour—dead, I am sorry to say, long years ago, when he was quite a young man—was one of the kindest-hearted men, as well as one of the truest gentlemen and most gallant soldiers it has ever been my lot to meet with during a life of three-score years. He was a few years my senior, both in the service and in age, and took upon himself all the details of the expedition.

We started as soon as morning parade was over—about 10 o'clock. We had not more than four or five attendants, which, for an Indian shooting party, was unusually small. With a view to the possibility that we might have to beat a very hasty retreat, we took care to provide a *tattoo*, or pony, for each of our followers; we ourselves being, as a matter of course, also mounted. Having got quietly clear of the lines, twenty minutes or so sufficed to take us to the river. The latter was a broad—but very shallow—stream, with a considerable stretch

1. Lieutenant Henry Seymour was familiarly known in the regiment as "Horace." Informant, Lieutenant-General J. W. Thomas.

of marshy ground on each side. It was very evident that if the Afghans did surprise us, the sportsman who was shooting on the bank furthest from Candahar would run by far the greatest risk of being cut off.

As a matter of course, my friend Seymour, like the plucky fellow he was, volunteered, and for some time insisted that he should take the post of danger. But to this I would not listen, and declared that, unless he drew lots for sides, I would at once go back to the cantonments. After some little discussion we tossed up, and the side where we thought the danger lay fell to me. We had arranged our plan of campaign against the snipe. We dismounted, having our horses near us in charge of our respective *syces*, or native grooms, who were mounted. Of the three followers who remained, we each kept one to carry our extra ammunition and to pick up the birds. The fifth, and last, we ordered to remain mounted, and to proceed slowly abreast of us, in order to beat up the snipe. That the latter were most plentiful, and by no means wild, there could be no doubt whatever.

During the ten minutes or so that we took making the above arrangements, not fewer than a score of birds rose—all more or less close to us—and, after a short flight, settled down again, showing by their tameness that they had no fear or anxiety about being shot at. It must have been about 11 o'clock when we commenced operations, and I have never seen or heard of snipe in such quantities, or so large and in such admirable condition. As fast as we could load and fire, we added to the number of the booty in our game bags. My friend, Seymour, who was a first-rate shot, must have bagged at least fifty birds in about twice that number of minutes. Even I, whose shooting left much to be desired, whose aim was by no means certain, but very much the reverse, killed no fewer than a couple of dozen snipe before we had been an hour on the ground.

As to labour or walking, there was little or none. The birds rose at our very feet, and as fast, or even faster, than we could load, fresh victims took the places of those we had knocked over. If, instead of two, there had been half-a-dozen sportsmen, and each of these had behind him a couple of attendants with spare guns ready loaded, there would have been sport and to spare for all. The condition of the birds was also something wonderful. If our sport could have lasted some four or five hours, we should no doubt have made, both in quantity and quality, bags which would have been historical in the annals of sport. As it was, notwithstanding that we were ill-provided with ammunition, had no good markers of the game, and also had to keep an outlook for the Afghans, who might at any moment be down upon us, we made much larger bags than we could have done on any ground that it was ever my luck to see in India or England.

We had got well to work, but halted for half-an-hour to eat a mouthful of lunch and smoke our cheroots, and had resumed our shooting, when a very unpleasant stoppage was put to our sport. Happening to look towards my friend Seymour, I saw that he was making signs to me in a most urgent manner. I was too far from him—the river being wide—to hear what he said, but I came to the conclusion that he was in need of powder or shot, or perhaps both. To the best of my ability I made signs, asking what it was he needed; but he shook his head and made gestures with his hand, which showed that it was something else—evidently more serious—that he wished me to notice. He had stopped shooting, and was looking through his binocular glasses at something on my side of the river.

At last what turned out afterwards to be a happy thought seized me, and I resolved to mount my nag and cross to where he was. I had hardly gone fifty yards in that direction, when I got a practical intimation as to what he wanted me to do, and whence the danger he had seen was to be expected. All at once, four or five bullets from behind whistled past me, causing me instantly to quicken my pace. I looked over my shoulder as soon as I got some little distance, and saw half-a-dozen Afghans, armed to the teeth, making after me as fast as they could. Fortunately, they were not mounted, so that I had the best of the chase thus far. In a very few minutes I had joined Seymour, who greeted me with "Now then, old fellow, we must ride for it; for there are a dozen or more of those ruffians following those who fired at you."

Our first care was to see that none of our followers were left behind. These individuals had, however, taken alarm in time, and were making their way towards Candahar much in advance of ourselves. Not that we were slow to follow them, for the first shots from the Afghans had been quickly followed by others, and, as we could now perceive, those who had fired at us were making their way to the river, and evidently intended, if they could, to capture us. As they were on foot, we had the best of the race, and galloped on towards the cantonments, feeling certain that we could not be overtaken; but we had very soon reason to take a less cheerful view of our position.

The ground between the river and the cantonments was, as is very common in Afghanistan, undulating to a degree seldom seen in any other country. So much so is this the case, that the pathways, or tracts—for they can hardly be called roads—look as if they were almost level, and hundreds of men or animals might be within a very short distance of each other, and yet have no idea whatever of the fact. We had just reached the top of a gently-undulating piece of ground, and were congratulating ourselves at being within reasonable distance from home, when all of a sudden we saw about fifty or sixty armed horsemen drawn up in line, and barring our further progress towards the cantonments. They were evidently waiting for us, and seemed certain they would capture us with ease. To be made prisoner by anyone is far from pleasant, but to be taken by the Afghans meant, as we knew, a cruel and prolonged death, so brutal in details that it could not be described in print.

About a month previous to our expedition, three young lads private soldiers in the 40th Regiment, had, in defiance of orders, gone out on a wandering expedition. Their bodies were found next day, not more than a mile from the cantonments. They had been murdered; but, as the medical officer who examined the corpses said, they had evidently been tortured in the most brutal manner it was possible to imagine before being put out of their pain.

Nor were these poor fellows the only example of what the Afghan savage will do in order to torment his enemy when living, and insult his corpse when dead. Such being the case, the prospect of being taken by the horsemen, who were so evidently on the lookout for us, was anything but pleasant.

"There is only one hope for us," said my companion, shortly after he saw the men in front of us; "we must do our best to ride through them, and make for the cantonments. Let us walk our horses quietly until close upon them, and then make a start for it. Our chance of escape is small, but it is the only one we have. If I fall, you will write to my friends and if you are killed, I will do the same to yours,"

Seymour happened to have with him a brace of double-barrelled pistols, he drew these from his holsters and gave one to me, saying, "In any case, let us sell our lives as dearly as we can, for to be killed on the spot would be infinitely better than to be taken prisoners by these cruel miscreants."

We had one thing in our favour; although our horses were not by any means large, they were both tolerably fleet, and would be able to hold their own for a certain distance. Another fact that Seymour reminded me of, was that at a certain ruin, a little more than half-way between where we were and the cantonments, there was very often a picket of Skinner's Horse, consisting of a *havildar*, or sergeant, and a dozen or fifteen troopers. "If either of us escape," he said to me—for it seemed far too much to hope for that both of us could by any possibility do so—"let him ride straight to that ruin, and bring down the picket of horsemen with him. It is just possible, although not very probable, that the one who remains with the Afghans may be saved."

Thus my plucky friend tried to make the best of what was, at the best, a very desperate position to be in. With a "Now goodbye, old fellow," from one to the other, we rode quietly on, having arranged that Seymour would give the word when we were to start off in a gallop, and try to shake off the enemy.

As we approached the Afghans, they evidently thought we intended to give ourselves up as prisoners. They shouted at and abused us after their fashion, using the most brutal epithets towards us in a sort of mongrel Hindostanee, so that we might understand them the better. Half-a-dozen shots were fired at us, but they went so wide of the mark that they were evidently meant to intimidate rather than to actually injure us. One thing—as we found out afterwards, when comparing notes—struck us both, and gave us very much better hopes than we had before dared to entertain of getting away safe if it came to a race for life; the horses of the Afghans were very dusty, had evidently come a long way, and were, compared with our own, very much done up.

"Now for it," said Seymour, as we got within thirty yards or so of the line—a line formed by single horsemen, some ten or a dozen yards apart—"now for it, old fellow; turn sharp to the right when you get near them, and go as hard as you can."

It is wonderful what effect the words of a cool-headed man have on desperate occasions, like the one I am endeavouring to describe. My plucky companion had—as he afterwards told me—seen at a glance that the Afghans were slowly closing in to the point opposite which we were advancing, thus leaving, as it were, their flank exposed. Towards, or rather at, that flank we rode, spurring for dear life to get clear of the ruffianly gang. In far less time than it takes to relate what happened, we *were* clear, and, what was better, we felt that we were increasing the distance between our pursuers and ourselves at every stride. The four or five horsemen through whom we dashed struck at us with sword and lance, but all to no purpose; neither our horses nor ourselves were touched. The enemy then tried to fire at us, but their doing this was so much in our favour. Every horseman, when he fired, had to stop his horse, and thus we had for the moment one pursuing enemy the less.

But what really saved us—for saved we were, and although poor Seymour did not live many years afterwards, I have survived forty odd years to tell the tale—was the superior freshness and speed of our horses. Half an hour's riding brought us safe to the cantonments. A few of our more intimate friends heard of the escape we had had, but, as disobedience of orders in the field is a serious matter, the affair was never talked about. During a campaign like that of 1841-42 in Afghanistan, when every man feels that his life is in his hands, and no one can tell what a day may bring forth, the private adventures of either officers or men are quickly forgotten, no matter how interesting they may be to those, or to the friends of those, chiefly concerned.

(Signed) M. Laing Meason.

MM

ALSO FROM LEONAUR

AVAILABLE IN SOFTCOVER OR HARDCOVER WITH DUST JACKET

THE 9TH—THE KING'S (LIVERPOOL REGIMENT) IN THE GREAT WAR 1914 - 1918 *by Enos H. G. Roberts*—Mersey to mud—war and Liverpool men.

THE GAMBARDIER *by Mark Severn*—The experiences of a battery of Heavy artillery on the Western Front during the First World War.

FROM MESSINES TO THIRD YPRES *by Thomas Floyd*—A personal account of the First World War on the Western front by a 2/5th Lancashire Fusilier.

THE IRISH GUARDS IN THE GREAT WAR - VOLUME 1 *by Rudyard Kipling*—Edited and Compiled from Their Diaries and Papers—The First Battalion.

THE IRISH GUARDS IN THE GREAT WAR - VOLUME 1 *by Rudyard Kipling*—Edited and Compiled from Their Diaries and Papers—The Second Battalion.

ARMOURED CARS IN EDEN *by K. Roosevelt*—An American President's son serving in Rolls Royce armoured cars with the British in Mesopatamia & with the American Artillery in France during the First World War.

CHASSEUR OF 1914 *by Marcel Dupont*—Experiences of the twilight of the French Light Cavalry by a young officer during the early battles of the great war in Europe.

TROOP HORSE & TRENCH *by R.A. Lloyd*—The experiences of a British Lifeguardsman of the household cavalry fighting on the western front during the First World War 1914-18.

THE EAST AFRICAN MOUNTED RIFLES *by C.J. Wilson*—Experiences of the campaign in the East African bush during the First World War.

THE LONG PATROL *by George Berrie*—A Novel of Light Horsemen from Gallipoli to the Palestine campaign of the First World War.

THE FIGHTING CAMELIERS *by Frank Reid*—The exploits of the Imperial Camel Corps in the desert and Palestine campaigns of the First World War.

STEEL CHARIOTS IN THE DESERT *by S. C. Rolls*—The first world war experiences of a Rolls Royce armoured car driver with the Duke of Westminster in Libya and in Arabia with T.E. Lawrence.

WITH THE IMPERIAL CAMEL CORPS IN THE GREAT WAR *by Geoffrey Inchbald*—The story of a serving officer with the British 2nd battalion against the Senussi and during the Palestine campaign.

www.ingramcontent.com/pod-product-compliance
Lightning Source LLC
Chambersburg PA
CBHW032048080426
42733CB00006B/202

9780857064905